Employee Risk Management

Employee Risk Management

How to protect your business reputation and reduce your legal liability

Helen Rideout

KoganPage

LONDON PHILADELPHIA NEW DELHI

Publisher's note

Every possible effort has been made to ensure that the information contained in this book is accurate at the time of going to press, and the publishers and author cannot accept responsibility for any errors or omissions, however caused. No responsibility for loss or damage occasioned to any person acting, or refraining from action, as a result of the material in this publication can be accepted by the editor, the publisher or the author.

First published in Great Britain and the United States in 2014 by Kogan Page Limited

Apart from any fair dealing for the purposes of research or private study, or criticism or review, as permitted under the Copyright, Designs and Patents Act 1988, this publication may only be reproduced, stored or transmitted, in any form or by any means, with the prior permission in writing of the publishers, or in the case of reprographic reproduction in accordance with the terms and licences issued by the CLA. Enquiries concerning reproduction outside these terms should be sent to the publishers at the undermentioned addresses:

2nd Floor, 45 Gee Street	1518 Walnut Street, Suite 1100	4737/23 Ansari Road
London EC1V 3RS	Philadelphia PA 19102	Daryaganj
United Kingdom	USA	New Delhi 110002
www.koganpage.com		India

© Helen Rideout, 2014

The right of Helen Rideout to be identified as the author of this work has been asserted by her in accordance with the Copyright, Designs and Patents Act 1988.

ISBN   978 0 7494 7160 6
E-ISBN 978 0 7494 7161 3

British Library Cataloguing-in-Publication Data

A CIP record for this book is available from the British Library.

Library of Congress Cataloging-in-Publication Data

Rideout, Helen (Business writer)
  Employee risk management : how to protect your business reputation and reduce your legal liability / Helen Rideout.
     pages cm
  ISBN 978-0-7494-7160-6 (paperback) – ISBN 978-0-7494-7161-3   1. Risk management.   I. Title.
  HD61.R514 2014
  658.3–dc23
                                                                                           2014015341

Typeset by Graphicraft Limited, Hong Kong
Printed and bound in India by Replika Press Pvt Ltd

Dedication

To my late parents, Jean and Fred Rideout.

CONTENTS

Acknowledgements x
Preface xi

01 Introducing employee risk management 1

  Introduction 1
  An overview 2
  Areas covered 3
  Improving legal compliance 4
  Enhancing HR's profile 6
  Safeguarding business reputation 7
  Chapter summary 8

02 The organizational context 11

  Introduction 11
  Organizational culture 11
  How culture influences risk taking 13
  Significance of the link between culture and risk taking 18
  Improving organizational culture 20
  Chapter summary 24

03 Pre-assessment groundwork 27

  Introduction 27
  Project planning 27
  Link to other disciplines and processes 34
  Drafting the business case 37
  Trade union involvement 43
  Chapter summary 44

04 Carrying out an employee risk assessment 47

  Introduction 47
  How to carry out an employee risk assessment 47
  Introducing horizon scanning 58
  Chapter summary 60

05 Recruitment 63

Introduction 63
Pre-recruitment 63
Hiring policies 70
Candidate screening 76
Specific recruitment needs 83
Chapter summary 88

06 Types of 'employee' and third parties 93

Introduction 93
Ageing workforce 93
Remote workers 98
Third-party threats 101
Interns 105
Volunteers 107
Young people 108
Chapter summary 110

07 Employee health and well-being 115

Introduction 115
Health issues 115
Sickness absence 121
Presenteeism 126
Chapter summary 128

08 Social media 133

Introduction 133
General problems 133
Problems by social media channel 138
Social media policy 145
Chapter summary 147

09 Information security 151

Introduction 151
Cybercrime 151
Bring your own devices (BYOD) 154
Cloud computing 156
File downloads 157

Online gambling 161
Data protection 162
Confidential information and 'know-how' 165
Chapter summary 167

10 Impact of HR function 171

Introduction 171
Role of HR 171
Learning and talent development 179
Managing poor performance 183
Whistle-blowing 186
Chapter summary 189

11 End of employment 193

Introduction 193
Unfair dismissal 193
Redundancy 205
Other concerns 212
Chapter summary 216

12 Avoiding common problems 223

Introduction 223
Project management pitfalls 223
Failing to manage change 225
Creating a risk-aware culture 228
Poor communication 229
Final thoughts 231
Chapter summary 233

Appendix 1: Project management checklist 235
Appendix 2: Business case checklist 238
Appendix 3: Employee engagement risk assessment 240
Appendix 4: Reputation risk assessment 241

Glossary 243
References 245
Further reading 249
Index 250

ACKNOWLEDGEMENTS

I am most grateful to both Peter Neville Lewis of Principled Consulting for generously giving me his time to discuss the relationship between ethics and risk, and the Institute of Risk Management for allowing me to reproduce some of its more recent work. A big thank you also goes to Lynn White from WDI Consulting Limited for her input to Chapter 2 on Organizational Context, and Graham Snuggs of Talent Assured for his help with Chapter 5 on Recruitment. Finally, I would like to acknowledge the contribution to Chapter 10 from Kevin Lovell, Learning Strategy Director at KnowledgePool, the managed learning service provider.

PREFACE

The purpose behind this book is to plug a large gap in the market by introducing the concept of employee risk management to employers. It is a simple process that allows organizations to identify, manage and reduce the potential threats and vulnerabilities that come with every employee (as well as other groups such as contractors, volunteers, interns and agency temps). This is from recruitment through to the end of the employment relationship. These threats include diverse topics such as managing: 1) employee social media use in order to safeguard business reputation; 2) the new problems that an ageing workforce will present over the coming years; and 3) concerns about remote working, such as data security, data protection risks as well as reduced productivity.

This book will be of most value to those tasked with reducing the risks that could harm the financial viability and reputation of their organization, as well as those who would like to be better equipped to predict emerging employee-related threats. Whilst some reference is made to UK employment law, the principles and ideas in this book can easily be applied to many other jurisdictions. For HR practitioners, this book covers the key aspects of an employee risk management approach from the planning stages through to the assessment's completion. It also offers a number of ideas to help HR become far more business savvy and to get involved in new areas. For risk professionals such as risk managers or internal auditors who are interested in employee risk as a project area, or a future audit topic, this book provides a one-stop shop of useful reference material.

Chapter 1 introduces the concept of employee risk management, whilst Chapter 2 places it within the organizational context. This is to establish the links between topics such as culture and ethics and how they influence the level of employee risk taking that is likely to be found within an organization. Chapter 3 covers pre-assessment groundwork, such as project planning and advice on how to present an effective business case to help gain senior-level support. Guidance on how to carry out the assessment itself is covered in Chapter 4, as is advice on how to incorporate emerging threats and horizon scanning into the process. Chapters 5 to 11 look at key topics such as recruitment, social media and the end of employment. Each describes the main areas that an organization should assess and why. Avoiding common problems, such as how to successfully manage and communicate the change, is covered in Chapter 12. Diagrams, checklists and a sample risk assessment are also included.

How employee risk management can help safeguard an organization's reputation: a theme continually revisited throughout this book.

Introducing employee risk management

01

Have you ever considered the damage that even one employee can do to your organization? Perhaps if Barings Bank had done so, a derivatives trader by the name of Nick Leeson would not have been able to bring down one of the world's oldest merchant banks in 1995. Equally, do you assume that groups of senior employees can be trusted to not act in a manner that will cost the organization millions or damage its reputation? Mid Yorkshire Hospitals NHS Trust probably thought so before it was forced to pay Dr Eva Michalak £4.5 million in compensation. This followed a campaign of bullying, harassment and sex and race discrimination orchestrated by several senior employees, including the human resources (HR) director. In the United States, JP Morgan Chase had to pay regulatory bodies £572 million (US $920 million) due to senior management's failure to deal with the threats presented by what is known as the 'London Whale' trades. The common denominator in all three examples is the existence of an organizational culture that allowed such risky employee behaviour to flourish.

Introduction

This is where an employee risk management approach comes in. Risk management is conventionally used to assess how threats and vulnerabilities, such as safety hazards, can affect individuals. But what it does not do is put the workforce at the heart of the assessment as the potential source of the threats. Adopting an employee risk management approach shows the harm that individual and group activities can have on unwary employers. Failure to identify, assess and manage these threats can increase the likelihood of legal liability and damage profit margins. In a nutshell, this is what the concept of employee risk management is about. The purpose of this book is to explain it, describe what areas it covers and show how it can help with HR-related compliance and good practice. A brief introduction is also included here on how the adoption of an employee risk management approach can enhance the profile of HR within an organization, along with a brief overview into how employee risk management can help safeguard an organization's reputation: a theme continually revisited throughout this book.

An overview

The concept of employee risk management comes into its own by focusing on how the actions of employees and others within an organization – such as the board, individual directors, contractors and agency staff – can harm an employer. It is not just limited to compliance issues, but covers a range of threats and vulnerabilities that can originate from the workforce: either as individuals or collectively. It does so by identifying, assessing and prioritizing these threats and vulnerabilities, and then devising a strategy to eliminate, reduce or otherwise manage those found. As a concept, risk management is usually associated with areas such as finance or health and safety. However, its principles can equally be applied to the management of employee risk in the HR context.

I have deliberately used the term 'employee risk management' rather than the better known 'people risk management'. This is because the former specifically refers to a situation where some kind of employment relationship exists, even if a loose one. So it refers not only to employees but other types of individual commonly found in organizations, such as agency staff and self-employed contractors and consultants. It has a broad remit as it covers all grades from the board down to the most junior employee. Outsourcing is also covered due to its increased use by many organizations in recent years. Whilst employers often see outsourcing as an easy route to cost savings, it is not a risk-free strategy. This is due to the reputation damage that may be caused by those who act in an organization's name and are assumed to be employees, but who are not on the payroll. Outsiders such as regulators, shareholders and customers are not included.

The word 'risk' has many definitions that vary according to the particular discipline that is assessing it. For the purposes of this book, I have used it to refer to the likelihood of an organization being harmed by a threat or a loss of some kind, and how serious the harm could be. Risk management itself refers to the process that systematically identifies, assesses and prioritizes these threats and then devises a strategy to manage them. However, its principles can also be applied to the management of employee risk. This could be as a standalone exercise or part of a wider enterprise risk review. For example, an employer may have already adopted a model of HR risk management as an internal review mechanism that is carried out by HR itself. Alternatively, it may be an area of interest for internal audit (where applicable). If so, employee risk could be seen as a component of a wider HR risk management strategy. Although risk is often seen as something negative for an organization, it can be positive if approached and managed effectively – in that it can lead to more innovative and better working practices.

Areas covered

As employee risk management covers any area where the activities of one or more individuals can harm an organization, its remit is potentially vast. For example, it could be one employee's poor password security that allows cybercriminals to infect the employer's computer network. Or it could be an interviewer asking illegal questions during a recruitment process, which then exposes the employer to a discrimination lawsuit. The availability of resources, or preference, will dictate whether an employer explores only one area of risk management, or multiple areas, at a time. Alternatively, the decision may be taken to invest time into carrying out an organization-wide review into how employee risk is managed. This book (in terms of layout and content) assumes that it is the latter. If this is not the case, however, and risk topics are being assessed in isolation, the chapters can easily be read on a pick and mix basis. Where a comprehensive organization-wide exercise will be undertaken, it is important not to underestimate the time involved in identifying the areas to include. Also, mapping them out will require input from other disciplines than HR in order to ensure that nothing important gets left out. There are several different ways of deciding what areas should be covered.

The first is to identify the different categories that comprise the 'workforce'. This includes the obvious groupings such as directors, employees, agency staff and self-employed contractors. However, it also includes those who are not considered to be workers for the purposes of employment legislation, such as genuine volunteers and interns. It can also include outsourcing, because in the eyes of customers, these third-party workers are effectively employees. The next stage is to identify the specific areas that will comprise the employee risk assessment. If it is to be thorough and look at an employer from the top down and inside out, it must consider a range of organizational factors, such as culture and the attitude to risk taking (see Chapter 2). It could also examine how the HR function is regarded. Without this, it will be difficult to obtain a full picture as to how well the policies and procedures it produces are viewed.

At this point, decisions on what else to include could be taken from different sources. One option is to look at regulatory requirements, such as compliance with anti-discrimination legislation, for example on age. Another is to examine 'employee' characteristics, such as ill health, obesity or remote workers. Alternatively, employment-related documentation could be reviewed, including the staff handbook and any outsourcing agreements that exist. Priority could then be given to known problems, such as poor disciplinary investigations and a weak social media policy. Alternatively, topic selection can be based on the employment life cycle. This would start with recruitment and work through different areas culminating with the end of employment. Last but not least is a different approach, which looks at key areas of concern. These could be based on those concerns already known to be an issue or suspected weakness in the organization, such as lack of employer control over employee use of social media. The best solution will be to combine these in order to arrive at the coverage that would best serve an organization's particular needs and budget (see Figure 1.1).

Improving legal compliance

A key advantage offered by an employee risk management approach is that it should reduce the likelihood of employment tribunal claims being brought (or threatened). This is because the focus moves to how those responsible for interpreting employment law requirements actually identify, interpret and follow them in practice (see Chapter 10). In this respect, this exercise also becomes a form of 'gap analysis' on how to move from the current state to a desired future state (see Chapter 4). If done well, it will identify any shortcomings in how quickly new or amended employment legislation and case law developments are reviewed and acted upon. It also offers a real-time picture of the level of employee risk that an organization actually faces: it moves the focus onto what an employee actually does in practice, rather than a theoretical review of what a company's mission statement and HR policies

FIGURE 1.1 Areas of coverage

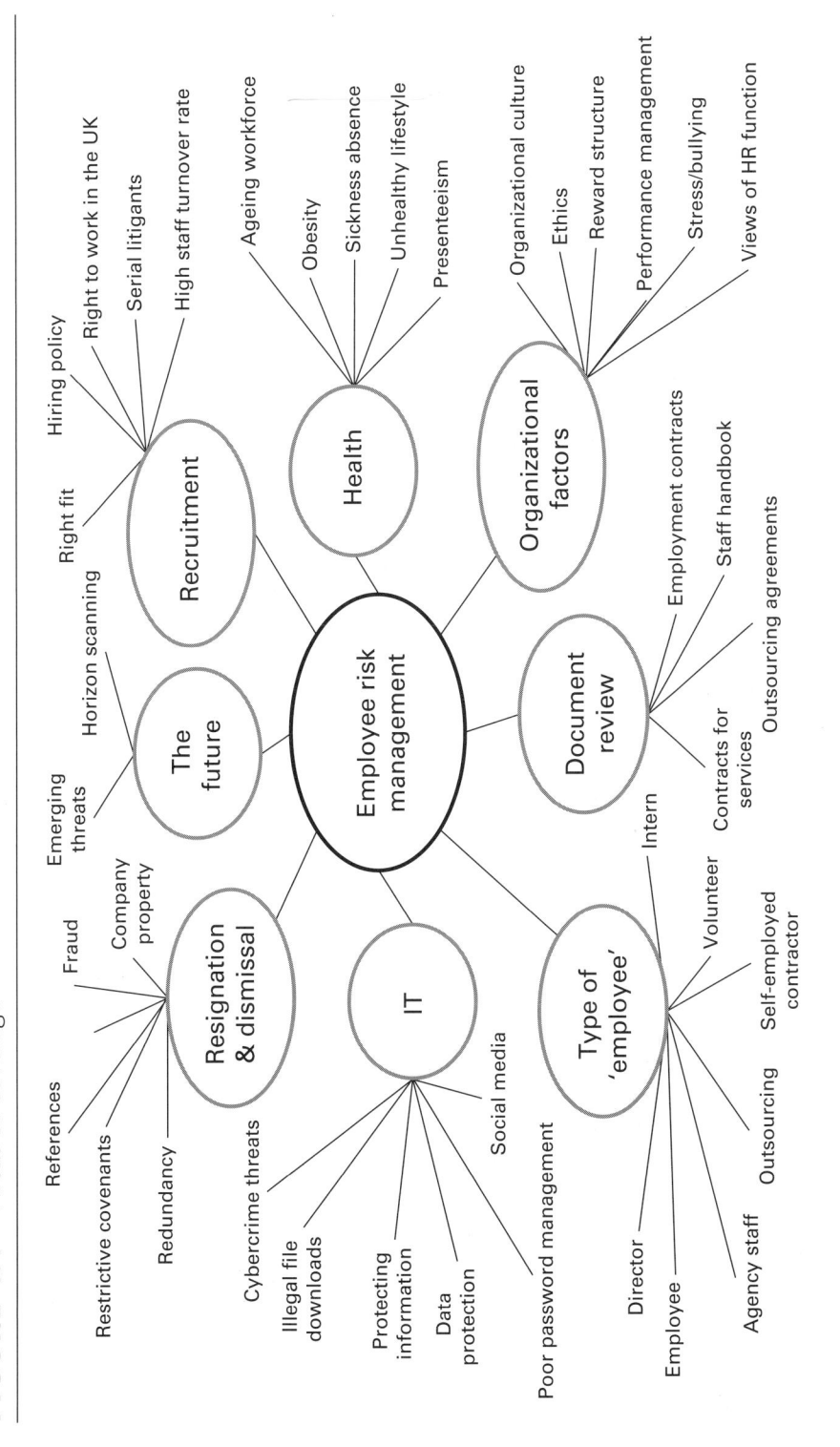

says happens. In other words, the best drafted procedures will not prevent tribunal and other civil court claims if they are not followed.

For example, a textbook disciplinary procedure may exist, but the reality could be a high number of disciplinary hearings and subsequent appeals. A risk management approach can unearth the following: 1) line management failure to deal with problems informally; 2) weak or biased investigations; 3) poorly conducted hearings; and 4) managers failing to follow procedure. If this is so, closer investigation is necessary. A risk-based approach will look for the existence of specific trends, such as a higher incidence of disciplinary hearings in some sites or departments over others. If so, it could be down to a more confrontational or bullying style of management. The risk assessment could continue by drilling down to looking at what training is provided to managers. This would not only be on carrying out a disciplinary investigation, but also on conflict management and the need for early intervention in conduct and capability matters. It could also look at wider issues such as what extra pressures managers may be under locally that do not apply elsewhere.

Enhancing HR's profile

The HR function could benefit from being the initiator of an employee risk management review. Providing it retains ownership of the process, it will provide an opportunity to demonstrate to the board its business acumen and value. This is especially the case for large companies that are subject to regulatory controls, such as Sarbanes–Oxley for public companies in the United States and CLERP 9 for their Australian equivalents. In the UK, listed companies are required to comply with the UK Corporate Governance Code (and other organizations may choose to follow its principles as good practice). The relevant section is Section C.2, which makes the board responsible: 'for determining the nature and extent of the significant risks it is willing to take in achieving its strategic objectives. The board should maintain sound risk management and internal control systems.'

It can be argued that the workforce could present a significant risk if various negative factors combine. For example, a disengaged workforce is more likely to perform badly, take time off sick and raise grievances. These problems are not UK-specific and will be costly in terms of money and time to any organization, making them of legitimate concern to shareholders. Thus HR can use the employee risk management process to enhance its standing and involvement in certain strategic areas, achieved via the promotion of specific recommendations made in its assessment procedure. So, supposing there is a high staff turnover of employees within four months of starting, HR could recommend that employer brand management is deployed to combat this (see Chapter 5). It would then position itself to lead the activity and, in so doing, start or continue to embed HR as a business function in its own right. This perception of HR is vitally important, especially as recent research by KPMG International, 'Rethinking Human Resources in a changing world' (2012), found that only 17 per cent of its respondents maintain that HR 'does a good job of demonstrating its value to the business' (see Chapter 10).

Safeguarding business reputation

Taking an employee risk management approach can also help to safeguard an organization's reputation, since it acts as an early warning system to the type of situation or behaviour that can lead to problems if allowed to continue. Since the rapid rise in the use of social media, the need to have a finger on the corporate pulse has never been greater. Criticizing an employer to anyone who will listen in the local pub is one thing. But a one-sentence rant on Facebook or Twitter can go viral and reach millions very quickly. In fact, IBM has recognized the potential impact of social media in its risk assessment process. As a consequence, it has added it as an extra dimension, which it has termed 'velocity', due to the speed of impact that social media can have on an organization in today's increasingly connected world.

Another advantage in taking a risk-based approach is that it can be used to focus solely on reputation risk. Equally, it could be named as one of several different areas that will be incorporated into a much wider review. In practice, the deciding factor will be how urgent it is to carry out a review into existing and emerging reputation threats for a particular organization. This can be answered by looking at whether or not there is already evidence of underlying problems that, if not dealt with, can leave an employer vulnerable. These could occur across the organization or be more localized within specific sites or teams. The key point here is that those making a preliminary assessment must be honest and not be tempted to ignore known or suspected issues. Whilst doing so might make for a more palatable report for the C-suite, it will only store up trouble for the future. This is simply because underlying threats and vulnerabilities will remain, irrespective of how they are glossed over.

For those unsure of what to look for, threats to reputation are more likely to occur if one or more of the following 'trigger points' are known to exist:

- disengaged employees;
- high staff-turnover rates;
- higher than expected levels of sickness absence;
- deteriorating employee performance;
- incidences of whistle-blowing;
- industrial sabotage, ie theft of confidential information;
- weak financial controls that have led to theft and/or fraud;
- key teams leaving to compete directly/work for competitors.

Chapter summary

In the context of employee risk management, an 'employee' includes the following:

- director;
- employee;
- self-employed consultant/contractor;
- worker;
- agency staff;
- outsourced staff;
- intern;
- volunteer.

Employee risk management:

- focuses on the potential harm that 'employees' can cause;
- looks at a wide range of threats and vulnerabilities, including those that are emerging;
- identifies, assesses and devises a strategy to reduce or otherwise manage these threats and vulnerabilities;
- can form part of a wider enterprise risk assessment;
- helps improve legal compliance;

- will help HR demonstrate business acumen;
- is leverage for HR involvement in new areas such as employer branding.

Identifying areas to include can be done by:

- types of 'employee';
- types of characteristic protected by anti-discrimination legislation, eg age;
- other characteristics, such as ill health, obesity or remote workers;
- organizational factors, including culture and attitudes to risk taking;
- documentation, eg staff handbook, employment contracts and contracts for services;
- mapping out key stages in the employment life cycle, eg recruitment and dismissal;
- key areas of concern, such as threats to business reputation.

Threats to reputation are likely to arise where the following trigger points exist:

- disengaged employees;
- high staff-turnover rates;
- higher than expected levels of sickness absence;
- deteriorating employee performance;
- incidences of whistle-blowing;
- industrial sabotage;
- weak financial controls that have led to theft and/or fraud;
- key teams leaving to compete directly/work for competitors.

Chapter 2 looks at the organizational context of employee risk management, including culture, its determinants and how it influences attitudes to risk taking.

The organizational context

02

Introduction

As a concept, employee risk management cannot be fully understood without placing it within the context of the organization itself. This is because such an entity, be it a company, government department or a charity, is largely its workforce. In turn, this workforce will be part of a unique culture that determines the type of individual employed. It is this culture that also dictates the prevailing attitude to risk in general. In addition, each individual will also have their own perception of risk that they will bring to an employer, as well as their own personal ethical values. The first part of this chapter looks at these factors and how they influence employee risk taking, both individually and collectively. It also examines how an organization's leadership can introduce its own threats and vulnerabilities into the mix, as well as how the perception of the HR function influences how it will be viewed internally. Finally, the chapter introduces some work produced by the Institute of Risk Management (IRM), which offers a framework for how the management of risk (including employee risk) can be improved.

Organizational culture

A brief overview

Organizational culture refers to the personality of an organization and 'how we do things around here'. According to Deal and Kennedy (2000), its main determinant arises from the business environment itself. In other words, an organization's reality in the marketplace is largely influenced by its products and services, customers, competitor activities, prevailing technology and regulatory framework. Values are also important as it is these that define what an organization stands for and what it establishes as standards for achievement. Where these values are strong, the organizational structure tends to be set up to reflect them. For example, companies that operate on high-volume turnover with low profit margins require tight cost control. This is reflected in the high status given to those operating on the financial side and their presence in top management positions. Where commercial success relies heavily on research and development (R&D), premium salaries and status are instead conferred on those working in these areas.

Other influences come from the language of anthropology. For example, those who strongly embody the organization's values are described as 'heroes' and become part of its mythology. This could be a charismatic founder, such as Virgin's Richard Branson or Apple's Steve Jobs, or an ordinary employee who invented a new process. There are also 'rites and rituals'. Rites show staff what is expected via rules and procedures; rituals include activities such as award ceremonies or after-work drinks. There may also be symbolism, such as corporate logos and status symbols. In all cases, their purpose is to reinforce the message of what the organization represents and how it defines success. Last but not least, there is the informal network. Sometimes referred to as a 'hidden' or 'cultural' network, it represents the main channel of communication. In other words, the source of what really happens rather than the official 'corporate-speak'. In fact, knowing who the right people are to get insight from is vital when doing the groundwork for an employee risk assessment!

Taken together, these elements are what differentiate one organization from another. For example, the underlying values and beliefs of a small charity will vary considerably from those of a commercial law firm operating in a highly competitive market. They will also be communicated in markedly different ways. For example, with a small charity, its CEO is likely to be the main source for transmitting its values, whereas a commercial law firm is likely to rely heavily on a slick induction process and glossy internal communications. There will also be established norms for behaviour and ways of working. Newcomers quickly learn what is expected of them via induction programmes and probation. If their face fits, employment is confirmed and the newcomer becomes an accepted part of the 'tribe'. Throughout their employment, they will usually be subject to regular appraisals, which, apart from assessing how well they perform in their role, will be another opportunity to reinforce organizational values and beliefs. Whether these are positive or not is another matter entirely.

How culture influences risk taking

The dangers of 'groupthink'

Organizational culture plays a key role in determining attitudes to risk taking. This is because culture is created by those at the top with the power to impose their own values and beliefs onto the workforce. One factor in influencing this is the degree to which groupthink operates amongst the C-suite or managing board. This arises where groups desire a state of conformity to the extent that conflict is minimized and healthy debate on acceptable levels of risk taking is discouraged. As a result, probable threats and vulnerabilities inherent in a specific course of action are either not considered, or ignored. Also, the group dynamics evolve to such a degree that any independent thinkers will be deemed to be showing disloyalty to the group. By discouraging dissension, the groupthink mentality is elevated to a state where its members start believing in their own invincibility. This leads to a belief that their leadership and decision making is the only way forward – and thus the group becomes increasingly isolated from its workforce. As a consequence, directors, both as individuals and collectively, can introduce many threats and vulnerabilities into their organization.

The reason that groupthink can gain a foothold is due to the homogeneity of the decision makers. Since the recent banking crisis, much has been made of the fact that the boards of many private companies are dominated by white middle-aged men from similar social backgrounds (in other words 'male, pale and stale'). One reason for this is that it is natural to recruit in your own image. This is a safety factor, as it is assumed that those who are similar will share the same values and beliefs. In turn, this further reinforces and perpetuates the groupthink mentality. Also, headhunters wish to keep the fees rolling in by forwarding the same type of candidates that they successfully fielded before. In fact, it was only after the global downturn that the homogeneity of boards was seriously challenged. For example, Christine Lagarde (Head of the International Monetary Fund) commented, 'if it was the Lehman Sisters, the crisis might look quite different'. This has led to pressure within the European Union for the introduction of quotas to get more women on boards.

The role of ethics

The type and degree of risk taking deemed acceptable is influenced by ethics. This is defined as the moral principles governing or influencing conduct. Naturally, the ethical tone will be set from the top and filter downwards. So if directors set a bad example, their behaviour will be emulated. A contributory factor here is the impact that an employee's own ethical standards will have on their behaviour and willingness to take risks. Peter Neville Lewis (IRM, 2012) has stated that 'managing risk is all about people making the best decisions. It is not just about strategy and tactics – it is even more about the judgements and behaviours of people.' He offers examples of several ethical businesses that continue to get it right. These include John Lewis in the UK, UPS and Southwest Airlines in the United States and Mondragon in Spain. All have been in business for many years without jeopardizing their existence through poor decision making and reckless behaviours. Plus, they have all developed sustainable and ethical business models, which have been integral to their success.

It also follows that the ethics laid down from the top can affect reputation. Unfortunately, this is something that organizations can overlook in terms of its impact on long-term business viability. One example is Ryanair, the budget Irish airline. In 2010 it had the dubious distinction of being named by Covalence, a Swiss research company, as one of the world's most unethical companies. Covalence had compiled a list of the most ethical by examining 581 companies using 45 different criteria and Ryanair came in at number 575. This was mainly due to its policy of levying hidden charges against its customers. Since then, Ryanair was voted the worst airline for customer service by *Which?* magazine. These two instances – along with shareholder criticism and two profit warnings in 2013 – made Ryanair's CEO, Michael O'Leary, finally realize that his credo of 'all publicity is good publicity' was not good for long-term business success. So, in autumn 2013, he announced the appointment of a marketing director, an end to its 'macho' customer-services practices and that he would become far less visible.

There is also a well-established link between a lack of ethics and its effect on greed. The example of Ryanair also applies here, but the best examples come from the recent banking crisis. In the quest for short-term financial gain that rewarded excessive risk taking, many banks lost sight of ethical values such as the pursuit of a responsible and sustainable business that looks to the needs of all its stakeholders, including customers. Yet, it was not always like this, as banks once used to be seen as respected and ethical institutions. So, in fact, it is more a case of disappearing ethics, which then triggered a loss of respect.

This was a theme of Greg Smith's resignation letter to Goldman Sachs published in the US media in 2012. Smith had been employed as an executive director and head of the firm's US equity derivatives business in Europe, the Middle East and Africa. In an article entitled 'Why I am leaving Goldman Sachs', published in the *New York Times* on 14 March 2012, Smith described what he believed to be the 'decline of the firm's moral fiber'. This, he argued, had allowed it to morph into a culture that he described as having become 'toxic'. He attributes it to a change in how leadership was viewed. It had moved from ethical concepts built around 'ideas, setting an example and doing the right thing' to a scenario in which – providing someone was not an 'axe murderer' – making enough money was all that mattered. Smith attributed this loss of the firm's culture to the influence of the president and CEO in place at the time of his resignation. Although Goldman Sachs responded promptly to defend itself, it is not known what damage the contents of this article did to its reputation and its client base, particularly given that it was followed up by a US $1.5 million advance for a book deal for Smith to fully expose the corporate culture at the bank.

A major problem for Goldman Sachs and other banks has been the link between high levels of risk taking and the resulting financial rewards. However, much of this is down to the short-term focus that dominates the City of London and Wall Street. The result is an organizational culture obsessed with immediate financial gain, rather than longer-term planning and effective risk management. Instead, individuals were actively encouraged to bring in as much money as possible, even though senior staff often lacked understanding of the product or the risk attached to it. If things went wrong later on, there were no repercussions for those involved. This is partly due to the culture of high staff turnover, which meant that there was no financial incentive for anyone to look at the long-term implications of their actions. Given this reality, HR lacked sufficient clout at board level to rein in the excesses of these reward systems. This short-termism can be found in many companies, albeit to a lesser degree.

This culture of greed had become so entrenched that the damage to business reputation was not enough to prompt decisive action from the top. A substantial part of this is down to the groupthink mentality and the leadership's physical isolation from the workforce. Instead, profligate pay awards are still in evidence. For example, the independent, non-party think tank, the High Pay Centre (2013), found that UK high-street banks paid nearly 1,000 senior bankers over £1 million in bonuses in 2012 alone. This was accompanied by redundancies and pay freezes for the rest of the workforce. Such a damaging culture inevitably had a negative impact on the rank and file worker. According to the Chartered Institute of Personnel and Development (CIPD), *Employee Outlook: Focus on Rebuilding Trust in the City* (2013), fewer than one in three employed in financial services (outside senior management ranks) say that they are proud to work in the sector. Over 1,000 employees were interviewed and 65 per cent believe that some individuals in their business are being rewarded in a way that encourages poor behaviour.

So it is not surprising that in 2013, the UK's Chartered Institute of Internal Auditors updated its guidance to its members working in financial services. It recommends that internal audit should extend its scope to specifically examine the risk and control culture of the organization. This involves assessing whether or not decision making and the 'tone at the top' fits with the stated values, ethics and policies of the organization. The advice given in the publication is to assess the attitude and approach taken at all management levels towards risk management. Interestingly, this expressly includes looking at poor customer treatment that could lead to conduct or reputational threats. It goes on to suggest that internal audit should evaluate whether or not the organization is acting 'with integrity' in how it deals with customers and interacts with relevant markets. The point about relevant markets is a nod to the massive fines levied on several banks by the EU regulator for the LIBOR and EURIBOR scandal. Deutsche Bank had the largest fine at €725.36 million. Others fined include Royal Bank of Scotland and France's Société Générale.

Relationship to how HR is perceived

The organizational culture will heavily influence how HR is regarded. If, for example, it is seen as merely a support function separate from the real decision making, there will be no HR presence in the C-suite. In fact, according to Groysberg, Kelly and MacDonald in their *Harvard Business Review* article 'The New Path to the C-suite' (March 2011), HR is still struggling to gain influence. In qualitative interviews with global business leaders, they found that whilst the top people-management roles exist, they are being populated by non-HR professionals from other disciplines such as corporate law, operations or marketing. This is largely due to the preference of CEOs for 'metrics-driven' leaders. In fact, this research found that the HR role was still viewed mainly as being administrative with HR directors mainly relegated to managing policies and cultural initiatives. In other words, HR is marginalized to more 'fluffy' activities that are not at the heart of the business.

The problem comes back to the organizational culture and the tone from the top. The harsh reality is that if the C-suite or equivalent decision makers have questionable ethics, and are inclined towards reckless behaviour, they are hardly likely to employ the type of HR director who will challenge it. If they do, that individual's tenure is likely to be a short one. There is also the question of remoteness, in that the more isolated senior management is from its workforce, the less likely that HR is to possess a high status. If senior HR staff lack access to the decision makers, and are unable to build relationships with them, the opportunity to be able to influence them is seriously limited. As a result, the C-suite or equivalent leadership are not exposed to the benefits that a good HR function can offer. A classic example of this is the banking sector, where HR lacked the proximity (and authority) to successfully challenge how the reward culture operated. Yet the paradox is that talent management is consistently a major concern of CEOs globally.

Impact of international culture

Another factor that influences the link between culture and risk taking is the particular country under the microscope. Given that cultures vary between countries this is reflected in how different organizations assess and view risk generally. For those operating internationally, it is vital that the differences that will be encountered are understood. The comparative work of social psychologist Geert Hofstede on national culture is useful here. Hofstede has created six 'dimensions' as a means of analysing different cultural values. In the context of propensity to take risks, some of the dimensions he outlines are more relevant than others. For example, he calls one dimension 'individualism–collectivism'. Individualistic societies are those that expect a high degree of self-reliance and for its citizens to look out for themselves and their immediate families. Naturally, this individualist outlook transfers itself to the workplace. So the UK, United States, Canada and Australia score highly here whereas countries such as China and Saudi Arabia score low. Collectivism is the opposite of this, with the dominant focus being on the needs of the group.

A second 'dimension' is 'uncertainty avoidance' (UAI). This reflects the level at which there is discomfort with uncertainty and ambiguity. Countries with low UAI scores demonstrate strong signs of maintaining rigid codes of behaviour and are intolerant of unorthodox behaviour and ideas. The UK is very accepting of uncertainty and is happy to 'muddle through' whereas Japan and Germany are not. A third dimension is 'masculinity–femininity', in which masculinity is concerned with the degree that a country is driven by competition, achievement and success. The UK and Germany scored highly here. In contrast, a feminized society is one focused more on consensus management and work–life balance. Examples of such countries are Sweden and Norway. Unsurprisingly, risk taking is far less acceptable in feminized countries than masculine ones. Just taking these three cultural dimensions and the UK as an example, it is easy to see how a high degree of individualism, high acceptance of uncertainty and a competitive work environment has created a culture where risk taking flourishes.

> **Key point**
>
> Hofstede's website (**http://geert-hofstede.com/countries.html**) gives a free overview of how over 80 countries score on five of his six 'dimensions'. The scores of up to three countries can be compared with each other on a bar chart. This provides a useful starting point for anyone needing background information on how well risk is perceived and tolerated by different nationalities.

Significance of the link between culture and risk taking

Taken together, the topics discussed above are significant because they determine how the leadership reacts to employee risk and how it approaches risk management generally – from minor issues through to those that involve regulatory breaches. In fact, one of the main influences on an organization's risk culture is what form this reaction to risk takes. Ideally, the culture should be one where the reporting of potential threats and vulnerabilities is actively encouraged at all levels of an organization. Done early enough, danger can often be averted. Even if it is not, it still presents a chance to learn from any mistakes by turning them into a learning opportunity. This can then be shared across the organization and used to devise better systems and practices. Equally, there may be opportunities that can be utilized by those organizations that move fast enough to exploit them before their competitors. A good example is organizations that quickly harnessed the power of social media as both a marketing and recruitment tool, rather than just seeing the downsides.

The global consulting firm McKinsey has examined the traits of strong risk cultures and the part that risk managers have to play. In its article 'Managing the people side of risk', published in McKinsey Insights in May 2013, Krivkovich and Levy found that a key trait is being able to respond to emerging threats quickly. Another is the ability to break through rigid governance mechanisms to get the right people on board to tackle them. They also recognize that acknowledging risk requires a certain confidence. Not only must the environment (and its senior management) be strong enough to support this approach, but the policy framework must also be robust enough. Such a culture is likely to exist in an organization that openly discusses risk and looks for emerging trends (see Chapter 4). Unfortunately, though, such transparency and forward thinking is uncommon. Instead, there is either a flourishing blame culture, or attempts are made to ignore or suppress what is happening.

A good example of suppression is the US retailer Wal-Mart and the allegations made against it by a whistle-blowing employee in 2005. These involved the payment of alleged bribes worth over US $24 million to Mexican officials. Their purpose was to facilitate the speedy purchase of construction permits that would enable Wal-Mart de Mexico to achieve rapid market dominance with their stores. The company sent in investigators who found evidence of payments, as well as the fact that Wal-Mart de Mexico's leadership had deliberately concealed their existence from Wal-Mart's US headquarters. In the report, the lead investigator recommended that the investigation be widened, as it was believed that both US and Mexican laws had been violated. Yet, following an independent examination by the *New York Times*, it appears that Wal-Mart's bosses shut down the investigation. Not only this, but no law enforcement official in either country had been notified of developments.

In an article entitled 'Vast Mexico Bribery Case Hushed Up by Wal-Mart After Top-Level Struggle' published in the *New York Times* on 21 April 2012, reporter David Barstow also said that no one was disciplined. In fact, Wal-Mart de Mexico's chief executive, who was named as the driving force behind the bribery, was promoted to vice chairman of Wal-Mart. Until media involvement in the affair, it appears that much time and effort had been spent on damage control rather than getting to grips with the scale of criminality involved. One example of this was a rapid modification of protocols for internal investigations. Its purpose was to give those being investigated more control over the process and to add layers of bureaucracy, such as requiring a cost-benefit analysis before agreeing to a full investigation. Only when the allegations against Wal-Mart were published, did Wal-Mart inform the US Justice Department of possible violations of federal law.

Improving organizational culture

All the examples given above are of environments where the organizational culture needs to be reviewed and changed. Until this happens, sufficient buy-in to the adoption of an employee risk management approach is unlikely. If it does occur, it will have only a limited impact as the senior level support essential to its embedding throughout the organization will be lacking. To combat this, two pieces of work produced by the IRM (as set out below) provide frameworks on what a healthy risk culture looks like. The first is a generic model on risk (see Table 2.1) and the other is a questionnaire on ethics. They have been chosen because: 1) they are straightforward and not complicated; 2) they are compatible with each other and the concept of employee risk management; and 3) both offer new opportunities for HR to proactively contribute to improving an organization's employee risk culture. Another advantage is that both models can be used together, as they complement each other.

The model is fairly self-explanatory. Developed by the IRM, it is called a 'Risk Culture Aspects Model' (Hindson: IRM, 2012). This model proposes eight 'aspects', grouped into four 'themes'. All must be in place to ensure that an organization has a healthy risk culture.

TABLE 2.1 Risk culture aspects model

Theme	
Tone at the top	Risk leadership: clarity of direction • senior management set clear and consistent expectations for managing risks • leaders role model risk management thinking and actively discuss tolerance to risk issues Responding to bad news: welcoming disclosure • senior management actively seeking out information about risk events • those that are open and honest about risks are recognized
Governance	Risk governance: taking accountability • management are clear about their accountability for managing business risks • role descriptions and targets include risk accountabilities Risk transparency: risk information flowing • timely communication of risk information across the organization • risk events are seen as an opportunity to learn
Competency	Risk resources: empowered risk function • the risk function has a defined remit and has the support of leaders • it is able to challenge how risks are managed Risk competence: embedded risk skills • a structure of risk champions support those managing risks • training programmes are in place for all staff
Decision making	Risk decisions: informed risk decisions • leaders seek out risk information in supporting decisions • the business's willingness to take on risks is understood and communicated Rewarding appropriate risk-taking • performance management linked to risk-taking • leaders are supportive of those actively seeking to understand and manage risks

Reproduced with kind permission of the Institute of Risk Management

Whilst this model refers to both risk in general and the existence of a dedicated risk function, it can easily be used in the context of employee risk. In fact, all four themes of: 1) tone at the top; 2) governance; 3) competency; and 4) decision making are revisited to varying degrees throughout this book (see Chapter 12 in particular). There is a possibility that where risk managers are employed, they may already be familiar with this model (especially if they are members of the IRM). The same applies to any internal audit team in place. If so, the model may already have been implemented in some form or other. Should this be the case, HR could suggest that this model's use be extended to formally incorporate employee risk. Should the model not be already in place, HR could propose its introduction by the board; even if only initially used in the context of managing employee risk.

Where there are also serious concerns over an organization's ethical standards, a questionnaire produced by Peter Neville Lewis for the IRM's document 'Risk Culture: Resources for Practitioners' (2012) can help get it back on track. Equally, it is a good benchmark for those employers who may wish to improve their organization's reputation. The questionnaire is called a 'risk and ethics culture assessment' (RECA) and its purpose is to ensure that the right standards are in place. This is to: 1) minimize risk; 2) protect an organization's reputation; and 3) maximize what Lewis refers to as sustainable profit. This model contains 10 questions that come with the advantage of having a global application and relevance (see box below).

Risk and ethics culture assessment, by Peter Neville Lewis

1. How well disciplined is your organization to meet the emerging public and regulatory demand for demonstrating risk-balanced and ethical decision making in the way you transact business with ALL your stakeholders in the global economy?

2. How clearly does your organization articulate and communicate its values in order to guide risk-balanced and ethical decision making at all levels? Where are the roadblocks to risk evaluation?

3. How well examined is your Values Statement to determine if these are based on true moral values like courage, self-discipline, fairness, trust etc rather than desired outcomes (eg reputation or efficiency)?

4. How committed is your organization to putting moral values and moral purpose, which affect ALL stakeholders, before just value for shareholders?

5 How strongly does your CEO (which might equally imply Chief Ethics Officer) champion a culture for balanced risk taking and decision making – A Culture of Enlightened Integrity?

6 How well emphasized in your Risk Register are 'RIGHT' (see below) decision making and effective measures to mitigate reputational risk caused by careless thinking? Is there a clear framework?

7 How open and properly supported at grass roots are your whistle-blowing culture and speak-up processes, to encourage people at all levels to speak the truth?

8 Have you identified or appointed independent Risk and Ethics Ambassadors at all levels to advise on and monitor risk and ethical dilemmas and to report to appropriate line managers (HR/Legal/Risk if appropriate)?

9 How clearly articulated is your organization's remuneration and reward structure to encourage and reward balanced risk taking and ethical decision making?

10 How firmly is your organization opposed to individual gain and corporate excess in its relations with ALL its stakeholders?'

Reproduced with kind permission of the Institute of Risk Management

Note

'RIGHT' stands for:

- **R-ules:** do we know and operate within them?
- **I-ntegrity:** do we act out ALL 10 moral values that could be held to make up integrity?
- **G-ood:** is our decision making intended to do good? For whom?
- **H-arm:** will our decision making cause unintentional harm? To whom?
- **T-ruth and T-ransparency:** can we stand behind our decision with a clear heart?'

In order to decide what would be the 'RIGHT' thing to do, Peter Neville Lewis created four questions to ask as part of the decision-making process. The first three are as follows: 1) Are you doing the RIGHT thing? 2) Are you doing it in the RIGHT way? and 3) Are you doing it for the RIGHT reasons? He points out that whilst the answer to all three questions may be a 'yes', is this enough? As an example, he points out that most totalitarian regimes would claim that this was the case. So too would many traders who were stoking the US sub-prime crisis. So this is where his fourth question comes in: 4) Is what you are doing based on the RIGHT (moral) values?

As far as an employee risk assessment is concerned, this questionnaire and the accompanying four questions can be used in different ways. Ideally, the assessment will cover the potential threats and vulnerabilities presented to an organization by its leadership (a recurring theme of this chapter). If so, they can be put to members of the board for a response. In the event that the assessment is to incorporate a review of how well the HR function operates (see Chapter 10), all 10 questions should form part of it. Where there is resistance to answering them, some of the points in this chapter can be used to argue the case for doing so. For example, potential reputation damage and diminished employee engagement due to a lack of ethical practices. The link can also be made with the growing need to have a formal corporate social responsibility agenda in place. This is a topic that is becoming increasingly important to younger workers, as well as consumers, and offers HR a good opportunity to assume a leading role in the process (see Chapter 10).

Chapter summary

Organizational culture is:

- 'how we do things around here' (Deal and Kennedy, 2000);
- mainly determined by the business environment itself;
- based on values that determine what the organization stands for;
- bound together by the informal or hidden network of communication;
- reinforced by appraisals, employee rewards and bonuses.

Organizational culture influences the acceptability of risk taking via:

- the extent to which the board is susceptible to 'groupthink';
- where independent thought is discouraged and leaders believe in their own invincibility;
- how physically isolated the top management become from the workforce;
- how homogeneous the board is in terms of being 'male, pale and stale';
- the ethics that the board bring with them, both individually and collectively;
- the manner in which business ethics are set from the top and filtered downwards;
- a link between a lack of ethics and greed that is supported by a short-term business outlook;
- having a weak HR function that lacks the clout to challenge rewards systems;
- a cultural view of how risk taking is viewed in the country that the enterprise operates in.

Organizational culture and how HR is regarded:

- research found that CEOs want 'metrics-driven' leaders in the C-suite;
- top people-management roles are taken by non-HR professionals;
- the more isolated the board, the less likely HR is to possess a high status;
- isolation means that HR lacks the opportunity to demonstrate its value;
- organizational culture and how HR is regarded:
  - will influence how well the workforce respects and follows HR policies;
  - determines whether HR is seen as value adding or merely a support function.

The link between culture and risk taking is significant as it:

- determines how senior management will react to unavoidable problems;
- influences whether or not staff feel they can report potential threats and vulnerabilities;
- defines whether or not serious problems are treated as a learning opportunity.

Improving the culture:

- is necessary to obtain buy-in to an employee risk management approach;
- board level commitment is needed in order to embed it throughout the organization;
- can be achieved by using the IRM's 'Risk Culture Aspects Model' – this looks at 'tone at the top', governance, competence and decision making;
- can be achieved by incorporating a risk and ethics culture assessment (RECA) into the organization.

Chapter 3 looks at the essential pre-assessment groundwork that should be covered before the project starts.

Pre-assessment groundwork   03

Introduction

Once the go-ahead has been given to carry out an employee risk assessment, some pre-assessment groundwork must be covered first. This is to ensure that the process goes smoothly and to identify possible problems from the outset. For this reason, this chapter considers a number of different areas that can cause difficulties if not anticipated early on. The first of these is the need to identify the most appropriate individuals to get involved in the project. The second is to see how this exercise links to other disciplines within the organization, as some relevant work may already exist. Equally, there may be other processes being used that the assessment can feed into, such as 'lean thinking'. If trade unions are recognized, a key consideration is whether they should be included and, if so, what form that involvement should take. Good project management skills are crucial, so the need for pre-planning is also covered, as is advice on compiling a business case to justify the project.

Project planning

Coverage

There is no single right way of approaching this task as the exact coverage of an employee risk assessment will be influenced by the nature of each organization and those working for it. As mentioned, the best starting point is to differentiate 'employees' into different categories. Apart from directors, employees, agency staff and self-employed contractors, other groupings can be included as appropriate. For example, if volunteers and interns are used, they should be added as they can still present problems. For example, the charity sector is more reliant on volunteers than other sectors and many of these are older people, such as those staffing charity shops. Equally, fast-paced industries such as publishing and fashion use a higher proportion of interns than is found elsewhere, and most are likely to be university graduates in their early twenties. Two very different groups – but each having the ability to present their own challenges if not identified and managed properly. Any outsourced functions should also be included, because poor management of the process has the potential to cause reputation damage (see Chapter 6).

Different types of working practices, such as remote working, can also be included, as they introduce vulnerabilities in terms of data security issues and maintaining productivity. Whilst apprentices and work experience students could be included, they are outside the scope of this book – the reason being that an employer's focus will be health-and-safety orientated due to their ages. However, some of the points made about young workers will also apply to them.

Once the different groups have been identified, one way of proceeding is to look at the various characteristics that an employee may possess and add them to a list. In the UK, this includes those with 'protected characteristics' covered under the Equality Act 2010. This refers to grounds on which discrimination is unlawful. It covers:

- age;
- disability;
- gender reassignment;
- marriage/civil partnership;
- race (caste discrimination will not be included until 2015 at the earliest);
- religion or belief;
- sex (including maternity and pregnancy discrimination); and
- sexual orientation.

Given that legislation governing these areas existed for several years prior to their amalgamation into the Equality Act 2010, most areas should be fairly well managed. If so, the decision may be taken to focus on those still causing difficulties. These concern characteristics that are subject to changing external factors that are affecting the wider population. For example, the realities of an ageing working population will soon start to make themselves known in terms of declining performance and challenges in succession planning. Equally, ill health is a growing issue in respect to soaring obesity rates, especially in the United States and the UK, due to an increasingly unhealthy and sedentary lifestyle, which is also resulting in more of the working population suffering from chronic diseases (see Chapter 7). In turn, this is likely to increase the costs to employers of providing health benefits as their take-up increases. In the UK, cutbacks to disability benefits are resulting in greater numbers of those with protected disabilities seeking jobs.

As a result, some organizations may find themselves dealing with disability issues for the first time, or in sufficient numbers to reveal that they have a weak approach in this area. Pitfalls include knowing what health questions can be legally asked and the making of reasonable adjustments. Closely related are the increasing costs of sickness absence to employers. So issues surrounding age and disability continue to evolve; meaning that they still present threats and vulnerabilities to many employers. For completeness, it is recommended that various organizational factors are included in the risk assessment. One of the most important is to examine the prevailing organizational culture and the impact that it has on risk taking (see Chapter 2). Closely linked to this is the system of reward in operation and the type of behaviour that it encourages. For this reason, any existing bonus system needs to be reviewed to see if the right outcomes are rewarded.

The same applies to performance management; the way an employer views risk will influence the behaviour that is encouraged in its workforce. However, given that performance management is integral to business success but is something that some managers still shy away from, it also merits inclusion in its own right (see Chapter 10). Connected to this is how senior management views and tolerates problems such as stress, which has increased in many organizations in recent years due to recruitment freezes, redundancies and pay cuts. The existence of a hidden or counterculture is also worth including, in respect to the damage that can be caused by a group of workers deliberately acting against their employer's interests. If such a culture exists, the reasons behind it will need to be explored – and will most likely be linked to a distinct lack of employee engagement.

Employee engagement has been defined by the CIPD as 'being positively present during the performance of work by willingly contributing intellectual effort, experiencing positive emotions and meaningful connections to others'. Whilst it is a term that has been in use at least since the early 1990s, it has assumed a new prominence as organizations look for extra competitive advantage. This is due in part to research that has shown the positive impact that employee attitudes can have on business performance. It is also a natural underlying theme of any employee risk assessment that is worth drawing out, given that the level of engagement is a strong influence on employee behaviour – be it for good or for bad. In practice, the more engaged the workforce is, the less likely it will be to indulge in behaviour that will damage the employer's reputation, for example by harming the employer's brand or by delivering poor customer service.

Any assessment incorporating organizational factors could also examine the HR function with regard to its reputation and the respect it engenders throughout the organization. If this is not included, it will be difficult to assess how well the documentation it produces is viewed and complied with in terms of whether or not it serves business needs, is readable and succinct. Non-compliance is more likely if the view of managers and staff towards HR is negative. In turn, this could result in employment tribunal claims and poor publicity. Another area to assess is any training provided and how well targeted it is in meeting both organizational and individual needs. However, if the decision is made to assess HR in this way, those from other departments should be involved to ensure impartiality. This must be considered when selecting those who will form the project team.

At this point, decisions on what else to include can be taken from different sources. If employment-related documentation is to be reviewed, it could include sampling employment contracts from different departments. Their existing clauses could be reviewed for effectiveness and any problem areas could be flagged up for further review. The same principle applies to other documents such as contracts for services. The purpose here would be to ensure that they are watertight and preclude any inference of an employee/employer relationship. Other important documents include the staff handbook, as each subject area could be examined. This might be done alphabetically, or following a prioritizing of areas meriting a closer investigation. For example, there may be known problems, such as substandard data protection compliance, poor disciplinary investigations and a weak social media policy.

Equally, topics may be chosen by viewing them in terms of the employment life cycle, the starting point of which is recruitment and its many pitfalls. This alone covers a variety of areas including the drafting of legally compliant job adverts and robust candidate screening. However, it will also include less obvious areas, such as the importance of having a strong employer brand. At times, there may be a need to make redundancies, and if so, there are several areas that can leave an employer vulnerable, such as weak selection criteria. The same principles apply to end of employment, which includes topics such as giving references, retrieving company property, as well as protecting trade secrets following a key employee's departure.

Another approach is to prioritize existing areas of concern, such as a growing awareness of the link between employee activities and the reputation damage to the employer's brand. In practice, a combination of approaches is likely to work best. This can be complemented by some brainstorming sessions with the project team.

Selecting the project leader

As with any sizeable task, good project management skills are essential, so the designated project manager should be an individual with previous management experience. Ideally, this will have been in a lead role, but if not, it should be someone who has had previous involvement in similar projects. They should also have been with the organization for several years in order to have a good grasp of its culture. Excellent analytical and interpersonal skills are also necessary, as communication with those at all levels will be required. This is always important, but given that this project is based around people issues, it is especially so. The individual chosen should also have sufficient seniority in order to give the project the necessary credibility in the eyes of the workforce. Without this, the entire project could quickly unravel.

Project team skills

Think carefully about the composition of the team that will carry out the risk assessment. For example, to give the project credibility in the eyes of the organization, it should involve at least one specialist from outside HR. One possibility is to involve someone in IT, due to the growth of both cybercrime and potential threats to business reputation from improper social media use. They would also be useful where there are concerns over data security. Although the number of team members depends on the remit, if there are more than four or five participants it can become unwieldy. It would also be useful to be able to draw upon advice from internal audit (in organization's where this exists). Equally, if risk managers are employed, it would make sense to involve them more fully in the process in order to benefit from their expertise. Such a move would also have the advantage that at least one project team member has a formal grounding in risk management. Other than this, team members should have a good balance of skills as follows:

- possess problem-solving, analytical and functional skills;
- be creative thinkers who can 'think outside the box';
- be commercially aware and able to incorporate cost-savings ideas into recommendations;
- have a good knowledge of the organization and its politics;
- be able to make good use of data to support their conclusions and recommendations.

Project objectives

It is vital that the right project is planned for at the outset. So a specification that will yield the best return on investment (ROI) needs to be created, in terms of the time and person hours involved. It is also important to show how the project will fit in with and further the organization's objectives. Given that the purpose of assessing employee risk is to protect business reputation and reduce potential legal liability, this should not be difficult to achieve. In terms of planning, this could be undertaken in various ways. One is to plan it around SMART or SMARTer objectives. The terms used here are only suggestions and can be replaced with others depending on preference. They are as follows:

- **Specific:** one reason that projects fail is because their objectives have not been properly defined at the outset. So if the overall purpose of the exercise is 'to assess the threats and vulnerabilities presented by the workforce in the HR context', first break down this statement. Start by defining what 'threats and vulnerabilities' refer to. For example, threats are known problems, whilst vulnerabilities represent areas where some weakness is thought to exist. Then, define who the 'workforce' is and what the 'HR context' refers to, eg a 'systematic review of all HR policies and procedures to see how well they reflect legal requirements and business needs'.

- **Measurable:** progress must be capable of being tracked and measured. That is the only way that the project team can measure if the objectives have been achieved or not. So, taking the above objective, the project can be measured by adding up the different HR policies and procedures. If the intention is to review compliance with relevant employment laws, then calculate how many apply to the organization and record the number. As each piece of legislation is reviewed, it can then be recorded as a percentage completed.

- **Achievable:** many projects fail due to a lack of realism as to what is involved, for example a project manager who agrees the project scope and timescale, knowing that it is under-resourced. So when deciding what is achievable, look at it from every angle and have evidence to back up the proposed remit and timing.

- **Relevant:** even with a topic whose purpose is legal compliance and protecting the employer's reputation and balance sheet, ensure that the objectives are relevant to the organization's needs. As well as current factors, look ahead for those that will have an impact, such as future legal changes. This is especially important if the intended project is pitched as being an extensive one covering lots of different areas and/or sites.

- **Timebound:** going back to the example of reviewing HR policies and procedures, it could be stated that varying levels of completion will occur over certain time frames. For example, 25 per cent of policies to be reviewed along with any recommendations to be complete in two months' time, 50 per cent to have been completed within four months' time, and so on: if there are 40 separate documents, this works out at 10 per month. Try to build in more time than will be needed, as it always looks good when something is completed early. Doing this will also take the pressure off, if any unanticipated problems arise.

- **Evaluated and reviewed:** once the project gets under way, it needs to be evaluated regularly. This requires a proactive approach and exists to ensure that the project remit continues to be relevant. It also acknowledges that there could be external factors that may require changes or additions to be incorporated. Similarly, one or more objectives may no longer be relevant. This may happen, for example, if a site closes due to unforeseen circumstances, or if some employment legislation is due to be abolished. It also allows for the smoothing out of any minor problems that arise.

Once a project outline has been drafted, consider how best to set out the assessment. This will depend on how wide its remit will be. For example, if several different sites are going to be assessed, it makes sense to make the findings and recommendations site-specific. Then, the layout could be based on individual departments listed alphabetically, and/or the specific area of focus, such as reputation risk (see Appendix 4 for an example), or employment law compliance. When deciding how to do this, the main motivator is the need to make the findings easily readable for the decision makers, such as the board. This means that there could be two versions of the same document. In this case, only those areas given a 'high' or 'medium' risk rating should be included. This is to ensure that the board's focus is only on the most important findings.

> **Key point**
>
> Before the project starts, a communication should be sent from a senior management sponsor saying what it is about. This will also endorse it in the eyes of the workforce.

> **Note**
>
> A project management checklist is provided in Appendix 1 on page 235.

Link to other disciplines and processes

Employee risk overlaps with other disciplines and processes (see Figure 3.1). So as part of the pre-assessment groundwork, look at what others in the organization have done. One reason is diplomacy and to avoid being seen to be encroaching on other departments' work. A second is practicality, as it is pointless to duplicate useful work that others have already undertaken. The logical place to start is with colleagues in areas that overlap with HR.

FIGURE 3.1 Potential overlap with other disciplines

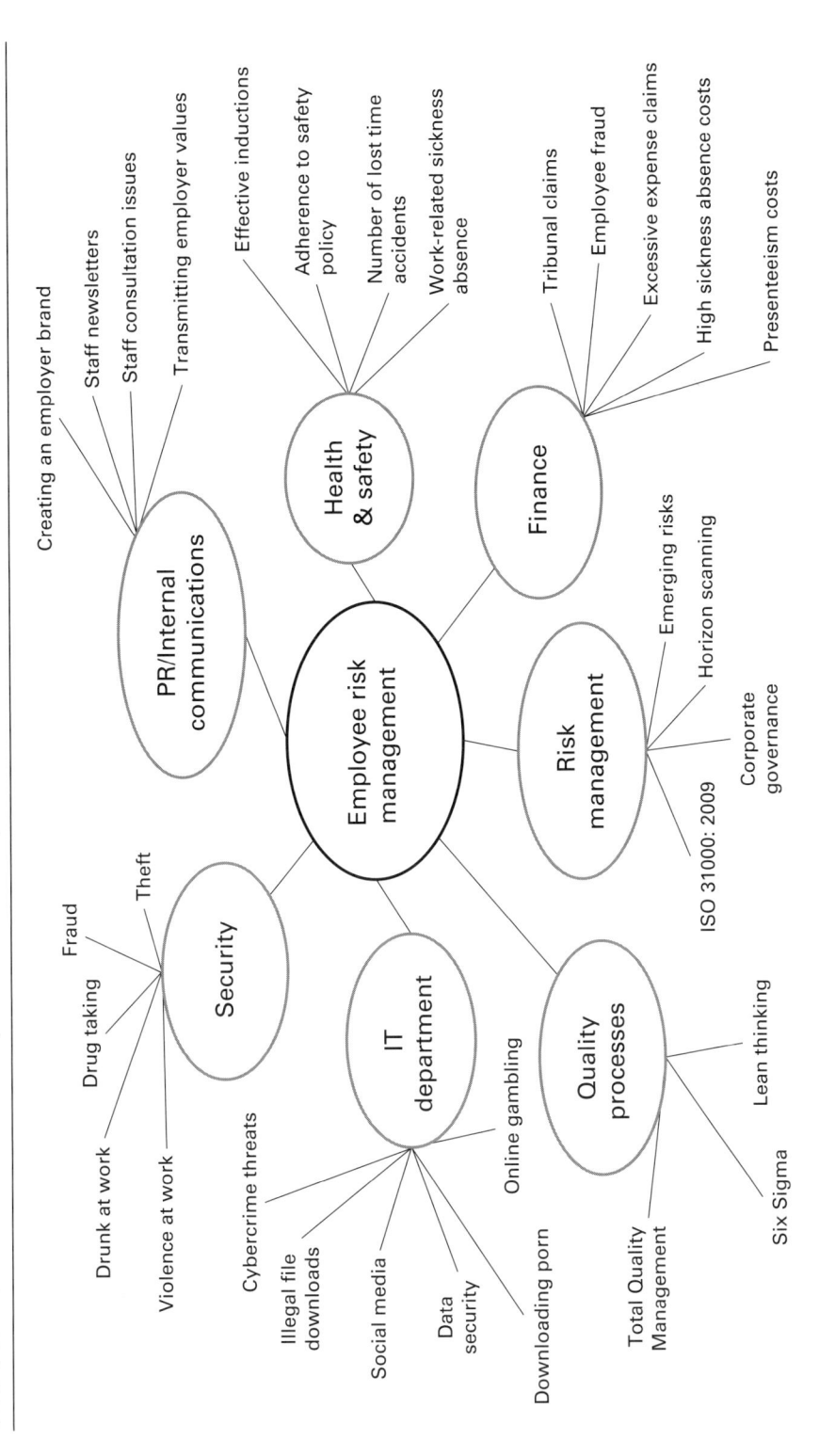

Apart from health and safety and IT, this includes security and finance. For example, security may have witnessed a spate of thefts or fraud. If so, this raises the question of how robust candidate screening is during the selection process. The finance department will also have a mutual interest due to the impact that high sickness absence and costly employment tribunal claims may have on the bottom line. Equally, if there is concern over an increasing expenses bill, finance can usefully input into how the claim process can be tightened up.

Once this has been done, consider other departments to see if there is a potential crossover, such as the internal communications/PR team. This could arise through their role in staff communication on topics such as brand awareness and internal newsletters. Their specialist knowledge would prove helpful where employee engagement levels are low, or, for example, where there has been bad publicity in the media about pay increases. This has been evident during the last few years in various sectors. It includes high salaries still paid to bankers, the culture of excess at the tax-payer-funded BBC and large salaries paid to charity chiefs despite falling donations. There may also be a good fit with other processes that have already been introduced into the organization.

One example is ISO 31000: 2009. Its purpose is to provide principles and generic guidelines on risk management that can be used by any sector. Equally, it can be applied to a diverse range of areas across any risk-based discipline. It is this feature that makes it possible to integrate the many different risk management processes used by different departments within the same organization. So, in other words, risk management objectives can be harmonized for operational, management and strategic tasks. This includes those focused on employee risk management as it can accommodate all three categories. For example, how employees carry out their activities in the course of their employment will count as operational. How they and any wrongdoing or risky behaviours are managed will fit under management; and some of the concepts outlined in other chapters, such as horizon scanning (see Chapter 4), sits nicely with strategy.

Another useful team to approach will be the one dealing with total quality management (TQM) – if such a team exists – or a similar process, such as Six Sigma. Whilst these two concepts have their differences in approach, both utilize various strategies to continually improve the quality of a process, product or service. One way of achieving this is through improving workforce quality. This could be achieved through improved: 1) recruitment practices; 2) induction; 3) targeted training; 4) employee engagement; 5) aligned reward strategies; and 6) team cohesion. These provide a natural fit for greater HR involvement in this type of process. One way of facilitating this is to focus an employee risk management assessment specifically on these six areas. The other is to apply the findings of a much wider assessment where they are relevant.

Another process to link into is 'lean thinking' (Womack and Jones, 2003). This is a set of principles that enables an organization to be more focused, efficient and agile in all areas from waste reduction through to producing better products and services. Lean is a process based on mutual cooperation so that all departments and employees work together. Its purpose is to improve work quality and to eliminate anything that does not add value to the customer. Although historically associated with manufacturing, its principles can be applied to any type of organization, including the public and not-for-profit sectors. It can also be applied to any function. Various findings from an employee risk assessment can potentially contribute to the 'lean' process. One example is better-targeted learning and development initiatives (see Chapter 10). Another is more streamlined policies and procedures. This fits in nicely with 'lean thinking', as more relevant and less bureaucratic procedures will free up managers and staff to focus more on servicing customers and clients.

> **Key point**
>
> The advantage to HR of investing some time in looking for links is that it achieves further integration into the organization as a core business function.

Drafting the business case

Format

Large-scale projects such as those spanning several sites or a wide range of areas are likely to require board approval due to the time commitment involved. This is not just for those taking part, but also for interviewees.

Therefore, a business case to justify the carrying out of an employee risk assessment should be compiled. It should specifically be built around the business drivers at work in the organization. For example, in a government department that has experienced a round of budget cuts, a key driver will be cost-cutting, whereas a technology company reliant on specialist staff must focus on employee satisfaction and engagement in order to retain those with key skills. The precise format of the draft business case will vary according to the type of project being proposed, but in all cases it should be broken down into several sections. This can be done as follows:

- **Purpose:** in this case the main purpose behind the project is to safeguard the organization's reputation and to protect the bottom line through employment law compliance. So, show what the current status quo is costing the organization. This can be done by calculating the outlay involved in any employment tribunals, both in terms of compensation awards, as well as an approximation of the management's time. Other costs that can be included are the direct and indirect costs of sickness absence (see Chapter 7) and staff turnover. Examples of damage to reputation can be evidenced in a temporary drop in share prices or in an online 'favourability' rating (see Chapter 8 for examples), where known.

- **Data sources:** when building the business case, remember that its overriding objective is to demonstrate what the benefits will be of carrying out an employee risk assessment. However, these benefits must be based on hard facts, not assumptions. This is where the use of data sets, especially 'big data', (if available) is helpful. If it is not available, input from IT staff may be necessary to ensure that existing data from different sources can be integrated in order to flesh out the proposal. Do bear in mind that the data used must be relevant. This means that it must pass the 'interesting, but so what' test (an example of how different data can be used is given in the case study below).

- **Methods:** explain why a risk assessment methodology is the best way of meeting the project aims. One already mentioned is that it can dovetail neatly into other processes, such as TQM. Another is that risk assessments are already used across the organization, eg for environmental or health and safety compliance. Another advantage is that this approach builds in a continual feedback loop that incorporates the identification of emerging risks.

- **Project risks:** be prepared to answer difficult questions as to what could derail the project and what contingencies are in place. The more preparation that has been done, the better its chance of success. What is important is for senior management to feel confident in both the project and the team carrying it out. An important factor in this is to gain a fairly accurate picture of costs.

- **Costs:** it will be impossible for these to be 100 per cent accurate, and the bigger the project, the harder it will be to predict the costs. Instead, estimate a ballpark figure. Do this by breaking down the project into three or four stages. Identify who will be interviewed and estimate how long each interview will take, eg one hour. Add on the interviewee's preparation time and set it against the hourly rate for that pay band: midpoint will do. Repeat the process for interviewers' time for preparation and interview. Also allow for processing the information, meetings, writing up the findings and presenting it. Then add on an extra 10–15 per cent as a safety margin. Although this is fiddly, this exercise will concentrate the project team and prevent them getting carried away with interviewing those who are not really necessary to the project's success.

CASE STUDY How data can be used to develop a compelling business case

In this scenario, the HR team in a large insurance company is aware that there is a high staff turnover and wants this topic to form part of the business case. The standard option is to limit themselves to including the annual turnover rates for each of the last few years in a simple table format. However, this will do little to interest the board in the proposal. The second option is to invest time in identifying linkages between different data sets in order to compile a more rounded and three-dimensional business case. For example, the same data on staff turnover could be analysed in more detail for the following information:

- **Department/team level:** break down the data into individual sites and departments as this could reveal some interesting trends that are currently unrecognized. If necessary, drill down further and look at employee leaver patterns from specific teams and shifts. This could reveal that one site or team has an abnormally high turnover rate, which is distorting the overall results. If so, further analysis can be undertaken into the area concerned.

- **Job roles/bands:** check if there is a fairly even distribution amongst leavers or if certain posts are disproportionately affected. For example, the high turnover rate at call centres is well documented, as working conditions are often poor. This refers to the physical working environment as well as job design, such as set scripts and a maximum allotted time per call. Poor working environments and job design are well-known stressors in themselves.

- **Sickness absence:** map sickness absence levels and the reasons for the absence against the leavers. Also look to see if there are higher rates of sickness absence generally within the sites, departments or teams with the highest turnover rates. It would also be useful to see if there were specific types of sickness absence that feature, such as stress.

- **Exit interviews:** review any exit interviews carried out for the reasons given by employees for leaving. The top three or four reasons given can best be presented visually, eg in a pie chart. Those presenting the business case should be prepared to explain what action they have previously taken, if any, on tackling the reasons given for leaving.

- **Related trends:** do this data analysis well, and a high turnover rate may reveal other trends that would be relevant to this project. One is staffing levels, if the patterns revealed overcapacity in some teams and short-staffing in others. Signs of overstaffing may be evidenced by employee boredom, stress from having too little to do (underwork also causes stress) and staff spending too much time surfing the internet. If so, HR can work with the affected areas to look at how overcapacity and undercapacity can be better managed.

Other data sources

Even if an organization does not utilize big data, IT colleagues can advise on what other information is available and how it can help build a better picture. So taking the example of presenting data on employee turnover, the marketing/PR department may have figures to show that customer engagement has markedly declined in the last few months amongst particular product or service lines. An analysis of leavers may reveal that this has coincided with a higher than normal attrition rate amongst those with customer-facing roles. Another example is where the finance department keeps records of employees who have attended workshops it has run on money management. This can be cross-referenced with results from exit interviews that give poor pay and conditions as a reason for leaving. For many organizations, this use of data represents a departure from what some HR practitioners are used to. Therefore, it means that a new mindset needs to be adopted in how available data can be exploited to carry out an employee risk assessment.

> **Key point**
>
> Making better use of data is a good example of how an employee risk management approach can lead to more innovative working practices.

> **Note**
>
> More information on potential data sources to use can be found in the business case checklist in Appendix 2 on page 238.

Terminology

It is also important that the right terminology is used rather than having traditional 'HR speak' seep in to the proposal. Examples include focusing too much on what may be seen as 'woolly' concepts such as having 'happier employees'. Whilst not diminishing the importance of this in any way, it will not resonate with the decision makers, as they are likely to come from financial and other analytical backgrounds. Instead, communicate in business language and clearly link the project's objectives to those of the business. In doing this, tap into developing trends where possible. For example, confidence in the job market is improving so staff retention is increasingly important. Accordingly, establish a link between how the project will create cost-effective recommendations that will boost retention levels. Then expand on this by demonstrating how it is intended that this will improve efficiency and protect the bottom line.

Once the identities of the proposed project team members are known, look at how much time they spend as a normal part of their job on the type of issues that will be covered in the employee risk assessment. That way, it won't look as though they are being removed too far from their job role. Where possible, also show how the project objectives will make them more efficient at their job. For example, those with responsibility for disseminating employment information throughout the organization are likely to do a better job if the current process is reviewed and the views of those receiving the information are formally considered. If the organization is a listed company, argue how this approach can help improve compliance with corporate governance requirements (see Chapter 1).

Identifying risk appetite and risk tolerance

One factor to consider when compiling a business case is 'risk appetite'. This is the level of risk that an organization actively wishes to engage in. It is something positive, such as a willingness to invest in a new product. A second element is 'risk tolerance'. This refers to the level of risk that might be accepted if circumstances dictate. According to the IRM, risk appetite usually operates within smaller parameters than risk tolerance. In turn, risk tolerance will be a small segment of what is known as the 'risk universe'. This describes all the threats and vulnerabilities that an organization could face, which are known or unknown. Where the organization's risk appetite is small, the more likely it is that the decision makers will quickly buy into the project. Where it is greater, the business case could be rejigged to show how its recommendations can strengthen the organization's ability to service its risk appetite.

> **Key point**
>
> Risk appetite and risk tolerance is unique to each and every organization; even those operating within the same industry.

Responsibility for identifying risk appetite is the board's responsibility. This applies to day-to-day operating conditions as well as projects and new ventures. Therefore, it is something that must be measurable, such as an increase in shareholder value. Risk appetite is complex because it is not fixed. Instead, there will be a greater appetite for some assessed risks than others, and at different times. Whilst its main association is with financial performance, it can be applied to employee risk management, as because many of the threats and vulnerabilities presented by the workforce have a financial impact. An assessment will identify what these are and can determine whether the resulting risk is low, medium or high (see Chapter 4). With help from risk professionals, risk tolerances can be applied to each area. In fact, it can be used to put a business case together in order to justify the move to an employee risk management approach. In doing so, it presents HR practitioners with another opportunity to demonstrate their business credentials.

Trade union involvement

If trade unions are formally recognized, the question will arise as to what involvement they should have in the process of employee risk management. In fact, some employers may question if they should have any participative role in this type of exercise at all. This could be for several reasons. First, such a review is likely to be outside the remit of any collective bargaining arrangements that exist with any recognized trade unions. Second, relatively few employers have adopted partnership agreements that could arguably contain an implied obligation to involve unions in this type of activity. Third, there could be a long history of mistrust and poor relations between the two groups, which would deter management from seeking union involvement. Yet, despite what may be valid reasons for their exclusion from the process, there may be even better ones for including them.

The main advantage for the inclusion of unions is that they can fulfil the role of the 'critical friend'. This works on the basis that whilst most are not intent on damaging the employer, they do hold an independent role. As long as their role is exercised legitimately, however, it is underpinned by employment law protection. This means that union representatives will not be subject to any groupthink mentality, but instead be free to ask provocative and challenging questions about the process. They can do this in a way that many employees will not feel able to do. Whilst this depends on the culture of the organization, there is a chance that those carrying out the assessment, or being interviewed as part of it, may be tempted to play it safe. For those running the project, this could be a tactic to steer away from contentious topics known to be sensitive to senior management. For anyone being interviewed, it could mean giving the answers that they think management wants to hear, rather than the truth.

For these reasons, trade union input should lead to a more vigorous exercise being carried out, as employees are more likely to be honest with their elected representatives than managers. This is especially the case in those organizations where there is already a culture of mistrust of management. These views can then be fed back into the project anonymously via union representatives to the project team. In some cases, it may unearth issues that management is unaware of, such as the emergence of an employee counter-culture that if left to fester could lead to declining productivity, bullying or higher staff turnover within a particular team. If so, the scope of the review can be tweaked as necessary in order to cover any new areas of concern. Such input can only ultimately add value to the project, especially given the financial constraints that many organizations are currently operating under. Union independence will also mean that the exercise will have more credibility in the eyes of the workforce.

Unions will likely seek guarantees that this exercise will not be used to punish their members. For example, that the organization's disciplinary procedures will not be invoked where members have been found to have breached the staff handbook or other rules in some way. If they do not receive such assurances, they may threaten to withhold their cooperation. Despite this, giving a blanket guarantee is not sensible as there could be incidences discovered of more serious misconduct. If so, it cannot be ignored, as that gives out the wrong message to employees. Instead, consider offering a guarantee that more minor misdeeds will not be acted upon, but any serious misconduct issues will be pursued. For example, a review of HR policies and procedures could lead to the unearthing of fraudulent expenses claims.

Equally, unions are likely to be resistant if they think that new practices will be introduced that make the working lives of their members harder, but for no tangible benefit to the organization. This is a fair point and should be borne in mind when thinking about what recommendations should be made following the assessment.

Chapter summary

When planning the project's coverage:

- a good starting point is to divide 'employees' into different categories;
- do not forget to include outsourced functions where applicable;
- also include different types of working practices such as homeworking;
- consider segmenting the categories to cover those protected by discrimination laws;
- focus on areas of discrimination law still causing problems, such as age;

- look at the prevailing organizational culture and its impact on attitudes to risk taking;
- include a review of the existing reward systems and performance management.

Other areas to include are:

- a look at how the HR function is regarded in terms of its internal reputation;
- a review of employment-related documentation;
- topics based on their order in the employment life cycle, eg recruitment and dismissal;
- any other ideas brainstormed by the project team.

When selecting the team and its manager:

- choose a project manager with good analytical and interpersonal skills;
- the project manager should have several years' service with the organization;
- the project manager needs sufficient seniority to give the project credibility;
- at least one individual from outside the HR function should be selected;
- choose no more than four or five participants;
- someone with formal risk management qualifications is a good choice, eg risk manager.

The project planning should be:

- designed to maximize ROI;
- built around SMART or SMARTer objectives;
- examining what overlap there is with other disciplines and processes;
- looking at what other relevant work has been carried out by other functions;
- seeing what other risk management processes it can feed into, eg ISO 31000: 2009;
- feeding into quality improvement initiatives such as TQM, Six Sigma or lean thinking.

Compiling a business case for larger projects:

- focus on the business drivers operating in the organization;
- show how it will benefit from an employee risk assessment approach;
- build the business case around:
  - purpose;
  - data sources;
  - methods;
  - project risks;
  - costs.
- base it on hard facts and not assumptions;
- analyse different data sets to support arguments;
- look at data from other areas of the organization to flesh out the proposal;
- use language that the decision makers understand, not 'HR speak';
- relate the project's objectives to wider business objectives;
- tap into emerging trends where possible;
- show how much time the proposed project team members already spend on these issues;
- try to show how the project objectives will make team members better at their jobs;
- link it to the organization's risk appetite and how it can support it.

Trade union involvement:

- provides the role of the 'critical friend';
- will be helpful where there is a culture of mistrust of management;
- can highlight the existence of problems that management is unaware of;
- could give the project more credibility in the eyes of the workforce;
- may result in a demand that the project will not be used to punish members in any way.

Chapter 4 looks at how to carry out an employee risk assessment. It also introduces concepts from the world of risk management that can enhance the process.

Carrying out an employee risk assessment

04

Introduction

There is no single right way to carry out an employee risk assessment. However, the key stages involved in the process are fairly standard across risk-based disciplines. This means that any resulting work should integrate seamlessly with that produced by other departments. The focus of this chapter, therefore, is on the processes involved in carrying out such an assessment. They apply irrespective of whether it is organization-wide or limited to targeting specific areas. However, what may be a departure is the introduction of some new ideas that can enhance the risk assessment process. The first is introducing horizon scanning into the mix, so that the exercise includes looking for signs of future threats and vulnerabilities. If done well, the knowledge gained can be converted into a SWOT (strengths, weaknesses, opportunities, threats) analysis. This will allow an organization to convert the knowledge gained into competitive advantage. The second is a concept called 'root cause analysis'. This can be run alongside the assessment where there are more complex problems that require a more in-depth approach.

How to carry out an employee risk assessment

The approach used is generally the same as for any other type of risk, though the terminology used can vary. For example, with health and safety, the first step refers to the identification of 'hazards'. Here, this has been replaced with threats and vulnerabilities. This is because the areas under review are not physical hazards, such as trailing cables, but practices and behaviours: for example, there may be working practices that leave the employer exposed to employment tribunal claims due to the bullying behaviour of managers. The process consists of the following six steps (as also shown in Figure 4.1):

- Step 1 – choose the areas to be reviewed.
- Step 2 – identify the threats and vulnerabilities.
- Step 3 – decide who (or what) may be harmed and how.
- Step 4 – evaluate the risks and decide on control measures (precautions).
- Step 5 – record the findings and implement control measures.
- Step 6 – schedule periodic reviews and update where necessary.

FIGURE 4.1 Carrying out an employee risk assessment

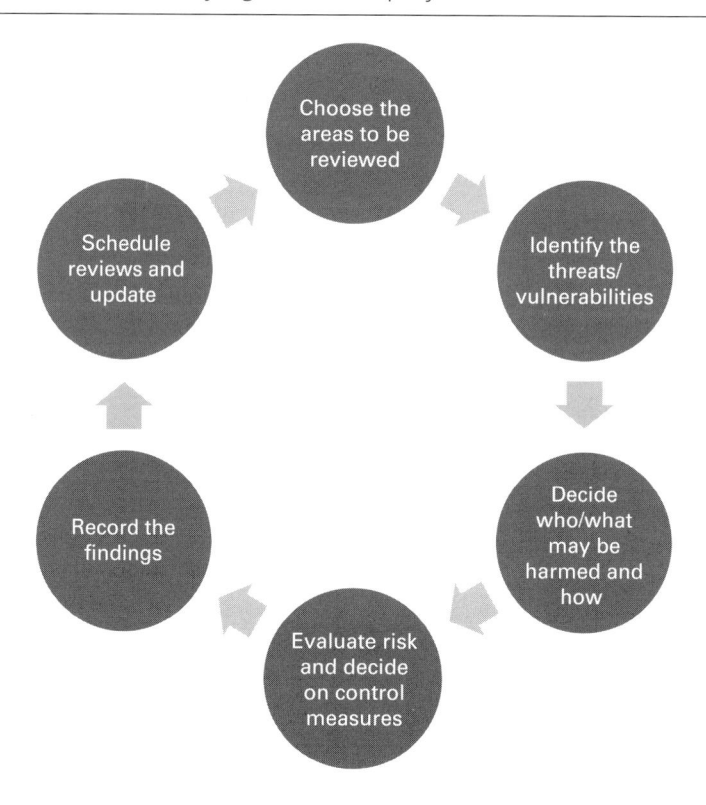

Step 1 – choose the areas to be reviewed

The first step is to decide the remit of the review. In other words, what type of employee risk will be included and what will be left out. To some degree, this will depend on the nature of the organization and its culture, particularly in terms of its approach to employee risk taking. For example, whilst many banks needed to review the link between reward and unacceptably high levels of risk taking, this is not an issue for public sector employers. Any decision will also be influenced by the existence of any known areas of vulnerability, such as an unusually high turnover rate in a particular department. Equally, it could include how well employment law changes are incorporated and filtered down to employees, or how well HR policies and procedures are followed in practice. So, it could include any area where employee activities and behaviours can present a threat. This may mean that a multidisciplinary team of professionals need to be involved, including for example IT and security.

Step 2 – identify the threats and vulnerabilities

Once the areas to be assessed have been chosen, the next step is to identify the threats and vulnerabilities from each one. For example, if one issue is poor performance, it may be that individual managers are a weak link in that they are reluctant to deal with emerging performance issues, or that some departments may have more of a problem than others due to poor leadership. This can be cross-checked by also reviewing sickness absence across the business as well as staff turnover rates. If another is concern over how employment law changes are managed, it will be necessary to examine how managers keep abreast of developments in this area. The following will also need to be reviewed: 1) what knowledge and qualifications in the subject is held by those responsible for disseminating information; 2) how they update their knowledge; 3) how frequently this is done; 4) how they choose what information to share with staff; and 5) how they communicate it: ie, is it engaging or too dry and legalistic?

In other words, those carrying out the risk assessment will need to get into the mindset of drilling down to find the root cause of a particular problem. This is instead of the usual tactic, which is to try to treat the symptoms. Unfortunately, treating the symptoms can have its drawbacks as it often ignores or fails to recognize the existence of a much deeper problem, which will only reappear again and again. The form of the problem may change but it will continue to have the same underlying cause. Also, because its origin has not been correctly identified, any time and money thrown at it will be wasted. As a consequence, hard questions may be asked as to why those tasked with solving the problems have failed to do so. Root cause analysis is a technique that can help with this – and more information on how it can be worked into the process is included at the end of this chapter.

Step 3 – decide who (or what) may be harmed and how

Once the potential threats have been identified, the next stage is to decide who or what could be affected and how. In most cases, the organization could be harmed. This could be via bad publicity or a damaging impact on profits, for example through employment tribunal awards or a loss of customers. If the organization is a charity, the impact could be a drop in donations. Another threat is a poorly drafted or non-existent social media policy. The harm would be to the employer's reputation by having no control over what staff can post, eg on Facebook, Twitter, or a personal blog. However, staff could also be affected. This could be through managers who are habitually lax in managing sickness absence, as the impact would be felt by those having to cover the work. If co-workers are already under pressure and working long hours due to a recruitment freeze/fear of redundancy, there is a greater chance that they could go sick with stress. It is important to consider the harm that could also be caused by third parties, such as self-employed contractors or agency temps.

Step 4 – evaluate the risks and decide on control measures

Next, evaluate the threats on the basis of the potential harm they could cause and the likelihood of this harm arising. There are different ways of doing this but 'low', 'medium' and 'high' should suffice for both: especially where non-risk specialists are involved. Another more colourful option is to use the traffic-light system, where icons with different colours are used instead of words. As to be expected, red corresponds to high risk, amber to medium risk and green to low risk. These two methods are suggested due to their simplicity of use and because the exercise becomes far less subjective with fewer options to choose from. If you were to start introducing lots of different options, such as numerical scoring systems of 1–5, or even 1–10, it is unlikely that two individuals will score the same threat or vulnerability in the same way. It also introduces unnecessary complexity into what should remain a fairly straightforward exercise. If the findings are passed on to an organization's risk managers or internal audit team, they will be able to change the findings into a more sophisticated format if they choose.

There are four main options available when deciding what control measures (precautions) to introduce. They are as follows:

- **Remove the threat:** sometimes, it is possible to eliminate the threat. For example, if concerns have been raised about employees downloading porn (increasing the risk of sex discrimination claims), access to such sites should be blocked by an organization's IT department. Equally, if there is concern about confidential information being downloaded on to memory sticks or similar, IT should be asked to disable all access to portable storage devices.
- **Risk reduction:** this is the most realistic option and could be done through training aimed at altering the employee behaviour that is creating or exacerbating the risks. One obvious example is to provide employment law updates to managers and staff, particularly in areas of discrimination law. Another is to ensure that the workforce is fully conversant with all HR policies and procedures.
- **Risk transfer:** another, albeit more limited, option is to transfer the risk. One example would be the purchase of legal expenses insurance. However, this is not without its own problems. For example, it would only pay out if the provider was contacted immediately an employment-related problem became apparent. Failure to do this will invalidate the policy.
- **Risk acceptance:** although short-sighted, this is a tactic used by some organizations with deep pockets. It is commonly found in the financial sector with claims under the same heads of damages appearing against the same employers again and again, eg sex discrimination-based claims. Rather than change the culture that creates the problem, these employers accept the risk and budget for tribunal claims accordingly.

Most control measures are likely to fall into the risk reduction category. Given that it is generally behaviours that need to change, many of these measures will revolve around tightening up on policies and procedures. However, that is only part of the solution, as training must be provided to staff and managers on what they can and can't do – and why. Where the threat or vulnerability is more complex, a good way to unearth the real problem is to use root cause analysis (RCA). This is a technique commonly used in environments such as production and safety. Its purpose is to identify a problem's origins so that steps can be taken to either eliminate it, or reduce the likelihood of it reoccurring. Its principles can also be applied to employee risk management as it can be used reactively to respond to events that have already occurred. It is also a good fit with the process outlined in Figure 4.1.

Here, there are likely to be two types of root cause. The first are organizational, where a system, process or policy is weak in some way. The second are human causes – these relate to individual or group actions and behaviours that cause problems, such as weak management or human error. The third is physical causes – but that is not relevant in this context. RCA has five stages to work through and, at the end of the exercise, there will be a diagram resembling a fishbone (as shown in Figure 4.2). This is not the finished risk assessment, but an ancillary document that is part of the process.

These stages of the RCA are as follows:

1 **Symptoms:** what are the specific symptoms of a known or suspected problem? For example, a high number of grievance hearings may have been flagged up as an issue in one department. This should be turned into a question, such as: why are there so many grievances? Doing this will help with the brainstorming process. This heading can be placed in a box on the right side of the page with a horizontal line coming off it and going across the page from right to left. They represent the head and spine of the fish retrospectively.

2 **Major factors:** this looks at identifying the key factors. So questions need to be asked such as: where is the proof that there is a problem? What is its timeline (ie recent – or long-standing due to no one wanting to tackle it)? What is its impact? Although these questions may unearth some unpleasant home truths, they do need to be answered fully and honestly. This is where interviewing key staff across the organization should pay dividends, as they understand the issues better than anyone. This exercise should also yield a valuable range of perspectives that cannot be obtained if those solving the problem are too remote. After completing this stage, there will be several lines coming off the main spine of the fish.

FIGURE 4.2 Root cause analysis

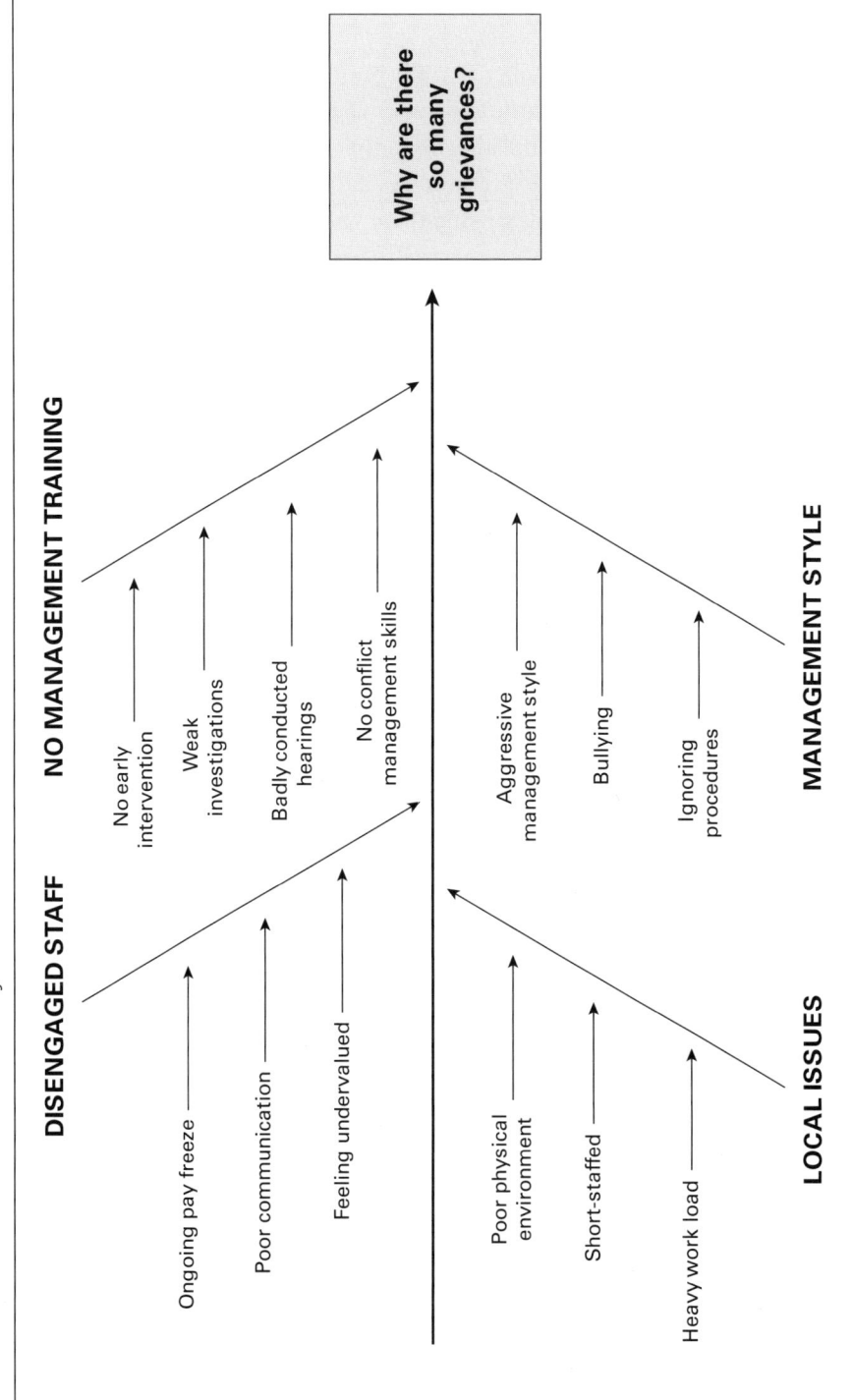

DISENGAGED STAFF

- Ongoing pay freeze
- Poor communication
- Feeling undervalued

NO MANAGEMENT TRAINING

- No early intervention
- Weak investigations
- Badly conducted hearings
- No conflict management skills

Why are there so many grievances?

MANAGEMENT STYLE

- Aggressive management style
- Bullying
- Ignoring procedures

LOCAL ISSUES

- Poor physical environment
- Short-staffed
- Heavy work load

3 **Possible causes:** these include those that are known as well as the prevailing conditions that allowed the problem to arise. Do not limit this exercise to one or two causes, but list as many as possible. Remember that the purpose of this exercise is to drill down and the mantra is always 'what, why, who, where and when?' So taking the above example as an illustration, the 'what' is the high number of grievances and the 'why' are the likely problem causes. Identifying these will require a look at 'who'. Here, it could be a manager with an aggressive management style who is causing friction. Identify the 'where' by pinpointing where the problem is occurring, such as in a specific site or team, and the 'when' by noting the dates of the grievances. This should result in a series of lines coming off each of those created in Stage 2. In the example shown in Figure 4.2 there are four possible causes: disengaged staff, local issues, management style and no management training.

4 **Analyse information:** this repeats Stage 3 but looks at the root causes, ie the real reason that a problem occurred. Political sensitivities have no place here. If the root causes are sidestepped or glossed over, the exercise will fail at this point. If done correctly, the result will be a diagram that shows all the possible causes of the problem under investigation. Once complete, a process of elimination can occur where, following meetings or surveys, certain lines on the diagram are crossed out (do keep the original diagrams, as over time they can form a database that can provide a starting point if this exercise needs to be repeated). What remain should be the causes that are the source of the problem.

5 **Recommendations/implementation:** this final stage asks questions about what can be done to prevent the underlying causes from reoccurring, as well as implementing the solutions that have been devised. However, with a slightly different approach, it can also add a bit more to the assessment, as a sub-process can be built in which formally looks ahead to predict how successful any suggestion will be. This is done by looking at the possible outcomes, both positive and negative.

An example of how this would work can be seen from the example shown in Figure 4.2. Under disengaged staff, one branch added via Stage 4 is poor communication. One easy answer to this would be for managers to introduce weekly team meetings with staff. However, this alone will be ineffective if the problems go much deeper. Whilst an easy fix might be tempting, looking ahead in this way will ultimately save time and money – this method seeks a solution that will actually work. In this scenario, far more will be required in order to tackle the underlying problems. For example, supervisors and managers will need training on the importance of two-way communication and how their body language influences how others interact with them. They will also require training in conflict management. Without these three recommendations, there could be more grievances, as the team meetings will just provide managers and staff with another opportunity to clash.

> **Key point**
>
> RCA is a technique that can be used in any HR context to identify the root cause of a particular problem. It does not only have to be used in large projects.

Step 5 – record the findings and implement control measures

Where the risk rating is more than trivial, the findings should always be recorded. In some disciplines, such as health and safety, this is a legal requirement. However, it is also advisable with employee risk assessments as it provides an audit trail. The assessment is usually depicted in a table format with a series of headings running left to right across the top of the page. Underneath these are the areas or topics that are being assessed. Many organizations use their own in-house format, with its layout and content varying according to the function using it. A suggested layout is included in Appendix 3, with some worked examples in order to provide an idea of what a finished assessment could look like. This can easily be adapted for an organization's own use.

Once this has been done, any control measures identified need to be implemented. Obviously, any areas noted as 'high risk' should be dealt with first, before moving down the list to those categorized as 'medium' and 'low'. It is also good practice to set a deadline for completion for each one. As part of this process, give specific managers responsibility for seeing that each control measure is actioned within its designated time frame. Giving ownership in this way makes it harder for matters to drift and not get done. If there will be a delay in implementation for any reason, such as for financial reasons, then this should be noted and a date set for review of the situation.

Step 6 – schedule periodic reviews and update where necessary

As a final step, periodic reviews should be scheduled in order to keep track of what progress is being made. Equally, if movement on implementing any recommendations has stalled, look at why this is. Consider possible underlying causes, such as resistance to change or an unwillingness to lose responsibility for functions that the assessment may have found would fit better elsewhere. The frequency of reviews will depend both on preference and how much outstanding remedial work needs to be done, but should normally be annual or biannual. The exception to this is where a lot of work needs to be done as a matter of urgency. Should this apply, quarterly would be more appropriate, at least until the action points have been dealt with. As a general point, feedback needs to be sought from stakeholders within the organization as to the effectiveness of the process and whether or not it is adding value.

One point to consider is that these reviews may identify the existence of emerging threats and vulnerabilities. These refer to those issues that are beginning to cause unexpected problems in the workplace, but where there may not be a framework in place for managing them. Social media is a good example, as many employers failed to keep up with the rapid growth in its development and use by their workforce. As a result, their HR policies and procedures lagged behind and they were not legally equipped to deal with the various problems that emerged, such as with employee blogs or Facebook use (see Chapter 8). For this reason, consideration of emerging threats that have appeared since the original assessment should be formally built into the review process. Together, the findings can be incorporated into a SWOT analysis, a basic example of which is given in Table 4.1.

TABLE 4.1 Example of a SWOT analysis

Strengths	Weaknesses
• Strong employer brand • Relatively low employee turnover in most areas of the business • Overall, there are good levels of employee engagement (evidenced by recent surveys and focus groups)	• Not enough resolution of capability/conduct matters informally • Key HR policies are too lengthy and can be ignored as a result. This leaves us vulnerable • No structure exists within the business to proactively look for emerging employee threats and vulnerabilities
Opportunities	**Threats**
• To increase the robustness of recruitment practices • To collaborate more with colleagues in IT and marketing on mutual areas of interest • To create a risk register across the business and better integrate risk management generally • To work with other departments to identify what data is collected and how its use across the business can be improved	• Loss of business 'know-how' to competitors and fraudsters due to weak data management • Insufficient control over employee use of social media. This could lead to reputation damage • Poor password security by many employees, leaving us exposed to cybercrime • The organization is ill-prepared to deal with a future workforce that is steadily ageing

> **Key point**
>
> Wherever possible with a SWOT analysis, make the points relevant to the organization as a whole, rather than keeping it too HR-centric.
>
> This neatly dovetails into what is known as 'gap analysis'. As a technique, it is used to determine what steps an organization must take in order to move from its current situation to a preferred future state. At its simplest level, it can be broken down into the following three steps:

1. **Identify the desired future state:** the starting point is identifying exactly where the organization wants to be following completion of the risk assessment. This could refer to a number of areas, such as a firm employing 50 staff wanting to achieve a 20 per cent reduction in one-day 'sickies' across the business. Where appropriate, use metrics such as percentages or costs, as they are measurable.

2. **The present situation:** next, an analysis needs to be carried out into the current state of play. This is likely to require input from a number of other individuals across the organization. It may also mean that a number of documents need to be studied, such as sickness absence records. In other cases, interviews and surveys may be necessary.

3. **Closing the gap:** this bridges the gap between the first two steps. So for a problem such as high levels of sickness absence, realistic recommendations for a 50-employee business may include tightening up procedures for employees ringing in sick, and introducing back-to-work interviews with line managers. For a larger organization with the relevant resources, it may involve outsourcing all sickness absence management to a company offering occupational health services.

Key point

The risk assessment process should be seen as an ongoing cycle rather than a one-off exercise that is undertaken and then forgotten about.

Introducing horizon scanning

In addition to those threats and vulnerabilities already on the radar, there are those that have not yet appeared on the corporate vista. These are the unknowns that could present huge dangers as well as opportunities if only there was a way to anticipate and prepare for their arrival. This is where the practice of horizon scanning comes in. Rather than being on the back foot and reacting to forced change, it is a proactive risk management strategy that gets organizations to look ahead to the next one to three years. If it can be hardwired into senior management thinking it can become a useful strategy for any organization, but especially for those operating in the global marketplace. This is because it offers the ability to translate what is learned from the exercise into a commercial advantage. It does this by using the information gained in order to avoid any identified threats and vulnerabilities, which could trap any competitors who are less proactive. The information gained can be distilled and depicted in a longer-term SWOT analysis.

So how should employers try to predict future threats with any accuracy? There is no one single answer to this. However, the best way is to use a wide range of resources in order to build up a picture of future trends. This is best done by a multidisciplinary team, which can have this activity built into their job roles. This gathering of 'intelligence' can include the following sources:

- **Future legal changes:** newspaper or journal reports on the employment legislation that the government of the day plans to introduce or repeal. It will also include keeping an eye out for the contents of the main political parties' manifestos for forthcoming elections.
- **Political landscape:** apart from current political developments, consider future initiatives that have already received some publicity. This could be anything from a personal crusade of a heavyweight politician, through to well-funded political pressure groups operating at national or international level.
- **Official statistics:** these are updated several times per year and provide a valuable source of information on employment rates by age and region.
- **Employment trends:** these are a regular feature on HR-related websites and mention topics such as the increasing number of those aged over 65 who are in employment, the numbers of mothers returning to work full-time or part-time, and details of skills shortages.
- **Demographic changes:** one known trend is the ageing population. As fixed retirement ages are disappearing, government statistics are already reporting that increasing numbers of workers aged 65 and over are choosing to remain in work.
- **Technological developments:** reports on new technology will continue to impact on organizations. This may be in terms of continuing to automate previously labour-intensive work processes. It may also mean advancements in computer technology that allows for more workers to work remotely.

- **Futurology reports:** futurology is the study of social, political and technical developments in order to understand what may happen in the future. Although more of a social science, 'futurologists' are increasingly writing articles in journals and speaking at conferences. Apart from the interest factor, their comments are worth a read as reference material.

Chapter summary

Six steps to carrying out an employee risk assessment:

- choose the areas to be reviewed;
- identify the threats;
- decide who (or what) may be harmed and how;
- evaluate the risks and decide on control measures (precautions);
- record the findings and implement control measures;
- schedule periodic reviews and update where necessary.

Control measures have four options:

- removing the threat, eg by preventing access to websites containing pornography;
- risk reduction, eg better compliance with employment law;
- risk transfer, eg a more limited option, but includes purchasing legal expenses insurance;
- risk acceptance – rather than changing the culture, set a budget for repeat tribunal claims.

Introducing horizon scanning:

- a proactive technique to help predict future threats and vulnerabilities;
- looks ahead to the next one to three years;
- if done well, can translate lessons learned into commercial advantage;
- uses a wide range of resources to build up a picture of future trends;
- best done with a multidisciplinary team.

Root cause analysis tackles underlying problems:

- it identifies a problem's origins so it can be eliminated or otherwise managed;
- it can be used reactively;
- organizational and human causes will be relevant here;
- it has five stages:
  - problem symptoms;
  - major factors;
  - possible causes;
  - analyse information;
  - recommendations/implementation.

Chapter 5 looks at recruitment and the various threats and vulnerabilities that a weak process can introduce into the organization.

Recruitment   05

Introduction

An organization is only as good as the people it employs. Get the recruitment process wrong and many potential threats and vulnerabilities will be introduced along with the new recruit. These can arise from numerous sources but some hiring practices are known to be more high risk than others. These include weak policies that result in a mismatch between what an employer actually needs in a recruit and the skills possessed by the person they end up employing. It also includes poor candidate checks: whether this be poor checking of applications, or an employee not having a legal right to work in the country. Other problems include candidates who exploit weak recruitment practices by bringing discrimination claims, as well as general poor hiring practices and strategies. In other words, recruitment can be a minefield even for well-prepared employers. With this in mind, this chapter pinpoints the key trouble spots that an assessment should look at, as well as some recommendations that can be made.

Pre-recruitment

Employment mismatch

The identification of potential threats and vulnerabilities should start as soon as a need to recruit has been identified. Simply relying on being able to filter candidates out at the application stage is far too late. There is a real danger of introducing a mismatch between what the job requires in practice as opposed to the type of applicant an employer thinks they need. One reason for this is that job roles often evolve over time, for example due to new working practices and internal reorganization. Yet despite this, old job descriptions and person specifications may be reused without a second thought. Another problem is the temptation to oversell a position in terms of promotion prospects and/or opportunities to gain new skills. Whilst this may achieve its objective of securing the best candidates, it is a short-term strategy, as once the employee sees the reality of the job and its limitations they will start to become disengaged.

If this is not resolved by their manager (either through picking up on the problem or having it brought to their attention), the employee's performance may start to noticeably decline. It could also have a negative impact on team productivity. This dissatisfaction may also lead to an increase in short-term sickness absence. If not tackled informally at an early stage, it could lead to capability proceedings. This is a specific process designed to support both managers and employees with performance problems. Apart from the cost to the organization in lost output, management time spent in trying to rectify the problem must also be included. Should the employee leave, there will also be the additional costs of finding a replacement. If recruitment for that post was outsourced to a recruitment agency, there will be extra costs to factor in of up to 25 per cent of basic annual salary. Other expenses include management time spent looking at what went wrong, recruiting for a replacement, plus the outlay for any training provided. Also, the departing employee's job will need to be covered by someone else, such as agency staff, until a replacement can be found. This all adds up.

Naturally these costs will vary from employer to employer and from country to country. However, according to the CIPD's Annual Survey Report 2013, the median recruitment cost of filling a vacancy in the UK was £5,000 for a senior manager/director-level appointment and an average of £2,000 for other employees (note that employers included different costs in their estimates). This is cheaper than in previous years and can be attributed to a move to less expensive recruitment methods. For example, just over two-thirds of employers now conduct recruitment in-house with an increasing reliance on social media channels such as LinkedIn and company websites. The decline in the use of recruitment agencies that gathered pace in the recession shows no sign of abating (in the UK at least).

Employers will already know if they have a high turnover rate across their organization or within departments, but there could also be other variables that have not been examined. If so, the risk assessment should consider the following so that a fuller picture can be developed:

- **Length of service:** there could be a higher than expected attrition rate at certain points during the employment relationship. For example, there could be an unusually high churn rate from those with less than six months' service. Alternatively, there may be a pattern that reveals a two-year or three-year 'itch'.
- **Team cohesion:** close-knit teams may not be as receptive to newcomers as they should be, particularly if the departing employee was popular. If so, there is a chance that a new employee whose face does not fit gets 'frozen out'. A similar outcome could arise where his or her personal values and work ethic run contrary to those of the team.
- **Underlying reason for departure:** the reasons that employees give for leaving might not always be truthful. This may be a reflection of an exit interview process that does not encourage openness and honesty. If so, those leaving are likely to give the answers they believe are expected, rather than the truth. Should this be the case, then the real reason behind resignations will remain unknown. This could lead to an artificially high turnover rate, as the employer lacks the knowledge to tackle the root cause.
- **Seasonal:** it may be that resignations show a seasonal pattern. Whilst this may be coincidence, it could also be down to specific weather-related factors. For example, in a stuffy open-plan office without air conditioning, departures could peak at the end of a hot and humid summer.

If an assessment finds that these problems exist, the recommendations made will need to be given a 'high' priority for action. Luckily, some of them can be implemented immediately. For example, if one or more employees have just resigned, talk to the present post-holder and their managers to find out what the job currently entails. Also, look at future business needs – if the job is still evolving, the next recruit should be someone who can grow into it. Do not leave this discussion until the present incumbent's exit interview, as this will be too late. As part of this process, the employee should be asked if they felt that sufficient training and support had been provided to enable them to carry out their duties effectively. In other words, maximize this opportunity to reassess what you want in the next post-holder. Part of this exercise involves looking at the mode of working. This is often overlooked as many employers tend to focus solely on the qualifications, skills and experience deemed necessary. Whilst important, this is not the full picture. Instead, also think about the job style. Does the job advert ask for a 'team player', whereas the need is for someone who will actually spend a lot of time working alone?

Another area that can cause problems for an organization is the potential disconnect between having a respected consumer brand and the realities of a particular job. For example, 'sexy' brands such as Apple, Google and Virgin are magnets for job candidates. Yet some of their vacancies will be less than glamorous, such as working in call centres or in a post room. If there is not honesty with job seekers at the outset about what the job really entails, there may be problems, due to the fact that in some cases, the harsh reality of the job will be far from the glossy image of the company that is sold to consumers. Once again, this could result in higher than expected employee turnover rates. In principle, this can apply to any employer, so any employee risk assessment should examine attrition rates across all departments as part of the preparatory work. It is also advisable to review the content of any exit interviews carried out. All too often, these get filed away and forgotten about, whilst any trends that have emerged get overlooked. As part of this process, check to see what use, if any, is made of such interviews throughout the organization.

Honesty is the best policy in this kind of assessment. So if the risk assessment highlights a mismatch, the recommendations will likely require a departure from an organization's current recruitment philosophy. This is where Minchington's (2010) concept of employer value proposition (EVP) can be introduced into the assessment. He defines an EVP as 'a set of functional and emotive associations and offerings such as career development, salary friendly working environment that is provided by an organization in return for the skills, capabilities and experiences an employee brings to the organization'. As this must be spot-on right from the earliest stage of the recruitment process, he says that an employer's EVP should answer a number of questions in regard to both job applicants and employees:

- Why should I join your organization?
- Why should I stay?
- Why should I give my best?
- Why should I recommend your organization as an employer and business?
- Why should I re-join (for ex-employees)?

Minchington develops this further by saying that EVP communication occurs at two levels. The first is what he refers to as being 'above the line'. These refer to online and offline communications and represent those activities that are likely to be actioned first. Online includes the recruitment section of an organization's website, its social media pages, podcasts, SMS job alerts and e-newsletters. Offline includes newspaper adverts, careers fairs, employee referral programmes and company events. In other words, the standard form of communications used today. Yet, whilst suitably glossy, they do not represent the realities of what working for a particular organization is really like. Instead, they fulfil the demands of a tick-box recruitment exercise.

This is where his 'below the line' activities come in. These are the ones that reflect the reality of working life in an organization and are revealed through the behaviours and actions of employees. In order to accurately depict this, there must be honesty in assessing the strengths and weaknesses of the current offering. This can be done by surveying staff on what they believe the EVP to be. Once complete, Minchington advocates that the focus should be on enhancing the strengths whilst eliminating any weaknesses. For example, if any flexible working or well-being initiatives are offered, then they should be promoted. Equally, if communication is poor in practice, strategies must be implemented to improve it. After this has been done, a multidisciplinary team needs to collaborate in order to communicate the revamped EVP consistently throughout the organization.

Once this has been done internally, attention can then move to external branding. One option here is to use **http://www.glassdoor.com**. For those unfamiliar with it, the US-based Glassdoor has several different functions. Apart from being a jobs site, it allows workers to post comments on the pros and cons of working for their employer. However, more importantly in this context, it allows employers to engage in promoting their brand to jobseekers. This is via entries that can include company information, photographs and links to other social media sites such as Facebook. It also allows for the monitoring of comments that have the potential to damage an organization's reputation – and gives employers the opportunity to respond to them. In fact, this website has tapped into the power of employer branding to the extent that it actively encourages employers to get their staff and job candidates to post comments.

For many employers, the notion of an employer brand will be a new concept. For others, it may be a good idea that has taken a backseat due to the much tougher trading conditions over the last few years. Yet according to global research carried out by People in Business and the research body CRF Institute, it is gaining traction amongst employers. This research took place between mid-December 2012 and mid-March 2013 and was published in July 2013. There were 271 valid responses received from large organizations in 32 countries including the UK, the United States, the European Union and BRIC countries (Brazil, Russia, India and China). Of interest is the fact that in 59 per cent of cases, it is HR that formally sponsors this initiative. The next closest is an executive director/CEO at 44 per cent. So this is another area that offers potential to any HR team wanting to develop their business credentials.

If this is an area of interest for an assessment, particular attention should be given to the impact of social media on employer branding. This is for two reasons. First, this research found that there has been a major shift in recruitment marketing towards what it describes as professional, social and referral networks. Second, social media is a powerful medium in allowing candidates to compare employer claims with employee opinion. Given the potential for divergence, it is crucial that the messages sent out match what employees are saying. If they do not, this can easily be discovered by accessing company pages on Facebook and YouTube. There are also dedicated websites to certain industries that contain gossip and opinion on what employers are really like to work for. Two examples are **http://rollonfriday.com** for lawyers and those seeking training contracts, or **http://wallstreetoasis.com** for those in the financial sector.

Discriminatory job adverts

The next area of potential vulnerability lies with the individual responsible for drafting the job advert. This is because candidates are protected from unlawful discrimination at the application stage. At present, the greatest threat is where it unintentionally falls foul of age-discrimination laws. Although this is less likely now due to greater employer awareness of anti-age-discrimination legislation, it is still possible. Whilst many clued-up organizations now avoid wording such as 'ideal for a first jobber', or specify upper or lower age limits for applicants, it is still possible to get caught out. For example, an advert that states that a vacancy is 'ideal for a new graduate' arguably implies that the target market is someone in their early twenties. If a mature student in their fifties applies after completion of a degree and is rejected without interview, he or she could argue that they are being discriminated against on the grounds of age.

In fact, potentially discriminatory job adverts have become a source of easy money to 'serial litigants'. These are individuals who bring baseless claims against employers. Unfortunately, their numbers have steadily increased as the groups given legal protection against discrimination have expanded in recent years. One particular area where this has arisen is with age-discrimination claims. Older and often highly experienced individuals trawl through job adverts to find and apply for entry-level positions that they are inevitably rejected from. They then claim age discrimination on the assumption that most employers will prefer to settle than go to the time and expense of litigation. Emboldened by their success, these individuals often repeat the process with other employers. For example, in the UK, a 51-year-old accountant with over 18 years' experience threatened employment tribunal claims against more than 22 employers if they did not agree to settle her claim. She had applied for graduate positions that required little or no prior experience and had netted over £100,000 via out-of-court settlements. Similar problems have arisen with race discrimination.

Whilst serial litigants tend to focus more on smaller employers or those less likely to have in-house employment law expertise, larger organizations should still be mindful of the existence of these people when assessing recruitment risks. At the time of writing, it is not known what lasting impact the tribunal-charging regime will have in deterring serial or try-it-on litigants in the UK. They may still make a direct approach to the employer in the hope that they will receive a settlement, rather than filing an employment tribunal claim. However, there are steps that can be taken that will reduce the likelihood of a claim. Where appropriate, these can be built into any recommendations made following the assessment. They are as follows:

- Check to make sure that the content of the advert is not potentially discriminatory, eg to require more years' experience than is really necessary. Instead, look more at the type of experience required, rather than length.
- On receipt of CVs/applications, flag up those where the candidates seem to be too perfect a fit in terms of qualifications and skills. Also watch out for those who are overqualified and live well outside a normal catchment area. It could suggest a serial litigant with no intention of wanting the position, but simply trawling in order to then make a claim.
- If psychometric testing is carried out, consider using it much earlier in the process in order to weed out the least suitable candidates.

This can be done via the use of short, internet-based tests that comprise the initial screening prior to submitting CVs and application forms.

- Maintain a complete audit trail of paperwork from receiving applications through to offering the job. Should an applicant then challenge the outcome, this documentation will form the basis of a defence (providing it reflects evidence of an objective process).

- If the organization is based in England and Wales and receives a tribunal claim, it can visit **http://www.serial-litigants.com/whatwedo.html**. This website was set up by an employment law solicitor in 2010 with the aim of searching employment tribunal databases to see what other claims may have been brought by the same individual. This service costs £60.

Hiring policies

Discriminatory practices

If an employer is not careful, they can come unstuck if their hiring practices are discriminatory in some way. In this area, the growing problem is known as 'lookism'. This refers to the policy of only hiring staff with a certain kind of look or appeal, and it has become increasingly common in front-facing sales roles, especially in the retail sector. Unfortunately, it can also prove incredibly costly as the US retailer Abercrombie & Fitch knows all too well. In 2003, the company was subject to a class action (*Gonzalez v Abercrombie & Fitch*). This involved several types of discrimination, including claims from ethnic minorities that its hiring policy directly discriminated against those who did not fit its white, all-American aesthetic. It was also claimed that where ethnic minorities, such as Latinas were hired, they were allocated jobs in stockrooms away from the public. This case was settled and Abercrombie & Fitch agreed to create a US $40 million settlement fund for the thousands of individuals who had completed valid claim forms.

On top of this figure was a requirement to pay an additional $10 million. This sum represented the lawyers' fees, and costs with monitoring compliance with the Consent Decree (settlement agreement) ordered by the US District Court for the Northern District of California. It contained numerous diversity requirements that Abercrombie & Fitch were required to integrate into its recruitment policies and programmes for both existing employees and future hires. Apart from the eye-watering costs involved, what is not known is how much damage has been caused to Abercrombie & Fitch's reputation. Whilst it has embarked on a number of store closures across the United States, it is not known whether this is purely down to the economic downturn or whether a contributing factor could be a loss of business due to its discriminatory hiring practices. This is also a good example of how damaging organizational 'groupthink' at a senior level can be. Not to mention the lack of an ethical approach to diversity.

Unfortunately, Abercrombie & Fitch had still not quite learned the error of its ways. In 2009 it was sued in the UK for disability discrimination at its London store. A 22-year-old law student born without her left forearm said that she was moved off the shop floor to work in the stockroom. This was because the company's visual team found that her appearance did not comply with its ultra-strict 'look policy'. Initially, she had been told that she could wear a cardigan to hide where her prosthetic lower arm met her flesh arm. However, this was found to contravene company policy, hence her being moved away from customer view. Unsurprisingly, she won her employment tribunal and was awarded around £8,000 compensation. This was for disability harassment and wrongful dismissal. Most of the reward was for injury to feelings.

Whilst 'lookism' is not illegal in the UK (it is in Victoria, Australia and some US states), a potential vulnerability is falling foul of existing anti-discrimination laws. In terms of direct discrimination, these will most likely include disability, such as facial disfigurement, or on the grounds of age. For example, Abercrombie & Fitch and its ilk are unlikely to think that a 50-year-old candidate will fit in with its concept of hip, young and athletic. Indirect sex discrimination may also become more of an issue in terms of 'fattism'. This term is starting to creep into everyday speech, but is already far more of a problem for women. The reason is that there is greater societal tolerance of fat men than women, who are still judged heavily on their appearance (hence the potential for sex discrimination). There have already been stories in the media concerning women who claim to have been rejected by recruiters due to being obese. However, where obesity is a side-effect of a protected disability, this could present organizations with the greatest risk in terms of an employment tribunal claim.

So to be on the safe side, an assessment should review the organization's hiring policies, though these are less likely to reveal discriminatory practices.

For this reason, it should also involve interviews with those responsible for making hiring decisions, to try to identify any practices that are potentially discriminatory on these grounds. As these employees will be more inclined to say what they think is the desired answer, this is a good example of where anecdotal evidence will help build a picture of what really goes on. Recommendations will need to focus on raising awareness of the link between 'lookism' and the underlying potential for discrimination-based claims. The best way to do this is to emphasize the fact that there is no upper limit to the amount of compensation that can be awarded, not to mention the bad publicity that may be generated.

Another area where hiring policies create problems is for those employers who promote 'refer a friend' schemes and/or encourage applications from employees' relatives. If this applies, the risk assessment should review how this process works in practice, as it could lead to allegations of favouritism if vacant posts are not advertised internally. If not dealt with, this could cause serious resentment, which in turn impacts negatively on employee engagement as well as damage team cohesion and productivity. There is also the problem of staff recommending inappropriate candidates, either to earn some easy money or to help out a friend. But worse still, it could lead to allegations of discrimination. These schemes can also create problems for those UK employers that do business with government bodies: s.149 of the Equality Act 2010 requires all public bodies to have 'due regard' to eliminating discrimination and the advancement of equality of opportunity. It is for this reason that tender documents ask questions on how recruitment decisions are made. If it is discovered that preference is given to friends or family of employees, it will be difficult to argue that this is consistent with an equalities agenda. Also, if certain protected groups are already under-represented in some parts of the workforce, these types of scheme may only serve to perpetuate this imbalance.

When making recommendations on how to reduce exposure to these potential threats, advise that any vacancy arising is open to all existing staff in possession of the necessary experience. Also make sure that full transparency is built into the selection process should a friend or relative be offered the position and an unhappy employee challenges it. Plus, the need to be seen to create opportunities for career advancement has assumed a new importance since the abolition of the default retirement age, as fewer workers can afford to retire.

Disability discrimination

In the recruitment context, an employer's concern will be hiring a new employee only to find that they take lengthy periods of sick leave due to a disability that is protected by legislation. Prior to the Equality Act 2010, UK employers reduced the likelihood of this happening by the use of pre-employment health questionnaires. These were usually issued to all serious contenders for a position and then used to quietly weed out those perceived as being a potential liability. However, since the Equality Act 2010 came into force, restrictions have been introduced on how employers can legally enquire about health or sickness absence. The situation now is that, in most cases, candidates should not be questioned on health issues prior to a job offer being made. If an interviewer risks it and the application does not proceed, the unsuccessful candidate may bring an employment tribunal claim. The onus will then be on the prospective employer to show that there was a non-disability-based reason for not proceeding with the application.

There are some limited exceptions to this rule in the early stages of the recruitment process. These arise where a prospective employer should ask certain health-related questions to ensure that a candidate:

- can carry out a 'function that is intrinsic' to the role, such as heavy lifting in a job that requires physical fitness;
- is able to take part in the selection process: ie in order to know if any reasonable adjustments are necessary, such as longer to complete written assessments due to dyslexia;
- may have a particular disability that may be an occupational requirement for a job, eg with a charity or a case worker assigned to those with specific disabilities.

Where none of these apply, health-related questions can only be asked after a job offer has been made. This may be done through a medical questionnaire and/or check-up. The problem is that if a concern comes to light, such as a disability that has led to a lot of sick leave, the prospective employer may want to withdraw the job offer. Unfortunately, this course of action will probably result in an employment tribunal claim unless reasonable adjustments are considered first.

Due to these potential pitfalls, the risk assessment should look at how disabled candidates are dealt with to see if there are any weaknesses in the process.

If the situation has not yet arisen, then a theoretical look at what would happen would be appropriate. Emphasis should be on ensuring that all those involved in the recruitment process are aware of what they can and cannot do. Where there are gaps, then the risk recommendation should suggest that training be given on disability awareness.

Interview questions

At interview, there are more potential pitfalls. One is a candidate who asks provocative questions in order to provoke the interviewer into making discriminatory comments. These are likely to be used against the employer if the candidate does not get the job. A classic example of this is the interviewee who voluntarily states that she is pregnant or wants to start a family in the next couple of years. Whilst this may not be evidence of a serial litigant, warning bells should be sounding. This is because any interviewer who indicates that it would be inconvenient for their business, and later rejects the candidate, is likely to receive a sex discrimination claim. The inference of sex discrimination is likely to have been raised, so the burden of proof will move to the potential employer to rebut it. To do this, the employer will need to show that on the balance of probabilities, the rejection was for a matter unrelated to the question about starting a family. Once again, defending such a claim will take time and money.

Equally, interviewers could accidentally fall into the trap of asking discriminatory questions themselves. Again, this is most likely to arise with female applicants of child-bearing age being asked how they plan on juggling work and children. It becomes a problem because it is still highly unlikely that men will be asked this question. For this reason, questions should be restricted to those that are competency-based and which test skills and aptitudes. Keeping the process objective in this way also makes it easier to provide objective feedback to any candidate who was unsuccessful. Those interviewing should also use a standard set of questions based on the job description and person specification being recruited for. Again, this will make the process more objective and make it harder to stray off topic into potentially discriminatory territory.

Discrimination against trade unionists

This has become topical following reports that employers across the European construction industry had introduced blacklisting (denying employment) to candidates on the grounds of activism or union membership. In the UK, it was discovered that 44 construction employers had paid a third-party company for access to a blacklist of 3,000 in 2009. As a result, the Employment Relations Act 1999 (Blacklists) Regulations 2010 were introduced. Their aim is to ban employers and employment agencies from compiling, distributing and using blacklists that contain information on trade unionists and activists. Compensation is payable in the UK and is subject to a minimum of £5,000 if a claim is brought in an employment tribunal. If it is brought in a county court, there is no minimum or maximum award. It is also possible for an 'injury to feelings award' to be made. Plus, there could be separate sanctions levied under the Data Protection Act 1998, since those featuring on the list will be unaware of the fact and will not have given their consent to their personal details being held.

In 2011, a delegation of blacklisted trade unionists and safety representatives held talks in Brussels with the European Union Commissioner with responsibility for employment, social affairs and inclusion. Its purpose was to discuss the potential for EU-wide legislation, as the problem of blacklisting by construction companies also extended to Ireland, France, Sweden and the Netherlands. But to date, nothing appears to have happened. However, new impetus may have been created when blacklisting hit the headlines again in 2013. This followed allegations that construction companies involved in the London 2012 Olympics and the Crossrail project adopted the practice. Unfortunately, employers in other Western economies are also leaving themselves vulnerable, such as in Australia. On 11 November 2013, Working Life reported that one of the largest construction companies in Australia had been taken to court by the Electrical Trades Union for pressuring subcontractors not to use shop stewards or safety representatives. Apart from heavy fines, there is also the reputation damage that can be caused to an employer, especially where safety issues are concerned.

Although mainly associated with the construction industry, employers in other sectors should also avoid the practice. This is done by avoiding what is known as a 'prohibited list'. This contains details of those who are currently members of trade unions or those who have taken part (or are participating) in union activities. It must have been created with the intention that employers or employment agencies would use its contents to discriminate during recruitment. In the UK, there is a reverse burden of proof. So if a candidate can show that his or her name was on a prohibited list and that employment was refused despite having the right skills, the employment tribunal must conclude that the reason for this was down to the blacklist. The potential employer would then have to show that the reason was unconnected, which may not be easy to do.

Even without blacklists, trade unionists enjoy legal protection when applying for jobs. More information on the type of employer behaviour that triggers this protection can be found in the UK Government's report 'Union membership rights of members and non-members' (2006). Produced by the Department of Business, Innovation and Skills (BIS), it covers the following:

- refusing or deliberately failing to deal with a job application or enquiry;
- causing the candidate to withdraw their application or not pursue it;
- refusing or deliberately failing to offer them the type of job sought;
- offering a job but on terms that no reasonable employer looking to fill the vacancy would offer, and which is not accepted;
- offering a position of the kind sought but later withdrawing the offer or by applying pressure not to accept it.

Employment tribunals have various powers, including being able to require prospective employers to pay compensation. It can also 'recommend' that they consider the candidate for a job. Any refusal to do so may lead to an increase in the amount of compensation owing, subject to an upper limit. For completeness, any risk assessment covering this area should look at what happens in practice. In countries where discrimination against trade unionists is outlawed in recruitment, problems can be avoided simply by not asking if candidates are union members.

Candidate screening

CV/application checks

When an organization employs someone, they may be entrusting this individual with money, confidential information and/or a significant investment in their learning and development in order to take up the role. But in all cases, they will be putting their business reputation in this unknown quantity's hands. So if the new employee lacks the qualifications and experience that they claim to have, significant reputational damage can be caused, which can take time and money to rectify. Apart from the costs of having to recruit a replacement employee, the fallout can also damage the morale of existing staff and the employer's brand too. For this reason, it is vital that organizations carry out due diligence checks on the CVs and application forms they receive. Unfortunately, since the job market has got far more competitive in recent years, checks have become even more crucial, as exaggerating or lying about qualifications and experience has increased.

In the financial services sector, these checks must be even more stringent and include checking for county court judgements, criminal convictions and other financial misdemeanours. If anything is found, it must be acted upon quickly. If Barings Bank had carried out better due diligence, it would have discovered that Nick Leeson had failed to disclose county court judgements for unpaid debts. Managers would also have found out that the Securities and Futures Authority refused to accredit him. Whilst an extreme example, it is a good one as it illustrates the damage that one man was able to inflict on a long-standing and highly respected bank. Another sector where stringent background checks are vital is in the NHS. Unfortunately, there have been several recent cases where fraudsters have slipped through the net. One case involved a former clinical director who lied about being medically qualified. Luckily, in the nine to ten years that he spent in strategic roles, he had no patient contact. However, he was imprisoned and ordered to pay back £270,000.

There may also be a tendency to be less thorough when recruiting senior staff, including directors. One reason for this is that there is an underlying assumption that due to their seniority, more recent employers would have carried out sufficiently robust background checks, either directly or via recruitment agencies. Unfortunately, this is not always the case. This is despite the fact that those at senior management level have far greater opportunity to commit wrongdoing, given that they are in positions of trust and are often budget holders. Given this dangerous combination, the potential to damage their employer is much greater than that of a junior-level hire. A good example of this is the Co-op Bank. Its reputation of being an ethical organization was in tatters when revelations of what its former chairman, Reverend Paul Flowers, got up to in his personal life were published in the UK media. Unsurprisingly, tales of alleged drug-fuelled orgies with rent boys led to an exodus of savers, not to mention the potential loss of new customers.

So any employee risk assessment that is revisiting the recruitment process needs to look carefully at what checks are made in practice. Just looking at what the relevant procedure says is not enough on its own. Unfortunately, with the time and cost pressures that now exist in many HR teams, it is easy for corners to be cut – with potentially devastating consequences. So one way of approaching the assessment is to take a number of different posts recruited for throughout the organization and review what checks were made. These posts should ideally be at different levels of seniority and in different functions. If there were problems, the risk assessment should take a blame-free look at what they were and what lessons have been learned.

The risk assessment will also need to focus on how CV checks comply with the data protection laws at work in the employer's jurisdiction. This relates to candidate verification and vetting, and how far an employer can reasonably go in making such checks. There are obvious privacy issues involved, due to the gathering of what is personal and possibly 'sensitive' personal data. Therefore, it would be sensible to review what information is provided to applicants on this (if any). For example, this would include what checks will be made and at what point, eg during the initial sift or when a job offer is made. So if an employer's policy is not to look at candidates' social media profiles until they have a shortlist, make this clear (as many candidates now provide potential employers with links to them).

Providing such information to candidates has also become necessary, however, due to the more damaging checks that some employers carry out that infringe privacy. These involved recruiters accessing candidates' social media profiles on sites such as Facebook, but not informing them that they were doing so. If they did not like what they saw, then the application would proceed no further. Yet the candidate would not know why. Whilst an employer might argue that public settings on these sites mean that a candidate by implication consents to these searches, this is legally dubious, certainly in the UK. Worse still is the practice that some US employers have adopted of waiting for candidates to arrive for interview before asking for their Facebook login and password details. There are several reasons why these practices are problematic. First, it is asking for information that would be considered excessive under data protection legislation. It also begs the question of why obtaining this information is necessary. In other words, what relevance does someone's leisure activities generally have on their ability to carry out the job being recruited for?

Facebook itself has something to say on this practice. Under the 'Registration and Accounts Security' section in its 'Statements of Rights and Responsibilities', it states that sharing a password or letting anyone else access a Facebook account is in breach of its terms of service, because it presents a security risk. The other problem for employers is that a candidate's profile often contains personal information, such as gender, age, religion and ethnicity. If an individual is not hired, the employer may be vulnerable to a discrimination claim as these are protected characteristics. It would then have to put resources into rebutting any inference that it used personal details to determine employment suitability.

Another reason is that many individuals were unaware that employers were adopting this process, or that the default Facebook setting was to public view. Also, Facebook, like MySpace, is a social medium and users tend to adopt a lax attitude to what they post on their 'wall'. Equally worrying is the risk of mistaken identity, especially where a candidate has a common name. Given that attaching photographs with CVs and application forms is not a common recruitment practice in the UK, the likelihood of this happening is higher. Thus the risk assessment should examine whether or not such vetting actually occurs. Apart from the issue of breaching data protection legislation, there is also the reputation damage that could arise if these practices became public knowledge. All it takes is for an agency temp, intern or disgruntled employee to compose a tweet or twitter post and it could go viral.

If the risk assessment reveals concerns in this area, the recommendations will need to focus on how validation and vetting practices can be tightened. For UK employers the easiest way of doing this is to abide by the Employment Practices Data Protection Code. This is produced by the Information Commissioner's Office, and whilst it has the legal status of guidance, following it will be enough to be legally compliant. Its principles can also be used by those in other jurisdictions. The recommendations should be as follows:

- Outline the verification process to candidates and tell them what methods will be used. Where vetting is also required (eg for working with children, or for reasons of national security), explain what this involves.
- Part of this process will include gathering references from a third party. How this works should be explained to candidates and their prior consent obtained.
- State that it is company policy to check any social media links offered up only at the point when a job offer is to be made. If any are checked before then (and many employers will check candidate

LinkedIn profiles), remember that the viewer may show up as having done so, depending on their personal visibility settings.

- Where any post-job-offer searches reveal inconsistencies, do allow the candidate to provide an explanation for these anomalies before withdrawing the offer.

One important lesson concerning background checks is never to assume that a previous employer has been thorough in carrying them out. In fact, it is better to work on the basis that none have been made. Various checks should be undertaken, which will to some degree vary on the level and type of position being recruited for. The precise order of checks may depend on the candidate numbers being shortlisted. Where numbers are few, the greater the number of checks that could be made before any interview takes place.

If problems have been found during the risk assessment, any recommendations could be based around the following:

1 **Sifting applications:** identify any gaps in employment dates and flag up for discussion if the intention is to invite the candidate to interview. Also check out any obscure universities or colleges that they claim to have attended. There are numerous bogus institutions that have been set up offering worthless qualifications. Where appropriate, make financial checks, such as searching the electoral roll for county court judgements. For director-level posts, check Companies House to confirm the status of any directorships as well as any disqualifications.

2 **Prior to interview:** when contacting the candidate to invite them to interview for managerial, professional or technical roles, ask them to bring the originals of key qualifications. The same applies to the roll number of any professional memberships that they claim to have. Explain that they will not be considered further without this information.

3 **During interview:** work through the candidate's application and talk about their last two to three jobs (where applicable). Ask about any gaps that are not easily explained and watch out for signs of discomfort. Where particular success and accomplishments have been claimed, ask for details and whether or not the relevant employer could support the statement(s).

4 **Job offer:** any job offer should be contingent on receiving satisfactory references. The same applies where Disclosure and Barring Service (DBS) checks are needed, ie for those working with children or vulnerable adults. Also verify candidate identity, because giving a maiden name or false address can invalidate certain background checks.

> **Key point**
>
> When corresponding with shortlisted candidates, point out that extensive background checks will be made. This is a free and easy way of weeding out some less than honest individuals.

If applications from foreign candidates are received, consider using a CV-checking agency that can verify foreign qualifications. One example is UK NARIC (**http://www.ecctis.co.uk/naric/**). This is managed on behalf of the UK Government and is the official source of advice to employers on qualifications and skills obtained outside the UK.

Employing foreign nationals

On the topic of foreign nationals, another minefield that an assessment should cover is ensuring that those employed have the legal right to work in whichever country is hiring. For countries in the European Union, there is a distinction made between workers coming from within the European Economic Area (EEA) and Switzerland as against those coming from outside it. EEA countries include EU members, plus Norway, Iceland and Liechtenstein. This group should have automatic entitlement to work, whilst all others will require permission. In the UK, any organization wanting to employ non-EEA nationals under the points-based system should apply to become a sponsor. This is managed by the UK Border Agency (UKBA). Without it, civil penalties of up to £10,000 per illegal worker can be levied against the employer (this may increase to £20,000 later in 2014). In the most serious of cases, they can also be found guilty of the criminal offence of knowingly employing an illegal migrant worker. This is usually done for financial gain and carries a maximum prison sentence of two years and/or an unlimited fine. Reputation damage can also result, as UKBA publishes quarterly 'naming and shaming' reports.

If an organization employs or intends to employ foreign nationals, the risk assessment should look at the steps taken to ensure that they have the legal right to work. For UK employers, this involves checking that the following are in place before an individual starts work:

- repeat document checks at least once every 12 months on those individuals who have a time limit on their right to work in the UK;
- that an individual is only employed for the type of work they are given permission to do and for the amount of hours that they are allowed to work;
- that recruiters know that it is no excuse to knowingly employ migrant workers illegally, regardless of any document checks carried out prior or during their employment.

Key point

An up-to-date list of acceptable documents to check can be found in the Home Office/UKBA's report 'Summary guide for employers on preventing illegal working in the UK'. The latest edition is April 2012. Other EU countries are likely to have similar requirements.

The risk assessment should also work through the recruitment process to ensure that it is fully compliant at all stages. The easiest way to do this is to remember that foreign nationals are protected from discrimination in the same way that UK nationals are protected. Yet whilst all those offered a job must be subject to right-to-work document checks, there are other steps that need to be taken with this group. The first is to ensure that offers of employment are conditional on them getting and maintaining permission to carry out the role that they are being employed to do in the UK. The second is to use the employment contract to reinforce this by putting the onus on the individual to maintain the necessary permissions. Also, make it a requirement for foreign nationals to give notification of any changes to their immigration status.

Another weak point for UK employers relates to the dismissal of those non-EEA nationals whose immigration status is about to expire and cannot be renewed. It is one of the limited areas where the relatively little-used ground of illegality can be used as a potentially fair reason to dismiss. The problem is that unless the employee does not have the necessary permission to work in the UK, the employer is at risk of an unfair dismissal claim. Merely believing that they lack the right is insufficient under this ground (based on current case law). Unfortunately, this is the position even where the employer carried out their own investigation by contacting UKBA itself. So one recommendation should be to use the other available ground for dismissal, which is 'some other substantial reason'. Here, dismissal is safe providing that the employer holds a reasonable belief that the employee lacks the legal right to work in the UK. In this case, a reasonable belief based on appropriate enquiries would suffice because the burden of proof is lower.

However, where dismissal is for 'some other substantial reason', employers will still need to follow a fair process. This will involve several meetings with the employee to look at ways of extending the right to work (assuming that this is what the employee wants). As part of this process, employers are expected to be more proactive in helping the employee secure the necessary immigration clearance. Whilst this might seem to be time-consuming, it will help avoid any later allegations of race discrimination. This could arise if the employee feels that the lack of assistance in obtaining further legal permission to extend their stay is on racial grounds.

> **Key point**
>
> It will also be necessary to give the foreign national notice. Therefore, a system must be in place to ensure that this notice is completed before the right-to-work expires.

Specific recruitment needs

Recruiting for skilled/senior roles

A different type of vulnerability for employers lies in what is often described as the 'war for talent'. This refers to senior, technical and specialist roles where the demand for employees with specific skills-sets is increasingly exceeding the available supply. According to the CIPD's annual 'Resourcing and Talent Planning Survey 2013' (in conjunction with Hays), managers and professionals/specialists and technical positions were the most difficult vacancies for employers to fill, followed by senior managers/directors. For manufacturing and production-based businesses, a lack of relevant sector/industry experience was a particular problem. One in six employers reported that a lack of candidates either caused or contributed to their recruitment difficulties. If this is not resolved, an organization's ability to survive and grow is hampered. This fact is acknowledged in the '16th Annual Global CEO Survey' carried out by PwC (2013). This research involved 1,330 CEOs in 68 countries and found that, overall, 58 per cent were concerned about the impact that skills shortages would have on business growth. In the previous year's research, this figure was 54 per cent. The problem is most acute in fast-growing markets such as Africa, where 82 per cent of CEOs are experiencing a problem.

Apart from the negative effect on an organization's ability to expand, these recruitment difficulties may create another problem: employers might panic and lower their standards in order to increase the supply of candidates. Now, unless the original person specification and competencies were unduly stringent or unrealistic to begin with, this could have a detrimental impact, the most obvious problem being that a poor-quality candidate might be appointed in a hurry. Unfortunately, there is no quick fix to this type of demand-and-supply problem. However, any risk assessment into recruitment practices could usefully test to see whether this is, or could be, a problem for the organization. Where senior candidates have been appointed into roles over the previous one or two years, a review could be made as to the progress (or otherwise) that they have made since they joined. This could be reviewed against their objectives.

With regards to recommendations, one could be that the current strategy for succession planning is reviewed in the near future. Whilst it will not solve situations where entirely new skills are needed, or there are other reasons to look externally, it will at least alleviate difficulties going forward. The risk assessment could ask the following 10 questions:

1 Have the skills, experience and personal qualities necessary to take the organization forward been correctly identified?

2 Are these subject to regular reassessment in order to ensure that they reflect current business realities, such as requiring specific language skills due to entering new markets?

3 Have managers who currently possess these attributes been identified?

4 Has an exercise been carried out into identifying a second tier who are showing signs of potential to acquire the relevant skills and qualifications?

5 If there are gaps, has a gap analysis been undertaken into identifying what areas these managers must develop in order to get where they need to be?

6 Are appraisals used to identify candidates for succession planning?

7 Have these matters been discussed in appraisals and are managers encouraged to put themselves forward?

8 Has a training needs analysis been carried out into what learning and development interventions will be necessary to get them up to speed?

9 Are these managers included in more complex-level activities and projects in order for them to gain the right experience?

10 Is there a formal system of mentoring potential high-flyers?

High-volume recruitment

At the other end of the spectrum are the problems associated with high-volume recruitment. Research published in September 2013 by Talent Q, a talent management and psychometric testing consultancy, found that the increased numbers of candidates chasing each job are resulting in the wrong people being hired. It surveyed some of the largest organizations in the UK who have requirements for staff in sales, service and customer-facing roles. One finding of concern was that 37 per cent of respondents admitted to knowingly hiring unsuitable candidates for the sake of filling a role quickly. Another is that because the expectations that the new recruits had in the job were not realized, they soon left. This was a problem for 48 per cent of respondents. Apart from generating high turnover rates, the recruitment cycle then restarts in order to hire replacement staff.

The implication that the high churn rates had on respondents are worth mentioning, as the costs involved are substantial: 60 per cent of those that relied on large numbers of front-line staff experienced an annual turnover rate of more than 20 per cent, but 32 per cent have a turnover of 31–50 per cent. Applying the CIPD figure of an average cost of £2,000 per employee hire, this will come at a price. They also have acknowledged the link between employing the wrong staff and the damage that it can cause to both the employer and the consumer brand respectively. After all, employees who are waking up to the harsh realities of their new job will not be giving the best customer service or successfully selling their new employer's goods and services.

Talent Q's report goes on to focus precisely on where the weaknesses lie during recruitment. It found that a major problem was that recruiters are unaware of the qualities they should be seeking in potential candidates. For example, when looking at recruiting for customer service and selling posts, they found that only 40 per cent of the population are likely to have good customer service skills, and only 37 per cent are likely to be strong on selling. Taking both together, only 12 per cent are likely to be strong in both skills. Whilst their report is being used as a marketing tool to promote psychometric testing amongst employers, it does raise an important question. This is to do with how many employers might hesitate to use this type of testing due to cost, but are willing to haemorrhage much greater sums of money servicing high staff-turnover rates.

If volume recruitment is being included in the risk assessment, it needs to look at what the existing turnover rate is and set approximate costs against it. It also needs to look at the comments made in exit interviews. Another area to consider is current working conditions. This does not just refer to pay and benefits, but what the physical environment is like. In other words, how attractive a place to work is it that people will want to work there? The danger for some employers is that they have become complacent during the recession. Once the labour market shows sustained signs of improvement, staff may vote with their feet and leave in much larger numbers. If so, this could have a highly damaging effect on an organization, as high-volume recruiting tends to be for front-line posts.

Recommendations can include the following, depending on each organization's own circumstances:

- to ensure that competencies for these roles have been clearly identified;
- to confirm that they have been properly communicated in any vacancies advertised;
- if the current interview process does not test candidates' practical skills, such as telephone manner or how they would deal with awkward customers, to introduce these tests;

- to align the employer value proposition (EVP) (see the section on 'employment mismatch' above) with candidate expectations;
- where the turnover is high, to consider changing recruitment practices, eg to include psychometric testing in order to weed out unsuitable candidates;
- to review the induction process if attrition rates are high during the first few weeks of employment.

Promoting internal candidates

Another risk factor to build into any employee risk management review is the thinking around promoting from within. The main problem here is the employer who bases such promotions around subjective rather than objective thinking, for example assuming that because an employee is a known quantity that they will automatically be suited to a more senior or lateral move. This is often done with the best intentions on the basis that an individual is somehow owed a promotion and that acknowledging them in this way will help maintain harmonious working relationships. Yet, the reality is often that whilst the employee is competent in their existing job, they lack the skills or aptitude necessary to successfully progress. A related problem with the same outcome is the manager who promotes in their own image in order to build or maintain a power base, rather than sourcing the best recruit for the job. If so, there is a risk that functional job skills will take second place to the ability to be a 'yes man or woman'. Whilst this may not harm an organization in the short term, it is hardly conducive for its medium- to long-term success.

If this is highlighted as a problem, the risk assessment recommendations should focus on introducing the same objectivity into internal promotions as those that would exist for external appointments. Doing this will also have the added benefit of reducing the likelihood of discrimination-based claims, such as those brought on the grounds of sex, race or sexual orientation. Given the number of different groups now protected under anti-discrimination legislation, a grievance (or a tribunal claim) could easily come forth from an unsuccessful internal candidate. A lack of objectivity and transparency in how internal promotions are carried out will unfortunately leave an organization vulnerable to a tribunal claim. For these reasons, the employee risk assessment should check to see if the points listed below are in place. If not, they can form the basis of the recommendations for improvement:

- Consideration of what skills, experience and qualifications are necessary to do the job, plus any wish list of desirable abilities, such as proficiency in a foreign language.
- Creation of a policy on promoting internal candidates. This should contain an undertaking that all job vacancies will be open to suitably qualified employees before looking externally. In the event that there is more than one suitable employee, it should outline what screening criteria will be used, such as sickness absence record (excluding any pregnancy-related sickness and that associated with a protected disability).
- Briefing managers on the importance of making hiring decisions based on an objective set of criteria rather than favouritism.
- Maintaining an audit trail to show that any internal promotion was made objectively.

Chapter summary

Employment mismatch:

- leads to disparity between what the job requires and the candidate recruited for it;
- can be caused by not updating old job descriptions and person specifications;
- arises due to a temptation to oversell a role in some way;
- often leads to employee disengagement that results in reduced productivity;
- if not dealt with effectively can result in disciplinary proceedings;
- may result in high staff turnover due to dissatisfaction in the job;
- may be caused by disconnect between the consumer brand and realities of a mundane job.

Discriminatory job adverts:

- can cause problems as protection from unlawful discrimination starts during recruitment;
- can leave the organization vulnerable; there are still some pitfalls around age discrimination in vacancies advertised;

- provide a good income for serial litigants who deliberately sue recruiting employers.

Hiring policies:

- 'lookism' is illegal if protected groups are discriminated against, eg by age, race or disability;
- 'fattism' may be discriminatory if obesity is related to a disability, eg treatment side-effect;
- if 'refer a friend' schemes are used, it is discriminatory not to also advertise internally;
- 'refer a friend' schemes may fall foul of the public sector equality duty;
- disability discrimination may arise if health questions are asked prior to a job offer;
- avoid asking discriminatory questions at interview, eg do you have family commitments?;
- blacklisting trade unionists is illegal in several countries, including the UK.

Candidate screening:

- job applicants may lie about skills, qualifications and experience;
- watch out for failure to verify the value or legitimacy of foreign qualifications;
- lack of thorough financial checks where required can lead to fraud/theft;
- do not assume that senior candidates have been thoroughly checked by previous employers;
- looking up candidates on social media sites such as Facebook breaches data protection laws;
- carry out checks to ensure that non-EEA nationals have the legal right to work in the EU;
- there are civil penalties of up to £10,000 for each illegal worker employed in the UK.

Specific recruitment needs:

- there could be talent shortages for those with specific skills-sets or qualifications;

- there could be risk of employers lowering standards to increase the supply of candidates;
- employers engaged in high-volume recruitment often choose the wrong candidates;
- choosing the wrong candidate leads to higher staff-turnover rate as disillusioned staff resign;
- there is a problem in that internal promotions might be made for subjective rather than objective reasons;
- there is a tendency for managers to promote in their own image, which can lead to 'yes' men and women.

Recommendations:

- analyse high staff turnover to look at other variables including:
  - length of service – it may peak at certain points, eg six months or two years;
  - team cohesion – if the face does not fit, new employees may be 'frozen out';
  - underlying reasons – exit interviews may not get the truth behind a departure;
  - seasonal patterns – eg weather-related factors such as swelteringly hot offices.
- when an employee resigns, ask what the job actually involves, as it may have changed;
- use this opportunity to reassess what you want in a job holder;
- maximize the information given by employees in exit interviews;
- create an employer brand through use of an EVP (employer value proposition);
- consider using **http://www.glassdoor.com** to aid with external branding;
- if 'refer a friend' schemes are used, ensure vacancies are always advertised internally;
- when drafting job adverts, focus solely on the requirements of the role;
- look at the type of experience that is necessary rather than length of experience;

- flag up applications where the candidate seems too perfect or lives too far away;
- maintain a good audit trail of paperwork in case of challenge by unsuccessful candidates;
- if sued, visit **http://www.serial-litigants.com** to see if the claimant has brought other claims;
- introduce briefings for recruiters on 'lookism' and its potential to breach discrimination law;
- ensure recruiters know when health-related questions can be asked at interview;
- avoid using a 'prohibited list' to weed out applicants who are trade union members;
- to inform shortlisted candidates as to what checks will be undertaken and when;
- check CVs/applications thoroughly and ask for originals of qualifications;
- ask for roll numbers of professional memberships;
- use UKBA's 'Summary Guide for Employers on Preventing Illegal Working in the UK';
- review strategy for succession planning based on 10 key questions;
- with high-volume recruiting:
  - ensure competencies for the roles have been clearly identified;
  - confirm that they have been properly communicated in any vacancies;
  - carry out practical tests of candidate's telephone skills;
  - align the EVP with candidate expectations;
  - where turnover is high, consider introducing psychometric testing;
  - review the induction process if turnover rates are high during the first few weeks;
- for internal promotions, ensure the process is objective rather than subjective;
- maintain an audit trail to show that any internal promotion was made objectively.

Chapter 6 looks at the different types of 'worker' and 'third parties' and the unique threats and vulnerabilities that each can introduce into an organization.

Types of 'employee' and third parties

06

Introduction

Apart from general threats and vulnerabilities presented by the workforce, different types of 'employee' present even more potential risks. For example, new challenges will arise as older workers remain at work for longer, especially in terms of dismissal (see Chapter 11). At the other end of the age spectrum, growing numbers of young workers are leaving school unprepared for working life. Other difficulties for employers can arise via remote workers, particularly in terms of managing data security. The same applies with third parties and ensuring that independent contractors are genuinely self-employed. Get this wrong and it can be expensive if they successfully claim 'worker' status. Equally, outsourcing is popular, but can backfire if the outsourcing company's workforce damages the hiring organization's reputation by their actions. Volunteers and interns can also present problems in certain circumstances. With these points in mind, this chapter looks at these different threats and vulnerabilities and considers how best to manage them.

Ageing workforce

Realities of an ageing population

According to December 2013 figures from the Office for National Statistics (ONS), 10 per cent of those aged 65 or over are in employment in the UK. This is the highest-ever number of people in this age group in work, and can be explained by the abolition of the default retirement age, as well as the reality that many people cannot afford to retire. In other cases, employees may simply enjoy their job and the sociability of the workplace. This trend is also being repeated elsewhere. For example, according to the Australian Bureau of Statistics, there were 3.22 million people aged 65 and over living in the country in June 2012; now comprising 14 per cent of the population, they are being encouraged to remain in the workforce due to falling migration and sliding population growth. In the United States, the 2010 census shows that nearly 22 per cent of men over 65 were in work and almost 16 per cent of women. Depending on the country, this can present a number of challenges to employers. The main ones are as follows.

Declining performance

With an ageing workforce, one problem that will start emerging more fully in the coming years is how to deal with declining performance in older workers. This refers to both mental and physical deterioration, which may gradually start to emerge once an employee reaches their late 60s. This is especially the case in the UK due to the abolition of the default retirement age: some of those who would originally have retired in October 2011 at 65 will now be approaching 68 in autumn 2014 with no signs of retiring. Unfortunately, the challenge for employers is that management time and effort will have to be expended by going through a performance management process. Any attempt to dismiss an employee due to poor performance could be met by a grievance or an employment tribunal claim. The same could apply where more subtle hints are given that it is perhaps time to retire, which could be construed as age-related harassment.

Any risk assessment should examine how older workers are currently being managed, or would be if any were employed in that age group. This means taking a good look at how declining performance would be treated in practice. Again, this is where honesty is required, as any shortcomings could result in the employer facing an age-based discrimination claim. In particular, those carrying out the risk assessment should be looking for evidence of a process where older workers would be performance-managed in the same way as their younger colleagues: age discrimination works both ways. Failure to do so could lead to arguments of bias operating in favour of older workers. Questions should also be asked on how performance issues are dealt with:

- **Sickness absence records:** would the employee's sickness absence record for the last one to two years be reviewed (going back any further is likely to be considered excessive under data protection principles)? The purpose of doing this is to identify the possible existence of medical problems that may harm their ability to carry out their job. This is more likely if the role is physical, but could suggest age-related ill-health problems, such as failing eye sight.

- **Appraisal history:** check if the manager would review the last few appraisals, which should be an accurate benchmark of performance. Equally, if shortcomings had been identified, there should be an audit trail of what action was taken to remedy them.
- **Training:** in some cases, declining performance may be due to an employee missing training on a new process or updated technology. So find out whether a manager would investigate this as a possibility before taking any further action.

Next, the risk assessment should see how a manager would raise issues with the older worker and at what point. An approach should be made as soon as there is evidence that a problem exists and that this is more than a temporary blip. Ideally, this approach should seek to resolve matters informally before adopting a formal process to improve performance (known as capability proceedings). Hopefully, an early intervention will be enough to resolve the problem, but if not, it will help provide evidence should formal capability proceedings become necessary. For completeness, the risk assessment should also review what options are on offer to older workers who seek a gradual, phased retirement. If no provision currently exists, recommendations could include the following:

- **Go part-time:** one possibility is a phased retirement that starts with the employee moving to part-time hours. Any task(s) that they are struggling with could be reallocated to junior employees who could benefit from the extra experience.
- **Mentoring:** another option is for the employee to change roles and mentor other staff. This would resolve the problem, whilst allowing the employee's knowledge and experience to be passed on and retained within the organization.
- **New role:** if there is a vacant position that is less demanding in some way, consider moving the employee into it. Although to some extent it is a 'stop-gap', it allows for their skills and knowledge to be passed on to others in the organization.

Another advantage of these solutions is that they also solve the problem of declining performance whilst allowing the employee to retain their dignity. This alone will reduce the likelihood of a grievance being raised or, worse still, an employment tribunal claim. As agreeing to one or a combination of these options will be a big step for the employee (and an admission that he or she is not coping as they once were), they should be given time to consider it. A trial period should also be offered. If agreement is reached, the employment contract and salary package can be amended to reflect the changes. If the employee refuses these options, advise them that formal capability proceedings will be brought if no sustained improvement is forthcoming.

Succession planning

Closely related to this topic is the subject of succession planning and development. This can present challenges for any employer, but especially for UK employers, as no set retirement age means possible 'bottlenecks' of employees in their late 60s or older. Unless the organization is expanding at entry level, this will prevent school leavers from entering the workforce. So, the assessment should look at what use is made of 'workplace discussions' as part of the appraisal process. These are recommended by the Acas guide *Working Without the Default Retirement Age* (2011). They provide a safe environment to discuss how older employees see themselves contributing to the organization, both now and into the future. If there are no performance issues, but the employee indicates that they want to consider their options, a discussion can take place on how they can get actively involved in developing the next generation.

As already mentioned, this could be through a transition to a mentoring or coaching role, on a part-time or full-time basis. Equally, it could involve a change of job that would allow for the employee's knowledge to be passed on to others. This will also combat the main criticism of succession planning in that there is often too much emphasis on planning and not enough developing of future talent. If this is not something that is already happening, then recommendations can be made along these lines. The same applies to having an audit trail from these meetings. Where necessary, any recommendations should suggest that the employee receives a written summary of the meeting. They should also suggest that these workplace discussions are held as part of the appraisal process.

> **Note**
>
> Whilst many other countries have fixed retirement ages, do bear these UK-centric points in mind, in case the decision is ever taken to follow the UK and dispense with fixed ages altogether.

Age-related insured benefits

Insured benefits linked to age will become a growing problem for UK employers especially. One illustration of this is the case of *Witham v Capita Insurance Services Ltd*, case number 2505448/12 (2013) – an employment tribunal case, it indicates how this type of case may be approached in future. The tribunal had to consider if stopping permanent health insurance (PHI) payments once an employee turned 55 was age discrimination. In this case, Witham had been denied the chance to join a more favourable PHI scheme that would have entitled him to continue receiving PHI payments until he reached 65. The situation arose because he was ill when the new scheme was introduced. As a result, he was not in 'active service', which was a precondition. The insurer was not prepared to indemnify his employer, Capita, in respect of PHI payments if the employee was not 'actively at work' when applying to join. The employment tribunal held that Capita had directly discriminated against Witham due to his age. Also, the less favourable treatment was not justified as a proportionate means of achieving a legitimate aim.

This is because the employer's stated aim of making PHI widely available as a workforce benefit (within the constraints of the policy age limits) failed, because only some employees were provided with PHI as a benefit. Also, denying Witham entry to the new scheme further went against this intention. Instead, the driving force was cost, given that payments ceased once the indemnity from the insurer was stopped. Unfortunately for Capita, the increased costs under these circumstances could not be considered as a proportionate means of achieving a legitimate aim. It also lost the indirect discrimination claim because the requirement for 'active service' as a qualifier to switch to the new PHI policy placed Witham at a particular age disadvantage. He was able to show that 92 per cent of those disadvantaged by this rule were over 45 – this was because they were more likely to be in receipt of PHI payments when the new scheme started. Therefore, they had a greater likelihood of being excluded from the more favourable scheme. Statistical evidence also showed that cost cutting was the main objective.

The ruling suggests that employers will face difficulties where any PHI (or other age-related insured benefits) is scheduled to cease payment at an age below 65, or the state retirement age applicable at the time. Any assessment into this area should check the terms of any PHI or similar benefit to see if the organization may be vulnerable to a similar claim. Checks should also be made to see if the age-related insured benefits offered provide similar benefits regardless of age (but see exception below). Unless there is an in-house expert, it would be advisable to contact the insurer or broker direct. If there are concerns, even if just in the longer term, the risk recommendations will need to apply some fresh thinking. One possibility is to change PHI policy terms to one that will pay for a specified period of time, such as five years. This would make it harder to allege age discrimination, as the benefit is based on a time period rather than age. Another option is to pay employees a cash sum so that they can make their own arrangements for long-term sickness cover.

> **Key point**
>
> Whilst UK-centric, these principles will increasingly apply to employers in other Western countries, as the effects of an ageing population start to be felt.

For UK employers with employees aged 65 and over, there is at least a partial 'get-out' clause provided by paragraph 14 of schedule 9 to the Equality Act 2010. This applies to insured benefits such as PHI, income protection, private medical cover and life assurance. It allows employers to cease providing access to insured benefits once employees reach 65, or the state pensionable age (whichever is the greater). This is to allow for the fact that the UK retirement age will steadily increase over the coming years. Such a proviso was introduced as the government realized that employers would withdraw the benefits from everyone due to the high costs of providing them to the over 65s. However, if these benefits are a contractual entitlement, withdrawing them from an employee aged 65 and over could result in a breach-of-contract claim in that the contractual position is entirely separate from age-discrimination laws.

Remote workers

Data security

Since the rapid evolution in notebooks, tablets and smartphones, it has become easier than ever for employees to work remotely. Whilst this is good for worker productivity, the flip side is data security weaknesses. According to research carried out on behalf of 3M in 2010, two-thirds of employees expose sensitive data when they work remotely. One problem is that passers-by (known as shoulder surfers) can see what people are working on in public spaces. For example, an employee could be developing a new marketing strategy or a presentation for a tender. In the time it takes to have a cup of coffee and a sandwich, anyone sitting nearby can get an eyeful of information. On a long plane or train journey, the situation is potentially far worse. The problem is enhanced by the ease of free Wi-Fi access. This makes it easy to turn a café, hotel, train station or airport into a temporary office. Unfortunately, free Wi-Fi is not secure, so someone can 'listen in' and see what websites have been visited and what passwords have been entered.

Homeworking can cause similar problems if the employee lets their family access a work computer. So the risk assessment should see what access is possible, such as being able to read business e-mails and documents. Other threats can be introduced via any downloads made. These could range from the downloading of porn, illegal music or film downloads as well as accidentally introducing viruses. If there are poor controls, they will need to be tightened (see Chapter 9). If this is a concern, the risk assessment should identify who works remotely. This will include those with a formal homeworking agreement, sales staff and those who travel abroad on business. Again, IT will need to identify what parts of the network these individuals have remote access to and whether existing IT security provisions are adequate. There is also the wider issue of the lack of employee awareness as to the potential problems. If this has not been covered in training, the risk assessment's recommendations could include the following:

- Running briefing sessions to remote workers on data security, as a high priority.
- Having IT produce some easy-to-read content for a staff newsletter. This should be aimed at all those who have access to computer networks either from home or remotely. It should include advice on limiting surfing on free Wi-Fi networks, the need to access only non-confidential information and to be mindful of who can see what they are working on.
- Ensuring that any policy on e-mail and internet use specifically covers 'dos and don'ts' for those who work remotely, even if only occasionally.

- Considering making it a disciplinary offence for an employee to allow a third party to use a computer or mobile device belonging to the organization. Although this cannot be policed, its purpose is to exist as a deterrent.
- Introducing a system that requires regular password changes.
- If a remote wipe function is in use by IT, checking that there are user agreements in place with staff.
- Considering purchasing privacy filters for laptops and tablets.

> **Key point**
>
> With remote wipe of personally owned mobile phones, written agreements are necessary. This is to ensure that there is no liability for any loss of personal data that arises when the device is wiped, eg following an employee's departure from the organization.

Productivity concerns

In a few cases, there may be concerns that those working remotely are less productive than those based on-site and working under the watchful eye of their employer. Though in practice, this is more likely to arise with homeworkers than travelling sales staff who operate in a target-orientated environment. If this is a concern, the risk assessment can examine what, if any, targets are set and what provision is made for regular face-to-face meetings. If there is a history of reduced productivity (eg in homeworkers), questions should also be asked about what use has been made of the organization's disciplinary procedures. If employees know what is expected of them – and that they have to account for themselves regularly – poor productivity should not be much of a concern. With homeworkers, the contract or homeworking agreement should also contain provision that it can be revoked if the employee abuses it. Taken together, this 'carrot-and-stick' approach should be sufficient.

Third-party threats

Agency staff

Whilst agency staff can provide employers with a rapid means of meeting seasonal or unexpected demand, they can also introduce their own threats and vulnerabilities into an organization. The first concerns the reputational damage that can be inflicted. This is something that is overlooked by many employers, as the imperative is often to recruit staff quickly and in large numbers. Yet, many temps are recruited into customer-facing roles, such as in retail or hospitality. Alternatively, they are engaged to work in call centres. However, from the perspective of current or potential customers, these agency staff will be seen as employees of the organization. So if the service provided is poor, it could damage the reputation of the organization. If there is a known or suspected problem in this area, the risk assessment should look at whether or not there is a link between any complaints made and the fact that the culprit is agency staff or an employee. Where a distinction is not currently made, a recommendation is that this information should be recorded.

The risk assessment should also look at a sample of different assignments to see what information is currently provided to agencies. This will determine if it is detailed enough to obtain suitable agency staff for the roles being recruited for. Questions should also be asked about the qualifications and experience required, and whether compromises are being made in this respect. Another area to review is what induction is provided upon arrival. This may be on a range of policies, including acceptable internet and social media use. Where necessary, any recommendations can focus on tightening up the recruitment of agency staff. They can be expensive when the agency's hourly charge is added on, so it is important that the right calibre of individual is recruited. In some roles, such as financial services, credit checks on the individual are necessary – the risk assessment must check that these are being made.

Another potential vulnerability concerns what information an agency temp is given access to during their assignment. For example, is computer network access set at a level that only the type of information necessary to do the job can be accessed? Or are the settings more lax? If so, it means that a temporary worker could access commercially sensitive information, which they could sell on. Fraud is another problem and, in this respect, temporary or contract staff often provide the biggest threats, due to the fact that they are likely have less loyalty to the organization but easy access. In fact, a good way for fraudsters to obtain information is via agency work, as background screening is often poor. So any risk assessment should look at the type of role that agency staff are used for and what checks are made. With the help of IT, see what access they have been given and whether or not this needs restricting in any way. If so, the recommendations will centre around how IT can tighten up on this.

Self-employed contractors/consultants

Self-employed contractors and consultants offer advantages in that they are often available at short notice, but do not increase the headcount. They also have the advantage of offering new skills and expertise. Many will trade under their own limited company (or equivalent), whereas some may freelance under their own or a trading name. The main threat here is the unintentional creation of a worker–employer relationship where the hiring organization did not intend one to exist. In the UK, if such a relationship was to be found by an employment tribunal, then the hirer would have to pay holiday pay. However, this is a greater risk with freelancers than with those who operate through a limited company, especially where the freelancers are ex-employees who have either opted for self-employment or were made redundant. In these cases, the HM Revenue & Customs (HMRC) may take an interest if it suspects that the self-employment is not genuine, but an attempt on the employer's part to evade a tax liability.

If the organization relies heavily on self-employed contractors and consultants, and there are concerns that they could accrue worker status via the back door, the risk assessment should examine the contracts for services and, where necessary, recommend the addition of the following:

- A statement that it is a contract *for* services. This is appropriate for a contractual relationship between a client and a contractor, rather than a contract *of* service that would exist between an employer and employee.
- That no 'mutuality of obligation' exists in that the self-employed contractor is not obliged to accept work and the hiring organization is not obliged to offer it.
- An outline of the skills and experience that led to the appointment being made. For example, that the self-employed contractor possesses skills that do not exist in-house.

- A statement to confirm that the contractor can provide substitute labour (though the hiring organization can insist on giving prior approval to the proposed replacement).
- Where applicable, the contractor must supply their own tools and/or equipment.
- A current certificate of insurance, such as professional indemnity.
- Although it is unlikely that this would arise in a medium to large organization, a requirement that invoices must always be submitted before payment will be made.

Another area to assess is non-disclosure agreements (NDAs). These are often issued to self-employed contractors and consultants in order to safeguard issues around confidentiality. If there is an in-house legal team, they will be best placed to do this. Where there is not, consider asking the organization's external legal advisors to review their content. One specific area to look at is whether or not an NDA is issued early enough in the process. For example, some organizations may need to share confidential information with consultants so that they can pitch a proposal. Although no appointment has been made, the information shared may still require protecting. A second check is how 'confidential information' has been defined. In other words, is it still relevant to the type of information that now needs to be covered? The business world is constantly evolving and it might be that the wording of any existing NDAs does not adequately reflect the latest developments, eg in digital media. Depending on the findings, any recommendations can centre on how these documents can be improved.

Outsourcing

Outsourcing refers to the transfer of business functions from a client organization to an external service provider, and is usually undertaken in order to reduce costs and workload. Typically, some activities lend themselves to outsourcing better than others. Commonly outsourced functions include call centres, IT, payroll and HR. When the decision to outsource is taken, a risk assessment should be carried out into potential providers. Normally the risk assessment's criteria will incorporate several areas including: 1) costs; 2) financial resources available for the contract; 3) contingency planning; 4) quality control; and 5) supply chain management. It should also cover the proposed service-level agreements (SLAs). But no matter how good this assessment process is, there will still be threats and vulnerabilities inherent in such an arrangement. For this reason, those responsible for managing any outsourcing contracts should be involved in this part of the assessment.

Of relevance here is the people aspect. This is because the same problems can arise as with agency staff. So once again, customers dealing with the outsourced functions will see those they are dealing with as employees of the organization that has their custom. So, if the quality of service or goods is poor, it will be the reputation of the organization that is put on the line rather than that of the external service provider. In some cases, poor-quality staff will result in goods or services being delivered late, be it to other organizations or private individuals. This is likely to affect customer satisfaction to the extent that some customers will take their business elsewhere. There is also the question of keeping shareholders happy, which is unlikely to be achieved under these circumstances. The problem is that where the motivator is cost cutting, the impact that third-party employees can have on reputation can so easily be overlooked.

Another concern is data leakage due to data protection breaches and fraud. The main vulnerability will be where the external service provider stores large amounts of sensitive data belonging to the client organization, such as financial information. For criminals, this is especially valuable and, given the current economic climate, they may find it quite easy to pay third-party employees to sell them client data. Also of relevance here are the number of other clients that are being serviced and whether or not there could be data mix-ups. For completeness, the following questions need to be asked from an employee risk management perspective:

- What screening is carried out on the outsourcing company's employees?
- What input does the client organization have on training those who will be providing goods or services to its customers and in its name?
- Is there a sufficient lead-in time to allow for any essential training to be given before the contract comes into force?
- Has the possibility of lower service standards for the first few months been acknowledged?

As the recommendations will largely involve contractual changes, they will be the domain of the department handling the outsourcing contracts. However, where one or more of the above four questions have been answered as a 'no', they can be turned into recommendations that, due to the people element, are reasonable for an HR department to have some input into.

Interns

Interns have been included here due to the difficulties that their lack of legal status have already presented to employers. A genuine internship is where interns are given the opportunity to shadow experienced employees and perform tasks under supervision. They may be unpaid on the basis that no work of value is being performed. However, it is customary to pay expenses, such as travelling costs. Since the recession began to bite in 2008, the demand for internships sky-rocketed amongst 16–24 year olds, due to high unemployment in this age group. Many employers in the UK and elsewhere responded ethically to this increased demand, but some saw it as an opportunity to use interns to carry out real jobs for nothing. Others were genuinely unaware of where the line was drawn on what tasks they could reasonably expect an intern to carry out. Once the media got hold of a few exploitation stories, it quickly became apparent that the use of interns was not without risk.

The first is the potential damage to an employer's reputation if they are publicly challenged for abusing the fact that so many young people are unemployed. This is not just through conventional media, but also via social media channels. A second danger is being reported to the authorities for failing to pay the national minimum wage. This has already happened in the UK in April 2013. Intern Aware, a campaign group, sent the government a list of 100 organizations that had advertised unpaid internships. This was forwarded to HMRC for them to investigate if they were genuine internships or not. In November 2013, HMRC announced an investigation into these employers. Should the internships not be genuine, organizations will have to fund back-pay of the national minimum wage (NMW) at the appropriate age rate. They will also be at risk of financial penalties of up to £20,000 and, in the most serious cases, prosecution.

In the UK, the Department for Business, Innovation & Skills introduced a policy of naming and shaming on its web pages those who deliberately flouted NMW requirements. This was introduced in 2011 as part of its business strategy on getting employers to pay the minimum wage. So, depending on the outcome of the HMRC investigation, it may be another route that could cause reputation damage to organizations. For these reasons, any organization still using unpaid interns should include them in their risk assessment and look at how they are being used in practice. This is not just in the UK, but in other countries with similar employment laws. The following questions need to be asked:

- Do the interns have set hours? If so, that indicates a worker relationship. Genuine internships are more flexible.
- Is the intern producing work or just shadowing experienced staff? If they are carrying out the type of task that would normally be given to an employee or agency staff, it is likely that they should be paid.
- Are demands being placed on them? As soon as an employer starts exerting control and issuing duties, they arguably become a 'worker' and accrue basic employment rights. This is because control is one of the tests of an employment relationship.

If the finding of the risk assessment concludes that insufficient distinction is being made, the following recommendations should be made:

- To identify how the intern's time will be spent. Mostly, this should be shadowing staff although allowing some time to practise carrying out some tasks is acceptable. However, feedback should be given, especially on those tasks that are more complex, such as writing a draft article for an in-house magazine.
- A basic intern agreement should be created to describe the situation regarding expenses, such as what will be paid, how frequently and if there is an upper limit. If there are perks, such as free lunches and invites to events, these should be mentioned.
- Any managers with responsibility for interns should be trained on the current legal position and the importance of not crossing the line into treating interns as workers.

Even where interns are paid, they could be working long hours, which can cause health problems. This is what happened to Moritz Erhardt, who was interning with Bank of America Merrill Lynch, when he collapsed and died in August 2013. He had been close to finishing a seven-week stint at its London headquarters but was said to have worked until 6 am for three days in a row. It was also reported that he had completed eight 'all-nighters' within two weeks. Once again, internships received bad publicity as other interns came forward with stories about the pressures faced by those competing for jobs. For example, there was mention of the 'magic roundabout': this is where taxis take interns home at 5 am, wait for them whilst they shower and change and then take them back to work. According to Erhardt's post-mortem, he died of epilepsy with lack of sleep likely to have triggered a seizure. Whilst investment banking is an extreme example, other industries, such as fashion, can involve long hours. For this reason, a review of hours should be recommended by the risk assessment.

Volunteers

Whilst volunteers offer real benefits to end-user organizations as unpaid labour, they can present their own problems. As with the self-employed, the main one is to avoid the accidental creation of an employment relationship where none is intended by the host organization. This could arise where the volunteer successfully argues that he or she has gained worker status due to a contract of employment having come into existence over time. What happens is that the volunteer takes the end-user organization's conduct as evidence that a legally binding agreement has been created. As part of this process, they will argue that something lawyers call 'consideration' has been exchanged. Consideration is a legal term that refers to the exchange of something of value, such as free attendance on non-job-related training courses, staff discounts or use of a workplace crèche when not volunteering. It also refers to the payment of expenses at a rate exceeding the actual costs accrued by the volunteer. All this arguably counts as pay and indicates an employment relationship.

Another contributing problem is when the end-user organization tries to exert control over the volunteer or otherwise create obligations. This might not happen immediately but, as the relationship develops, an organization may slip into trying to formalize working hours into a fixed pattern. In a similar vein, never try to dictate when a volunteer can and cannot take leave. Even if they appear happy for control to be exerted in this way, it may be because they are hoping to accrue basic employment rights, such as the right to receive the national minimum wage or paid annual leave. The only areas where it is safe to set out obligations are: 1) where there are statutory requirements, such as health and safety laws that must be followed, or: 2) the organization's own HR policies on key areas such as internet and e-mail use.

Where volunteers are used, the risk assessment should review how the system works. If necessary, one recommendation could be to introduce 'volunteer agreements'. These should focus on the 'hopes' for how the arrangement will work. It should avoid use of words such as 'employer', 'contract' and 'disciplinary' as these suggest an employment relationship. In fact, it should go further and expressly state that there is no intention on the part of either party to form a legally binding contract. It should also provide that the agreement can be cancelled at any time by either party and that only those travel expenses incurred will be reimbursed. As with agency staff and outsourcing, any volunteer who deals with customers or the public will often be assumed to be an employee. Yet they may receive little or no basic training. So for completeness, the risk assessment also needs to review what induction training is given. If it is not provided, or is poor, the obvious recommendation is to introduce or improve it. This can be justified on the grounds of minimizing reputation risk.

Young people

According to figures produced by Eurostat in 2013, 23.5 per cent of 16–25 year olds in the European Union are unemployed as of March 2013. Unsurprisingly, the worst-affected country is Greece, with just over 59 per cent of under-25s out of work. Spain follows with 55.9 per cent and Italy is third with 38.4 per cent. The UK stands at 20.1 per cent, with Germany and Austria having the lowest at 7.6 per cent each. As a comparison, the United States was included, with 16.2 per cent of this age group unemployed. This is no doubt due to the global economic crisis and the debt situation in several eurozone countries. Unfortunately, employers are understandably wary of recruiting those who have been unemployed for a long time. So a vicious cycle is created. There is also another problem, especially in the UK: the growing concern over the readiness of young people for working life. A key issue continues to be low educational standards when compared to other countries. For example, according to the 2013 annual Legatum Prosperity Index, the UK was rated 30th out of 142 countries for education. It was beaten by Hungary, Latvia and Lithuania.

The best countries were New Zealand, followed by Australia and Canada. Other research by the Organization for Economic Co-operation and Development (OECD) showed that out of 24 countries, England was rated 21st for maths and 22nd for literacy. So it is not surprising that Sir Terry Leahy, former CEO of Tesco, stated that too often employers are left to 'pick up the pieces' of poor schooling. This referred to the practice where some UK employers were providing school leavers with remedial maths and English skills. Unfortunately, the complaints have extended to the general lack of work readiness displayed by school leavers. The CIPD's *Employers are from Mars, Young People are from Venus* (2013) found that youngsters lack the ability to market themselves to employers. Its recommendations tended to focus on how employers should adapt their expectations for this age group. Yet it overlooks the fact that in the current economic climate, many employers do not need to spoon-feed young people in this way, as apart from those young people who can market themselves effectively, entry-level positions can easily be filled by experienced workers who simply need a job or who want to downshift.

This reality was acknowledged by the Work Foundation in its report 'Beyond the business case: the employer's role in tackling youth unemployment' (2013). It acknowledged that a moral duty on the part of employers to employ youngsters is not the same as having a compelling business case to do so. Any employee risk assessment covering this area should look at the number of workers in this 16–25 age group who have been recruited into the organization. This could look at a period of the last two to five years and should identify: 1) what, if any, problems have been experienced, such as poor-quality applicants; 2) if there have been enough young people applying; and 3) whether or not these candidates have the right qualifications and skills. Such an exercise is necessary in order to identify current or emerging problems in the supply of young talent. After all, it could be that media reports are masking the fact that there are already the beginnings of a supply problem.

Even if this is not the case, it is advisable that employers in countries with high youth unemployment should earmark it as a future threat to monitor periodically, due to the potential impact on successfully building a future workforce. The key aspect here is having the opportunity to mould adaptable young recruits in a way that will best suit the organization. Part of this is cultural, as young people can be trained into systems and processes unique to their employer, as well as its organizational culture. It is also because young people have what the report describes as 'digital literacy', which means that they can learn how to use multiple IT systems more quickly than older workers. Coupled with being more flexible and open to change, these are the skills and traits that employers will increasingly need as the pace of change increases in the coming years. One way around this is to consider offering work experience, or sandwich placements, to the 16–18 age group. Such a scheme could also fit nicely into any corporate social responsibility (CSR) initiatives already in operation.

Chapter summary

An ageing workforce means:

- an increase in the average age of employees;
- a rise in both worker ill health and the amount of sickness absence taken;
- UK employers preparing themselves for people to work into their late 60s and beyond;
- employers being prepared to do more performance management of older staff;
- treating older workers in the same way as younger workers;
- a challenge in succession planning;
- an increase in phased retirements, such as switching to part-time working;
- a likely increase in the cost of providing age-related insured benefits.

Remote working pitfalls:

- two-thirds of employees expose sensitive data when working remotely;
- the increased availability of free unsecured Wi-Fi increases the threat;
- homeworkers can give their family access to work computers and their contents;
- downloading porn or copyright material on to work computers;
- introducing viruses on to an employer's network via this type of download;
- reduced productivity on the principle of 'out of sight, out of mind'.

Paid third-party threats:

- reputation can be damaged as a result of their activities, especially in customer-facing roles;
- poor-quality control in their appointment if there are time pressures;
- the stealing and selling of sensitive commercial information, eg by agency staff;
- fraud due to lack of loyalty to an organization;

- unintentionally creating an employment relationship with self-employed labour;
- creation of an unwanted tax liability if an employment relationship is found;
- poorly drafted NDAs that do not fully protect the organization;
- poorly performed outsourced functions can cost in terms of loss of business;
- outsourcing could also lead to data leakage problems.

Unpaid third-party threats:

- the uncertain employment status that interns present to employers;
- damage to the host employer's reputation if seen to abuse interns;
- some employers are at risk of prosecution for using interns as workers;
- the danger of allowing interns to work long hours, which can cause health risks;
- with volunteers, the need to avoid creating an accidental employment relationship;
- reputation damage through poor training of volunteers in dealing with the public.

Young people:

- have problems with marketing themselves to employers;
- are unprepared for working life, eg they lack basic skills;
- are the future workforce, so a lack of supply could cause problems in a few years.

Recommendations:

- early intervention is best with older workers who are struggling in their role – try an informal approach, at least initially;
- consider options for a phased-retirement, such as switching to part-time working or mentoring others;
- give older workers time to consider their options and a trial period in any new role;
- UK employers should use employee appraisals to find out employee's retirement plans;

- written records should be kept of any 'workplace discussions' with older workers;
- look at changing age-related insured benefits to payment for a fixed period only;
- remote workers should be briefed on data security issues;
- ensure that any e-mail/internet use policy covers dos and don'ts for remote workers;
- make it a disciplinary offence to allow third parties to use work computers;
- introduce a system of regular computer password changes;
- if a remote wipe function is used by IT, ensure that user agreements are in place with staff;
- consider purchasing privacy filters for laptops and tablets;
- ensure that weekly/monthly targets are set for homeworkers in order to allay productivity concerns;
- issue homeworking agreements to contain a clause that can revoke the arrangement;
- tighten up pre-employment screening of agency staff;
- restrict agency staff's access to the computer network to only what is necessary;
- review and tighten up contracts for services for self-employed contractors;
- update any non-disclosure agreements in place;
- tighten up any outsourcing contracts at the point of renewal, for example:
  - better screening of outsourcing company's employees allocated to the contract;
  - more input on training these third-party employees;
  - increased lead time before the contract goes live in order to allow for this training.
- ensure that unpaid interns are mainly shadowing staff and not 'working';
- create an intern agreement to set out the relationship and position on expenses;

- train managers with responsibility for interns on the relevant legal issues;
- review the working hours of interns to ensure they are not excessive;
- introduce a volunteer agreement that states that no employment relationship is intended;
- provide training where necessary in order to avoid reputation risk (or safety breaches);
- check the quality of applicants in the 16–25 age group over last two to five years and flag current or emerging problems in recruiting young workers;
- monitor unemployment levels of young workers as it could have a future impact.

Chapter 7 examines employee well-being and engagement. This is against the backdrop of the global economic downturn and the realities of an ageing and increasingly unhealthy workforce.

Employee health and well-being   07

Introduction

Many organizations have mission statements proclaiming that 'our employees are our most important asset'. Yet, it is debatable as to how meaningful such declarations are, especially in recent years. This is due to the impact that the global economic downturn has had on employees in terms of redundancies, pay freezes and demands to do more with less resources. Apart from taking a toll on health and well-being generally, this pressure can lead to sickness absence and stress in the longer term. If there are concerns over job security, it can instead lead to 'presenteeism' (turning up to work whilst sick). Add an ageing and increasingly unhealthy workforce to the mix and there is a potentially toxic combination facing employers in the future. This chapter focuses on these interrelated areas and how they can be tackled. The emphasis is on emerging or underlying problems that many employers are not aware of, rather than more established health and well-being issues.

Health issues

Obesity

One literally growing problem is obesity. According to the OECD's 'Obesity update 2012', in the developed world more people than ever before are now obese. Until 1980, obesity affected fewer than 1 in 10 people. Since then, rates have doubled or even tripled, with the result that in 19 out of the 34 OECD countries, the majority of people are now overweight or obese. Its projections estimate that in some member countries more than two in three people will be overweight or obese by 2020. Obesity arises where an individual's body mass index (BMI) is 30 or above (25 or over is overweight). However, in some countries, its progression appears to have halted. Examples include Japan and Korea with obesity rates of 3–4 per cent at one end of the spectrum, with England towards the other with 22–23 per cent. Increases in obesity rates of between 4–5 per cent have occurred in Mexico and the United States, taking their figures to over 30 per cent. The figures for those who are deemed to be overweight are unfortunately far higher.

With childhood obesity, the same study found that one in five school-aged children across all OECD countries is affected by excess body weight. However, in the United States, Greece and Italy the figure is closer to one-third. Unfortunately, it is easy to see how this situation has arisen. One is the adoption of an increasingly unhealthy and sedentary lifestyle based around the TV and computers. Another is the cheapness and ease of availability of junk food. Not only is it cheaper than fruit and vegetables but BOGOF (buy one get one free) deals in supermarkets are often for junk food. Portion sizes have increased and some retailers actively promote unhealthy eating; the UK newsagent WH Smith was criticized for offering McDonald's vouchers as an incentive for parents purchasing their 'back-to-school' ranges. Given that these children are tomorrow's workforce, this issue should be flagged up by employers as an area to monitor.

At this stage, any risk assessment incorporating health issues should consider if overweight or obese employees are already presenting problems. This could be in terms of sickness absence or difficulty in carrying out their job due to their increasing size. Input from occupational health would also be valuable here (where applicable) to provide figures on any obesity-related sickness absence so that its current costs can be benchmarked. However, due to the data protection laws that operate in most countries, this information must not identify individuals. It would also be useful to know how many days of sickness absence in the previous two years is wholly or partly attributable to obesity. At this point, one recommendation is to check the effectiveness of any employee health and well-being initiatives already in place. These may range from an on-site or subsidized gym membership package through to healthy eating and weight-loss initiatives.

Chronic diseases

Many countries will experience an ageing workforce over the coming years. For example, according to a 2009 report produced by Bupa entitled 'Healthy work: challenges and opportunities to 2030', the average age of the UK workforce will increase from 39 in 2007 to nearly 43 by 2025. This is due to changing demographics and the presence of those in the workforce who are past state retirement age. As a result, the incidence of ill health among workers will also increase. For example, this research found that 40 per cent of those with one long-term medical condition say that it affects either the type, or the amount of work that they can manage. This is because the ageing process is linked to various common diseases. These tend to involve either frequent episodes of absence, such as for musculoskeletal disorders, or lengthy absences for other ailments, including cancer. The average number of days lost to sickness is also statistically higher for this older age group. Although this research is UK-focused, its findings will also be reflected in other countries to a greater or lesser degree.

Obesity is also contributing to the increase in chronic disease. According to the World Health Organization (WHO), within the next six years, medical conditions such as heart disease, diabetes and strokes will become responsible for 70 per cent of all deaths. Soon, this will start to have a knock-on effect for employers, and many will need to review what support is offered to staff to help them manage these conditions. For example, greater flexibility in allowing time off for hospital visits may become necessary. In other cases, working patterns may need to change. Two examples of this given in the Bupa report are diabetics, who require regular meal breaks, and angina sufferers who cannot work alone for long periods. However, on the plus side, Bupa found evidence that older workers can be more productive than their younger counterparts. This is due to better job satisfaction and being able to exercise more control over how their job is carried out.

Bupa's research also highlighted a growing need for awareness training amongst managers on how to manage teams that will increasingly include those with chronic conditions – and how best to accommodate them. The financial justification will lie in enabling those with long-term health conditions to remain in work. The alternative is the payment of sick pay for several months before the employee is dismissed; plus the costs of the management time involved. There will also be a societal cost, as in many cases these employees will go on to whatever state benefits operate in their country.

Adequately tackling these problems will require far more than employers being prepared to increase or refocus their spend on employee health and well-being. Instead, it requires government and third-party health provider intervention. Bupa recognized this and produced a follow-up report entitled 'Healthy work: evidence into action' (2010). Still valid, it recognizes that the realities presented by an ageing and unhealthy workforce cannot be managed by employers alone. However, it does look at what employers can do to respond to these future challenges. Its recommendations can be applied internationally and can be incorporated into the employee risk assessment as follows:

1 **Health profile:** if not already in progress, analyse the workforce's health profile by: 1) age; 2) amount and categories of sickness absence; and 3) the numbers participating in any health initiatives. These could include smoking cessation or weight-loss programmes. Again, due to data protection compliance, such data will need to be anonymous.

2 **Cost-benefit analysis:** to review existing health interventions to ensure that money is being targeted at those that produce results. Staff feedback on this would be valuable, eg via staff-satisfaction surveys. This will identify those initiatives that employees support, as well as those that are less popular.

3 **Future needs:** talk to occupational health on how to best target resources to manage the realities of an ageing workforce. Also, the organization's mindset needs to start adjusting so that it becomes more adaptable to changing worker needs in the coming years.

4 **Clear objectives:** irrespective of whether any health interventions are altered in the months following this assessment, ensure that they have clearly defined objectives that can be measured, eg percentage of employees who started a smoking cessation programme as against the proportion who have still quit smoking six months after the programme's end.

> **Key point**
>
> Employers acting on the recommendations for action put forward by Bupa will benefit in that the outcome will show if an organization's health and flexible working initiatives need to evolve to better reflect workforce needs.

Mental illness

The Bupa (2009) report mentioned above ('Healthy work: challenges and opportunities to 2030') also suggests that mental illness is a growing problem in both sickness absence and costs to the UK economy. In fact, mental illness is set to become the second largest source of ill health in the UK by 2030 (second only to musculoskeletal disorders, such as back pain). It is also something that can be aggravated by poor job quality and long working hours. According to Mind, the mental health charity (**http://www.mind.org.uk**), one in six workers currently deals with stress, anxiety or depression. It also found that the main cause was work. As a global issue, the World Health Organization recognizes that mental health is a growing concern, and so in 2013 it launched its 'Comprehensive mental health action plan 2013–2020'. This has been accepted by the World Health Assembly to take forward in member countries. One of its four objectives is to focus on prevention, so over the coming years, expect government schemes and initiatives in this area.

As with obesity and chronic disease, the risk assessment should identify the current levels of sickness absence that can be attributed to mental illness, such as anxiety. It should also examine what support is available to staff and whether it is adequate. Input from occupational health professionals is likely to be necessary here. Depending on the findings, one recommendation could be built around improving management awareness of mental illness and its symptoms. Due to the stigma still attached to mental health problems, much of it goes undetected. This is until an employee finds themselves suddenly unable to cope, which can result in lengthy sickness absence. Training targeted specifically at employers is increasingly being offered by mental health charities, so it is worth looking at setting up some in-house training.

Stress

The Health & Safety Executive (HSE) defines work-related stress as: 'The adverse reaction people have to excessive pressures or other types of demand placed on them at work.' Whilst stress is not a new phenomenon, it has become a global problem following the economic downturn. Workspace provider, the Regus Group, surveyed 1,000 corporations across 15 countries and found that workplace stress levels have increased. Although this research was undertaken in 2009, it is still relevant as the reasons behind the rise in stress levels remain in evidence today. The main finding was that an average of 6 in 10 workers in major global economies had experienced increased workplace stress in the two years leading up to 2009. China was the worst affected, with 86 per cent of people feeling this way. The increased focus on profitability was the main stressor across countries including the UK, the United States, Canada, Australia and Germany. Other causes included pressure from customers, risk of unemployment and a lack of administrative support.

The issue here is that many employers are turning a blind eye to both the problem and its extent. With the redundancies and pay freezes/cuts of the last few years, it has been an employer's market, and as a result, stress has been a latent problem that workers have kept quiet about, fearing for their jobs. Yet whilst this tactic may seem to have paid off, there is a tipping point. This is already starting to reveal itself in different ways. One is the increase in sickness absence (see the section on this below). A second is that once confidence in the job market is sustained, staff will look for other jobs. Replacing these staff will cost the employer money, not to mention the loss of the know-how that will leave with them. Also, staff will feel totally disengaged from their employer – and productivity and loyalty will diminish as a result. Once lost, this is hard to regain, especially as some employers still underestimate how costly stress can be to their organization.

Non-work factors are also becoming more relevant to how stress affects the working population. One example is the emergence of the 'sandwich generation'; adults who have ageing parents as well as children (and possibly grandchildren) who are dependent on them in some way. Increasingly, these children are adults who either cannot afford to leave home, or still rely on their parents financially. Many working people also have financial worries of their own, due to the increased cost of living and below-inflation pay rises. In other cases, spouses or partners have been made redundant and have been unable to find stable employment. In the UK, there has been a rapid growth in those wanting full-time employment but having to accept part-time work. This has been coupled with an increase in the use of contracts, including those operating on a zero-hour basis (a type of on-call arrangement where an employee only gets paid for actual hours worked).

Whilst the risk assessment could look at what sickness absence is stress-related, the figures are unlikely to give the true picture. An unknown percentage of stress-related absence will be attributed to other ailments, particularly where the employee self-certifies the reason for their absence. In an environment with poor job security, no employee will want their employer to know that they are stressed, as it suggests they cannot cope. The risk assessment should also look for evidence of the following points and base any recommendations around them:

- **Work–life balance:** encouraging staff to take their full annual leave entitlement and to use their designated lunch breaks. The same applies to monitoring their working hours (UK employers must comply with the Working Time Regulations 1998).
- **Monitor workloads:** whilst increasing workloads have been a reality for many organizations during the economic downturn, the situation needs reviewing. Workers should not be expected to continue indefinitely doing more with fewer people resources. It is in situations like this where underlying ill-health problems will become apparent.
- **Staff feedback:** evidence that managers know the mood of their staff. As this relies on managers interacting with staff rather than sitting tucked away in an office, it is likely that many will fall short here. Apart from talking about work pressures, good managers should be able to see if certain aspects of the job are conducive to stress.
- **Stress awareness training:** look at what training is given to line managers on how to identify stress symptoms in their staff. Also review which stress management techniques are taught to the workforce, if any.
- **Employee assistance programmes:** checks should be made on what use is made of these and if they are well advertised. However, they should never be seen as a way of allowing employers to get complacent and avoid tackling stress problems.

Sickness absence

According to research by PricewaterhouseCoopers (PwC), the annual cost of sickness absence for UK employers has increased to nearly £29 billion in 2013 from £27.8 billion in 2011. It surveyed 2,500 firms and found that the average sickness absence per employee was 9.1 days in 2013 (up from 8.7 days in 2011). Typically, public sector workers took the most sickness absence with an average of 11.1 days. In contrast, workers in technology firms took the least with an average of 3.4 days. Unfortunately, the UK topped the global scale as these figures are higher than those for Western Europe (7.3 days), the United States (4.9 days) and the Asia-Pacific region (2.2 days). This level of absence was found to account for up to 93 per cent of the UK's total cost of unplanned absenteeism for 2013. The remainder consisted of compassionate leave and industrial action.

These figures from PwC are much higher than that revealed by other UK research such as the CBI/Pfizer 'Absence and Workplace Health Survey'. In comparison, however, the latter only surveyed 153 organizations as opposed to PwC's 3,500. Plus, PwC favours large firms in its research and they have higher rates of sickness absence due to operating more generous company sick-pay schemes. Small UK businesses are far more likely to rely on statutory sick pay, which is only triggered on the fourth day of sickness absence. Similarly, the less generous sick-pay provisions in the United States and Asia Pacific region will explain the far lower rates recorded in these areas. But what is interesting is that, according to official figures from the Office for National Statistics (ONS), sickness absence fell in the UK during the economic downturn, when workers feared most for their jobs. One less obvious explanation for sickness absence creeping up again is that the pent-up stress that many workers experienced has led to new ill-health problems. Many workers adopt their own coping mechanisms such as excessive drinking, smoking and cheap comfort food, which can also cause poor health.

One particular problem with sickness absence is the days off that are falsely claimed as sickness when they are actually being taken for personal reasons (known as 'sickies'). Aon Consulting surveyed 7,500 employees from 10 European countries, including the UK, France, Germany and Spain, in order to find out the extent of the problem. Although this research was published four years ago in 2010, it is useful as it offers a European comparison. It found that Spanish workers were responsible for 22 per cent of the 122 million sick days that were taken in 2009, with UK workers contributing 21 per cent. In contrast, the Danish were the most reliable workers at 4 per cent of this total (interestingly, Denmark offers good flexible working to employees). Aon estimated that these practices cost €40 billion for the employers in the 10 countries surveyed. Yet, if anything, these figures are likely to be an underestimate, as many workers will not admit to faking sickness absence.

Of those who admitted to falsifying sick days 58 per cent said that they would not feel forced to if they had flexible working hours or social days to take for personal non-medical reasons; and 15 per cent said that more interesting tasks would keep them at work. Yet whilst many employers will understandably want to clamp down on any sickness absence that is not genuine, the use of draconian measures on their own may not be enough. Such measures may deal with absences clustered around major sporting events or bank holidays, for example, but will not deal with all the underlying causes, such as a desire for more interesting work. So where this type of sickness absence is a known or suspected problem, one recommendation would be to add some questions to any anonymous staff-satisfaction survey carried out into health and well-being. These should focus on identifying the full range of reasons for the taking of sick leave that is not genuine. Only then, can effective measures be taken to deal with all aspects of the problem.

Whilst the response is likely to be an underestimate of the true picture, sickness absence costs can be applied against the resulting figures. Ideally these will represent both the direct and indirect costs of sickness absence. For example, direct costs will be the wage bill for the period that an employee is off sick, plus the costs of hiring any agency staff to cover their job. Indirect costs represent the costs of management time in dealing with the sickness absence, as well as any negative impact that it has on customers; it also includes productivity losses. Where agency or other cover is used, indirect costs will also represent the time spent on inducting them into the job. Once a ballpark figure has been calculated, it should help to support any recommendations that need to be made on the basis of the findings.

> **Note**
>
> Aon Consulting also produced 'The European sick leave index: fresh insights into sick leave absence' (2010). It offers detailed comparisons between four EU countries: Belgium, France, Germany and the Netherlands. The aim is to extend it to cover more countries including the UK and Spain. It can be found at **http://img.en25.com/Web/AON/Aon-ESLI-Report.pdf**.

Apart from an increasing likelihood of losing staff as job markets improve, there is another reason to revisit how sickness absence is currently managed. This follows research undertaken by Ellipse and Professor Cary Cooper (2012) entitled 'Sick notes: how changes in the workplace and technology demand a rethink of absence management'. It found that for 72 per cent of workers, the way that a company treats sick employees influences how they view the company (this increases to 85 per cent in the 18–24 age group). Only 15 per cent of employees stated that it had no impact at all. This link to employer brand and employee engagement is an important one for employers, as gaining a good reputation for looking after staff will aid staff retention. The reason is that many employees expect their employer to invest in their well-being; especially given the constraints on pay rises. In turn, this approach links back into business ethics (see Chapter 2) and how an ethical approach is now seen as integral to an organization's corporate social responsibility agenda.

Given the impact that sickness absence has on both the bottom line and maintaining efficiency, any assessment covering this area should examine what use is made of return-to-work interviews by management. These are highlighted due to their effectiveness in cutting high levels of sickness absence. For example, according to research carried out by XpertHR in 2010, 94 per cent of the 166 employers surveyed use return-to-work interviews; 68 per cent report that their organization's absence rates have fallen as a result. Whilst they may not always be the sole cause of this reduction, they have a key role to play. However, this research also found that for 48 per cent of employers, their use is not consistent. The main reason is that line managers lack: 1) the time; 2) buy-in to the process; or 3) the confidence to carry out return-to-work interviews – with a major factor being hesitancy to hold what could be difficult conversations with employees.

These concerns can be resolved with the training of line managers. This should include estimates of how much sickness absence is currently costing each manager's department in terms of both direct and indirect costs. Do this well and it should trigger a cultural shift to show managers that they should do more than simply police sickness absence. Instead, if these interviews are done correctly, they can help to improve employee engagement – because with the right approach, they can show employees that they are valued. These interviews will also provide an opportunity to discover if there are underlying work or personal reasons for the absence, and they also allow for a discussion to see if there are any temporary adjustments that can be made for the employee. Also, in some cases, a referral to occupational health may be appropriate. If so, it can be made promptly and may avoid further sickness absence. So, bearing these points in mind, the risk assessment should look at what use is currently made of return-to-work interviews by asking the following questions:

- Are return-to-work interviews used consistently across the organization?
- If not, why not?
- What training, if any, has been provided to managers on their use?
- Is this training given to new managers on joining?
- Where return-to-work interviews are used, are they used promptly on an employee's return?
- Are any problems that have been identified, such as excessive absence, dealt with?
- If so, how are suspicious absences dealt with?
- Is employee confidentiality respected at all times?
- Are the results of these interviews fed back and absence trends monitored?

Any problems in using return-to-work interviews probably rest with line managers. The recommendations must focus on how to make them work. The first point is that they should only last 15–20 minutes. Any longer and managers will see them as a burden; any shorter and their benefits are lost. Briefing sessions on the format and their benefits should be run, because having high levels of sickness absence takes more time to manage than carrying out these interviews. There is also likely to be employee suspicion surrounding the interviews. So another recommendation is to sell return-to-work interviews to employees by tapping into their resentment at the extra work generated by those who are not thought to be genuinely sick. Also, work the employee engagement angle in that it helps to ensure that employees are well enough to return to work. Finally, a standard form should be created in order to maintain consistency in approach. Managers should also be briefed on the need for good data security, as any medical information will count as 'sensitive personal data' in many jurisdictions, including the UK and Australia.

> **Key point**
>
> Where the sickness absence policy is contractual, consultation will be necessary before return-to-work interviews can be introduced.

Presenteeism

A paradox is that whilst an employer may introduce initiatives that successfully reduce absenteeism, it often contributes to another problem known as 'presenteeism'. This refers to attending work whilst ill, but being less productive or engaged as a result. It arises because strategies such as return-to-work interviews may drive down overall sickness absence figures, but fail to solve the problem of worker ill health. The issue here is the mindset that many managers adopt when approaching these interviews. If it reflects an organizational culture that considers absent staff to be skiving, the problem of ill health – and the presenteeism it leads to – remains unresolved. As mentioned above, the drop in sickness absence due to the global economic downturn and fears of redundancy in recent years led to staff turning up to work whilst ill. Even though sickness absence has started to increase again, it seems that presenteeism is a growing problem. This tends to confirm the above research findings that the prevalence of ill health amongst workers is increasing.

According to 2013 research of over 1,000 UK workers carried out by the insurance company Canada Life, 93 per cent of employees said that they have gone to work despite being ill; 76 per cent stated that they turned up as they did not feel sick enough to justify going absent. However, 31 per cent said that a heavy workload precluded them from taking time off, and 19 per cent felt pressurized by colleagues to turn up. Perhaps it is not surprising that the research also revealed a trend for extreme presenteeism, with 33 per cent of employees saying that they would go to work with flu. Predictably, this led to 81 per cent of those surveyed catching illnesses from colleagues; and 82 per cent admitted to performing worse whilst unwell. Unfortunately, it is difficult to get an accurate picture of how much presenteeism actually costs a particular organization. This is due to the difficulties in calculating it with any accuracy, as it relies on the individual making a subjective assessment on how less productive they are, eg due to back pain.

Nonetheless, 2011 figures from the Centre for Mental Health have estimated that presenteeism from mental health alone costs UK employers £15.1 billion per annum, as opposed to £8.4 billion for absenteeism. Unfortunately, research figures for physical ailments vary hugely and it is often unclear as to how they have been calculated. However, taking Australia as an example, a Medibank report published in July 2011 estimated that in 2009–10, the total cost of presenteeism to their economy was estimated to be AUD $34.1 billion. This was based on an average of 6.5 working days of productivity being lost per employee each year due to presenteeism. This equated to a 2.7 per cent decrease in GDP for 2010. But whatever the actual figures may be for an organization, the lack of being able to calculate them with much accuracy does not detract from the fact that presenteeism can come with a heavy cost for employers.

With this in mind, the risk assessment must be honest about how the taking of sick leave is viewed. If employees are pressurized to turn up whilst sick, or workloads are heavy enough to make this practice likely, then this fact must be acknowledged. The more heavy-handed the approach is, the more likely it is that a presenteeism problem will exist. Unfortunately, it also means that the organizational culture is not conducive to employees being able to talk about the extent of the problem. But even if they are, measuring the associated loss of productivity with any accuracy is difficult. There are two options here. One is to carry out an anonymous staff-satisfaction survey into existing health and well-being provision and add on some questions about presenteeism. The second option, which is probably more realistic, is to simply accept that there could be a problem and focus on changing the culture. If the assessment covers this area, ask the following four questions:

- Does the organization focus on absenteeism at the expense of a more holistic approach to managing ill health?
- Have managers been briefed on what presenteeism is and how it can harm productivity?
- Do managers understand the relationship between presenteeism and its potential to increase sickness absence levels?
- Do employees experiencing ill-health problems feel supported by the organization, eg in terms of time off for hospital appointments or a change of hours?

Depending on the findings, the recommendations should suggest a move away from an overemphasis on absence management towards an approach that puts employee health and well-being centre stage. However, it is important that there is clarity over what any repositioning towards well-being is meant to achieve. From an employer's perspective, the objectives are likely to include: 1) reducing the direct and indirect costs of sickness absence; 2) improving productivity; and 3) enhancing employee engagement. Once this is clear, it will be possible to assess how current initiatives contribute to this and how successful they are. Input from the occupational health team on this is important, but it does have its limits, since their knowledge is based on those employees who have been referred to them, not those who have not. Therefore, some extra questions can be added to a staff survey in order to find out what the workforce thinks of current initiatives, as well as what well-being means to them personally. This will also have the benefit of getting their buy-in to the process, which contributes nicely to the third objective of enhancing employee engagement.

These objectives are all measurable in some way. For example, employee engagement can be benchmarked over annual staff surveys with trends mapped out. If not already undertaken, another recommendation is to define what well-being includes. This could incorporate the areas covered in this chapter, as well as others affecting employee health. For example, some employers provide advice on financial management, as money problems are a key source of stress to employees. If so, this could be brought under the well-being banner.

Chapter summary

Obesity:

- in 19 out of the 34 OECD countries, most of the population is now overweight/obese;
- by 2020, more than two in three people will be overweight/obese in some countries;
- one in five school-aged children across all OECD countries is overweight;
- obese employees tend to take more sick leave.

Chronic disease:

- will increase as the average age of the workforce rises – in the UK, the average age of the workforce will increase from 39 in 2007 to nearly 43 by 2025;
- involves frequent or lengthy episodes of absence;
- is on the increase due to rising levels of obesity;
- heart disease, diabetes and strokes will become responsible for 70 per cent of all deaths;

- employees must rethink how they will support staff with medical conditions in the future;
- more flexible working will be required in order to accommodate staff with medical conditions.

Mental illness:

- is set to become the second largest source of ill health in the UK by 2030;
- can be aggravated by poor job quality and long working hours;
- work is the main cause of stress, anxiety or depression.

Stress:

- has become a global problem following the economic downturn;
- the main stressor was the increased focus on profitability;
- employers are still turning a blind eye to the extent of the problem;
- many employees have feared for their jobs so have kept quiet about stress;
- once the job market improves, fed-up workers will look for new jobs;
- replacing them will cost money and the loss of their know-how;
- non-work factors also impact on employee stress levels;
- a growing problem is employees with aged parents and dependent children;
- many people are forced into part-time roles or zero-hours contracts (in the UK);
- few workers will admit to sick leave caused by stress, so will give other reasons.

Sickness absence:

- according to PwC 2013 research, UK employees top the global scale for sickness absence:
  - UK employees took an average of 9.1 days sick leave;
  - Western Europe's average is 7.3 days;
  - US employees average 4.9 days;
  - Asia Pacific region averages 2.2 days.

- UK sickness absence is now increasing after falling during the recession;
- UK workers take the most 'sickies' out of the 10 countries surveyed by Aon Consulting;
- how companies treat sick workers influences how the workforce views their employer.

Presenteeism:

- arises where workers attend work whilst ill and are less productive and engaged;
- often increases due to initiatives to reduce sickness absence;
- does not solve the issue of ill health but instead moves into the workplace – also explained by employees having a too-heavy workload for them to go off sick;
- infects other employees due to people turning up ill at work;
- is hard to calculate but has the potential to be more costly than sickness absence.

Recommendations:

- check the effectiveness of any employee health and well-being initiatives that are in place;
- analyse the workforce's health profile, eg by age and involvement in health initiatives;
- review existing health interventions to ensure an optimum return on investment;
- look at future workforce needs and where resources will need targeting in future;
- employer mindset must adapt to accept the reality of ageing and an unhealthier workforce;
- ensure that any health and well-being interventions have clear/measurable objectives;
- consider an in-house workshop for managers on mental ill-health awareness;
- encourage staff to take their full annual leave entitlement and designated breaks;
- carry out proactive monitoring of employee workloads;

- brief managers on how to identify potential work stressors;
- arrange training on stress awareness for both managers and staff;
- review any employee assistance programmes to see what use is made of them;
- identify the underlying reasons as to why staff take non-genuine sickness absence;
- introduce or improve the use of return-to-work interviews – they only need to last 15–20 minutes:
  - any longer and they become a burden; any shorter and the benefits are lost;
  - briefing sessions should be run on how to conduct the interviews;
  - sell them to staff by showing how they will improve employee engagement;
  - create a standard form in order to maintain a consistent approach;
  - be aware of data protection laws relating to how the completed forms are kept;
  - if the sickness absence policy is contractual, consult with employees/unions first.
- move the emphasis from absence management towards health and well-being;
- define exactly what is meant by well-being and to state its objectives;
- carry out a staff survey into what the workforce wants from a well-being initiative;
- where presenteeism is a suspected/known problem, focus on changing the culture;
- consider moving from absence management to a focus on employee health and well-being;
- define exactly what well-being initiatives include and are designed to achieve.

Chapter 8 looks at social media and the harm that failure to manage employee use can cause. This includes reputation damage as well as questions over ownership of LinkedIn contacts.

Social media

08

Introduction

Social media refers to a wide range of software applications that can be accessed via devices such as computers and smartphones. It includes social networking sites (Facebook), business networking applications (LinkedIn), blogging applications (Wordpress) and micro-blogs (Twitter), and video-hosting websites (YouTube). The commonality here is the ability to allow for the sharing of information and interaction with other users. Yet whilst this has provided new business opportunities, it also presents problems. These relate to how employees use social media both during and outside working hours, but also includes other areas, such as ownership of LinkedIn contacts. This chapter looks first at the general problems that can arise. Then it moves on to those specific to particular types of social media. Finally, it looks at how these threats and vulnerabilities can be managed by the use of an extensive social media policy and the areas it should cover.

General problems

Reputation damage

The advantage of the internet has been its ability to give an organization a global platform for a fraction of the costs of conventional advertising. However, the flip side is its unique potential for reputation damage. Updates to social media feeds, such as Twitter, reach followers immediately, and they can then be re-tweeted just as fast. Here, the problem lies in what material an individual may upload. Organizations put considerable trust in those tasked with generating what is known as user-generated content (UGC). Unfortunately, the wrong content – be it posted deliberately or unintentionally – can seriously harm an organization's reputation. This problem is heightened by the fact that whilst content can easily be uploaded via a mouse click, it is impossible to completely erase any uploaded content that is undesirable in some way.

However, a bigger problem is what employees and others post on their personal accounts, such as Facebook. One example is the sacking of a prison officer at Wandsworth Prison in London and the disciplining of four others in November 2013 for posting photographs of themselves on Facebook wearing T-shirts saying 'We Have Madeleine McCann'. The pictures were up for two months before prison bosses were told about them.

There are also other questions related to social media. How far can an individual go in expressing their views about their employer in their own time? How should employers deal with the fact that, in some cases, employees have created a website or Facebook page for the sole purpose of criticizing or embarrassing their employer? Closely related to this point, is how far non-employees, such as third parties, can go in making derogatory remarks. These groups include self-employed contractors and agency staff.

Trolling/harassment

The issue of trolling hit the headlines in the UK over the summer of 2013. Although this was mainly related to abuse of female campaigners and politicians on Twitter, it did raise international awareness of the devastating impact that 'trolls' can have on their victims. Unfortunately, this can occur via any social media platform and, thanks to the relative anonymity of the internet, is a growing problem globally. Although it is possible for trolls in England and Wales to be arrested under the Malicious Communications Act 1988, it had not ever been used in this context. That has now changed. Apart from covering conventional written communications, this act also covers those made electronically. It is a criminal offence to send messages to another person that are indecent, grossly offensive, threatening or false. The key word is 'sending' – as the messages do not have to be received by the recipient. Penalties are up to six months' imprisonment and/or a £5,000 fine if the intention behind the message was for it to cause distress or anxiety to the recipient.

This has the potential to affect employers in terms of liability for employee actions. Such a scenario could arise if an employee used work equipment to troll, harass or otherwise cyberbully colleagues, especially if done during working hours. The concept of vicarious liability (which is also recognized to varying degrees in other jurisdictions such as Australia and Canada) makes an employer liable for the acts of its employees if done in the course of employment. So it is likely that this behaviour would count. This makes employers even more vulnerable, as they also have deeper pockets than an employee. Therefore, they will be the ones most under threat if the victim in question decides to sue. Even if the victim does not go to the police, he or she could seek redress under the Protection from Harassment Act 1997. Following the House of Lords (now the Supreme Court) finding in *Majrowski v Guy's and St Thomas' NHS Trust* [2006] UKHL 34, it was confirmed that this could be used against employers as well as individuals.

What is not yet known is whether an employer could be vicariously liable for an employee's trolling of a third party with no connection to the workplace: for example, if an employee logs into a personal social media account using a work computer during a lunch break and uses it to threaten violence towards another poster. Legally, this is still a grey area. However, it is likely that the risks to the employer will be reduced, the more remote from the organization the victim is. So the riskiest area is likely to be trolling/harassment of an organization's customers and suppliers who have a clear connection to it. But no matter the legal jurisdiction, the safest bet is for the risk assessment to review the content of any existing social media policy in place. It should look for sections that expressly ban this type of behaviour as well as making infringements of the policy a serious disciplinary offence.

Potential for libel

In the UK in October 2013, Sally Bercow, the wife of the Speaker of the House of Commons, was ordered to pay £15,000 damages for libel following a tweet to her 56,000 plus followers on Twitter wrongly implicating the former Conservative Party treasurer in a sex abuse scandal. As was foreseeable, many of her followers re-tweeted her message to their own followers. Originally, Lord McAlpine intended to pursue many of these individuals through the courts. However, in February 2013, he announced that he would drop defamation claims against those Twitter users with fewer than 500 followers. Although Bercow was sued as an individual, this raises the question of what would happen if she had used a work account. At the time of writing, this is unanswered. However, it is possible that libellous remarks could be made via tweets on behalf of an employer. Another question is at what point does someone become an opinion former via Twitter? Lord McAlpine's actions (presumably following legal advice) suggest that it is triggered at

500 followers. This is something for organizations to bear in mind when considering how much time to spend on monitoring content.

To successfully avoid liability, an employer would need to show that the employee was behaving in an unauthorized manner. This will not be easy to do in practice, due to the concept of vicarious liability. In other words, the employer would have to show that the content uploaded was so far removed from what the employee was paid to produce that it could not be said to have occurred within the course of employment. Unfortunately, issuing a disclaimer on tweets (and blogs) to the effect that the views given are that of the writer and not the employer will not work either. This is for the same reason. Given that this is an emerging area of the law, both in the UK and globally, the risk assessment should look at what training is given to those with responsibilities for UGC. If third parties were used to produce the content, such as freelancers, these matters will need to be covered by the contract for services between the parties.

Ownership of user-generated content

Unsurprisingly, many organizations have tapped into social media due to its global reach. This could be for a variety of reasons, such as having a Facebook page for marketing purposes, or providing company information via a blog. Yet, in both cases, someone needs to provide the text. The question is what happens if an individual has created UGC that proves to be a problem for the organization. This may be because it breaches business confidentiality in some way, such as by including information that is not meant to be in the public domain. Equally, it could also be by bringing the employer's reputation into disrepute, be it intentionally or by accident. One example is using a corporate social media channel to criticize the employer or to give a deliberately poor response to a customer complaint. Should this happen, there is every chance that it will go viral, especially if the employer is a household name.

Where junior staff or non-employees, such as interns, have responsibility for creating UGC, the risk assessment should look at whether or not the content is vetted before it is posted for public viewing. Apart from human error, it only takes one disengaged employee a matter of seconds to cause lasting reputation damage. Having that extra filter can do much to reduce the likelihood of this happening. One risk assessment recommendation more appropriate for larger organizations who make substantial use of this medium is to put a manager in charge of social media output. He or she would then be responsible for approving any UGC created in the employer's name, before it is published. This should do much to reduce the problem of unsuitable content or having sensitive commercial information published. Even small- to medium-sized organizations would benefit greatly from having at least one 'go-to' person to run an eye over content.

The risk assessment should also look at what disciplinary sanctions are in place to deal with this type of problem and whether staff are aware of them. If nothing suitable is in place, the existing disciplinary framework should be extended to cover these scenarios. It should then be added to the social media policy. This will describe the circumstances that warrant disciplinary action and what the likely sanctions will be, such as a first written warning for misconduct. If dismissal is a possibility, for example for going as far as disclosing trade secrets belonging to the organization or a third-party client, this must be made clear. However, any decision to dismiss must be a reasonable one in all the circumstances. One way of helping to ensure this will be to link the misconduct to a breach of the social media policy. The same applies to bringing the organization into 'disrepute'. However, this needs to be defined, as its meaning is subjective and will mean different things to different employees. So a check needs to be made in order to ensure that any policy that is in place actually defines what is meant by this term.

Reduced productivity

The negative impact that uncontrolled access to social media has on productivity rates has been subject to much debate. Estimates on the time spent on these sites tend to average one to five hours per week per employee. In fact, a 2012 survey of 1,000 workers in the United States and Canada found that nearly one-third spent at least one hour per day accessing social media sites such as Facebook and Twitter. This research was carried out by Intelligent Office, who also found that one-quarter of those polled would not work for an organization that banned or blocked social media sites. In this respect, it suggests some cultural differences between how social media is viewed within the United States and Canada, as opposed to the UK and elsewhere. This could be due to the fact that the former see social media access at work to be more of an automatic entitlement.

Whilst the productivity argument is compelling, there are counterarguments to suggest that an outright ban on social media use is unduly restrictive. This is due to the resentment it will cause, given that social media is now an integral part of many employees' lives. Also, according to Australian research by the University of Melbourne (Melbourne Newsroom, 2009), some personal use at work can actually improve individual productivity by up to 9 per cent. Dr Brent Coker surveyed 300 workers and found that 70 per cent engaged in what he called 'workplace internet leisure browsing' (WILB). This allowed employees to 'zone out' temporarily in order to regain their focus between tasks. Another side to this debate is to reconsider what is meant by productivity. Given that it is measured in terms of output, allowing some moderate use of social media does not in itself preclude staff from being productive. Another point is that time-wasting employees existed long before the advent of social media. So it could be argued that it has just replaced the water-cooler chats that they previously indulged in.

Also, blocking access to social media via an organization's computer network will only encourage employees to use their own personal devices instead. Some employees may even see an outright ban as a challenge, particularly if they are feeling disengaged and unmotivated. So rather than penalize sensible users, the best way to deal with the few time-wasters is via the disciplinary process, assuming that an informal chat does not resolve matters first. If disciplinary sanctions, such as proceedings for misconduct, do become necessary, it should act as a salutary warning to others not to abuse any fair-use policy on social media. Any employee risk assessment into social media should review the current policy (if any) on access at work to see if it works as intended or if it is actually counterproductive. It also needs to look at whether or not the organization has productivity issues with how social media is currently accessed and used, and how any problems are dealt with.

Problems by social media channel

Blogs

A 'blog' is an online diary that shares the opinions and thoughts of its creator with anyone who reads it. With the rapid growth in internet use in the last few years, a blog's audience may be substantial. As with other forms of social media, it is this ease of access that could leave employers vulnerable. This is because an employee, or even a non-employee such as agency staff or a volunteer, could use their personal blog to bring an organization into disrepute. In fact, one of the first cases occurred whilst blogging was in its infancy. In January 2005, an employee of Waterstones, the UK bookseller, was dismissed for gross misconduct on the basis that some of his comments had brought the company into disrepute. This was because on at least one occasion he had referred to it as 'Bastardstone's' and had made comments about his manager, who he called 'evil boss' (his equivalent to pointy-haired boss who features in Scott Adams's Dilbert cartoons). He brought an unfair dismissal claim against his former employer.

He was successful for several reasons. The first was that he had not directly identified the branch that he worked for. Second, his blog was clearly described as being satirical. Third, any references were confined to complaining about annual leave and his poor working relationship with his boss. Finally, but most important, was the fact that Waterstones had no policy on the writing of blogs by its staff. Neither was there any mention of it in its disciplinary policy as being an offence of gross misconduct. The reason was that at the time, Waterstones had not identified blogging as an emerging threat, or if it had, it had failed to respond to it. Although many employers now cover blogs in their HR policies, the employee risk assessment should review how well it is dealt with. Some boundaries must be created, the main one being able to retain some control over content in so far as it impacts on the employer. Therefore, any policy can reasonably ban the following either on the grounds of risks to reputation, or to prevent the loss of confidential information:

- any direct or indirect identification of the organization;
- any information on what work employees or colleagues undertake;
- any reference to or criticism of colleagues, suppliers or customers by name;
- divulging information that could reasonably be described as confidential in some way;
- using work computers to write blogs;
- the updating of personal blogs in work time.

If these points are not already covered, the recommendations should suggest that they are added to the social media policy. Once these and any other changes outlined in this chapter have been made, the changes and the reasons behind them need to be communicated to the workforce. Again, retain the right to make breaches a disciplinary offence.

Facebook

Employer misuse of Facebook in the recruitment process has already been covered in Chapter 5. So this section looks at the end of the employment relationship. In the last few years, dismissals connected with employee use of Facebook started to enter the employment tribunal system. In the UK, one of the youngest victims to be dismissed was a 16-year-old who had been sacked because her boss had seen her describe her first day in her job as 'so dull' on Facebook: he had been surfing the internet and found her comments after she had spent only three weeks in the job. Virgin Atlantic also dismissed 13 crew members for describing its customers as 'chavs' (ie uncultured and lacking in intelligence) and for claiming that the airline's jet engines had to be replaced four times per year. Apparently, a Facebook group had been set up where these and other comments had been made. Unsurprisingly, these dismissals were made on the grounds that their actions had brought the company into disrepute.

This type of dismissal has raised interesting questions about the extent of an individual employee's right to privacy under Article 8 of the European Convention on Human Rights (ECHR). This was considered in *Teggart v TeleTech UK Limited* NIIT 00704/11. Teggart (T) had been employed in his employer's call centre in Northern Ireland. He had posted several crude comments about a female colleague that referred to her alleged promiscuity. However, he did so using his personal Facebook account, on his own home computer and in his own time. Although these comments were not seen by the victim, they were read by a number of mutual colleagues who he was 'friends' with on Facebook. But instead of removing them, once she had become aware of them, he posted more vulgar comments. Once his employer had been informed, T was subjected to disciplinary action and dismissed.

He challenged his dismissal in an industrial tribunal (Northern Ireland's equivalent to an employment tribunal), citing unfair dismissal and a breach of privacy under Article 8 of the ECHR. He also claimed breaches of Article 9, which includes a right to freedom of thought, and Article 10, which covers the right to freedom of expression. All of his claims failed. The dismissal was found to be fair and a reasonable response to treatment that clearly breached the employer's 'dignity at work' policy. But what was more interesting was the tribunal's response to T's privacy claim. It stated that he had no right to expect it, given that his comments could easily be copied by others and forwarded on. Therefore, T could not invoke the ECHR in his favour. Even though this case was heard in Northern Ireland and is not binding in England, Wales or Scotland, it does provide a good idea of how similar arguments invoking human rights will be treated, not just in Great Britain but also in the EU.

This can be contrasted with the approach increasingly being taken in the United States by the National Labor Relations Board. Federal law protects the rights of most private sector employees to discuss work-related matters if the aim behind it is a 'concerted activity' to improve wages, working conditions or benefits. If so, their comments will be protected as free speech. What has happened is that attempts by employers to introduce an outright ban on comments that criticize them in some way has been deemed illegal, if these posts fit the above criteria. In fact, companies such as Costco and General Motors have been forced to reinstate workers who had been dismissed for making such comments. However, this approach has been heavily criticized for taking legislation enacted in the 1930s and trying to force-fit it to a digital age that it was never designed for.

LinkedIn

With 225 million members, LinkedIn is well established as the premier business-networking website. So, given the networking and marketing potential it has, it is not surprising that many employers encourage their staff to create site profiles and populate them with connections. Whilst a director or employee remains with the same employer, there is no problem. However, when they leave, the question arises as to who owns the connections made during the course of employment. Is it the individual or the employer? This question has arisen because the information held goes beyond that which is in the public domain. For example, not only are contact details present, but there is usually detailed information about a connection's current and previous job roles as well as access to their connections (in most cases). So the question increasingly being asked is whether these LinkedIn connections could be considered confidential information belonging to the employer. This is on the basis that the opportunity to accumulate them was provided by the working relationship.

In the UK, this question was first considered in *Hays Specialist Recruitment (Holdings) Ltd & Another v Ions & Another* [2008] EWHC 745 (Ch). Mark Ions had left Hays in order to set up his own rival agency. As part of this process, he had taken his LinkedIn connections with him, which included Hays clients. Hays had brought a case in the high court to seek what is known as pre-action disclosure. In other words, confidential information that Ions had taken with him that was in breach of his employment contract. It was ruled that these connections were capable of being considered confidential information belonging to Hays as the employer. All then went quiet for five years until *Whitmar Publications Limited v Gamage and Others* [2013] EWHC 1881 (Ch). As with Ions, this case also involved competing with a former employer, but concerned a specific LinkedIn group. This group was owned and maintained by the employer and the ex-employees had tried to use its contacts to further their new business. It was held that LinkedIn contacts could be considered confidential information and the actions of Gamage and the others was theft. An injunction was granted.

Until the legal position is clarified further, any risk assessment into use of social media must look at what safeguarding provision already exists. This means that employment contracts of directors, senior and specialist staff will need to be checked as a priority. Also, checks should be made of HR policies on social media and the use of confidential information to see if they cover ownership of LinkedIn contacts. If they don't, the following recommendations could be made:

- Potentially high-risk staff should be identified. This should cover anyone already subject to restrictive covenants in their contract. However, this would also provide the ideal opportunity to check that all personnel who need to be covered, actually are.
- Existing restrictive covenants should be reviewed to see if they adequately identify the type of information the organization wishes to protect. It should cover specifically LinkedIn connections gained through employment and state that they will be considered to be confidential information belonging to the employer.
- If employment contracts need updating, those affected need to be consulted on what the changes are and why they are being implemented.
- The social media policy should be checked to make sure that it includes a statement on how the organization views the ownership of LinkedIn contacts. If it is lacking, something needs to be added. Once this is done, any additions or alterations made should be communicated to all staff, eg via team meetings.

YouTube

YouTube is a video-sharing social media website with a global audience. According to its own statistics it has over 1 billion unique users each month with 100 hours of video being uploaded every minute. As it gains in global popularity, 70 per cent of its traffic now comes from outside the United States. With these figures, it is unsurprising that it has become a popular advertising tool amongst employers. This is not just to promote goods and services, but also as a recruitment tool to attract new staff. But in its success as an advertising medium, also lies its potential to damage an organization's reputation. This is something that Domino's Pizza found – to its cost – when two of its employees decided to prank the company. The video made in 2009 showed one of them preparing a new Domino's product whilst carrying out a number of unhygienic acts. Even though the video uploaded to YouTube was poor quality, it was clearly made in a Domino's kitchen.

Before the video was withdrawn from the site, it had received over 1 million hits, which put it on the first page of YouTube featured videos. Unfortunately, the impact on Domino's reputation was instantaneous. According to US media reports, Domino's 'favourability' rating had dropped by over 50 per cent. Also, the huge advertising and marketing costs it had incurred in launching a new product had been effectively wasted. What is even worse in this situation is that neither employee had set out to deliberately damage their employer's reputation. One of them e-mailed Domino's to say that it was meant as a joke. However, this begs the question of what would happen if there was a concerted effort by employees to harm their employer. Luckily for Domino's, it had the financial resources and the PR backup to deal with this situation, but a smaller organization would not. The two employees were dismissed and Domino's was believed to have brought a civil action against them for brand defamation.

Still on the theme of reputation damage is the fact that unhappy customers are able to upload video reviews on YouTube. Another example of how this can damage employer reputation and profit margins also came from the United States in 2009. In this case, Dave Carroll, a musician, blamed United Airlines for breaking his US $3,500 Taylor acoustic guitar. After spending nine months unsuccessfully trying to get compensation, he penned a song that became an instant YouTube hit. Entitled 'United Breaks Guitars', his video featured his friends posing as baggage handlers and flight attendants. According to *The Times* newspaper, the video had been viewed nearly 3.7 million times and prompted many other disillusioned customers to post their tales of woe. It also sent United Airline's share price into temporary decline, allegedly by up to as much as 10 per cent. Some bloggers reported that this cost shareholders around US $180 million. Needless to say, United Airlines have taken steps to improve their customer service and, with a nice touch of irony, have used Dave Carroll's song to do it.

Any risk assessment should start by looking for evidence of an awareness of these dangers at senior level. Next, is to see what measures are in place to protect online reputation. Common measures include having a video presence on YouTube that provides information and gets the organization's values across. Others will include social media and the internet generally, eg an online facility for dealing with queries and complaints within 48 hours. Online channels for two-way communication are also important. One valuable input from HR will be to review what training is provided to the individuals involved in this particular process, as well as those in customer-facing roles generally. This is, of course, what let down United Airlines so badly. HR will also need to review what the organization's social media policy says about employee use of YouTube.

Twitter

Twitter can present employers with a similar problem to LinkedIn. This arises where an employee 'tweets' as part of their job role. Once again, the question is who owns the followers that have been amassed? Is it the employee who obtains the followers, or the employer? This situation arose in 2011, when a US Twitter user was sued by his former employer for taking his followers with him when he changed jobs. By the time of his departure, Noah Kravitz from California had accumulated 17,000 followers during his employment with PhoneDog, a mobile-phone review website of which he was the editor. When he left, he renamed his account in his own name. In response, his former employer sued him for US $340,000 (£217,000). Their argument was that these followers amounted to a customer database and each follower represented a monetary worth to them. This was calculated on the basis that each individual was worth US $2.50 per month over an eight-month period.

Unfortunately, there is still no answer to this question because both parties settled at the end of 2012. All that is known publicly is that Kravitz got to keep his Twitter account and his followers. However, until this question is answered by a court of law, organizations should take their own steps to try to safeguard any company Twitter accounts. To this end, the assessment should examine what provision there is for this. So look for evidence of the following:

- Whether or not there is any statement as to who owns the followers amassed under an organization's Twitter account.
- Is the account in the organization's name or that of the individual tweeting?
- Does the social media policy or the employee's employment contract include a statement that clearly describes who 'owns' the followers?
- Has there been any attempt to categorize Twitter followers, eg as customer lists? Going as far as referring to them as trade secrets or confidential information is unlikely to hold up, as they are accounts that are in the public domain.
- Is there any control exercised over what is 'tweeted'? The more professional and work-orientated the tweets are, the more likely it is that the followers will be deemed to be the property of the employer.

> **Key point**
>
> Whilst it may not hold up if a similar court case to *Kravitz v PhoneDog* was to take place in the UK, the fact that steps have been taken to identify ownership of Twitter followers can only help an employer's case.

Social media policy

Due to the nature of threats presented by social media, any employee risk assessment recommendations should focus heavily on either the introduction of a social media policy, or on tightening an existing one. Without this, there will be no safeguards on employee behaviour. This is necessary as it cannot be assumed that staff will exercise common sense and restraint in use of social media. Also, given the potential legal liabilities and the high risk of reputational damage, it is foolhardy not to lay down some boundaries. As a basic principle, any social media policy should aim to balance the needs of an employer with the rights of employees to be able to express themselves. It should incorporate the following elements:

- **Policy purpose:** in the introduction, there should be an explanation as to why a social media policy is necessary in order to protect the organization's reputation, both as an employer as well as its consumer brand. It is important that workers are made aware of the impact that their actions can have, both on their employer and their colleagues.

- **Personal use:** the policy should make absolutely clear the situation on personal use of social media during work time. If it is allowed during lunch breaks, or other designated breaks, this should be clarified. Where a more relaxed approach is adopted, there should be a statement setting out what is considered to be reasonable use during the working day. Equally, it should be made clear what the disciplinary sanctions will be if this facility is abused.

- **Content:** the content section should describe what staff cannot include when posting social media content. This applies to their use of both work and personal social media accounts. So it should ban: 1) any activity that will bring the organization into disrepute, with a definition of what 'disrepute' means; 2) the use of any material that could give away the organization's identity, such as company logos (or modified versions) or photographs of products; and 3) potentially libellous comments made from any work social media account, or on a personal one if it identifies the employer in any way.

- **Cyberbullying:** there should be a complete ban on any behaviour that could be construed as cyberbullying, both inside and outside work. It should also be explained what it refers to, such as trolling and harassment. A link to an organization's 'dignity at work' (or similar) policy should also be provided. This is important – as being seen to take all reasonable steps to prevent any abuse from taking place will be a defence to this type of claim.

- **Content ownership:** the policy should also set out ownership of both LinkedIn contacts generated through the course of employment as well as Twitter followers. It should also explain why the organization stakes a claim to them.

- **Disciplinary sanctions:** breaches of the policy should be linked to the organization's disciplinary procedures. This way, staff will know exactly what is expected of them and what possible sanctions they could face if they break the rules.

- **Monitoring:** if any monitoring is carried out into employees' use of e-mail or the internet, there are privacy issues that will need to be dealt with. Whilst legal monitoring is permissible, the social media policy should either provide an outline of what form this takes, or it should clearly refer to a monitoring policy.
- **Social media manager:** if this post exists within the organization, the name of the post-holder and an outline of their duties should be included.

Chapter summary

Social media includes:

- social networking sites, such as Facebook and MySpace;
- business-networking applications, such as LinkedIn;
- blogging applications, such as Wordpress;
- micro-blogs, such as Twitter;
- information sharing, such as Wikipedia;
- video-hosting websites, such as YouTube.

General problems that can arise from social media use:

- reputation damage;
- trolling and harassment;
- potential for libel;
- uncertainty over ownership of user-generated content (UGC);
- reduced productivity.

Blogs:

- are an online diary that shares the opinions of its creator;
- can be used by an individual to damage their employer's reputation;
- their use may not be properly controlled in an employer's social media policy;
- the main risk is a blogger identifying the organization in some way and criticizing it;
- employees can accidentally (or deliberately) divulge confidential information on blogs.

Facebook:

- groups and pages can be set up by staff to criticize their employer;
- employers including Virgin Atlantic have sacked staff for damaging its reputation through Facebook;
- employee attempts to invoke the right to privacy for their comments on Facebook have failed;
- US employees try to use 1930s law to protect their right to criticize employers on Facebook;
- this US legislation was not designed for the digital age so it causes problems for employers.

LinkedIn:

- has 225 million members globally and increasing;
- there is debate over ownership of LinkedIn contacts made during the course of employment; UK courts say that these may be confidential information belonging to the employer;
- many employers have not updated their restrictive covenants to include LinkedIn contacts.

YouTube:

- has over 1 billion unique users per month;
- 70 per cent of its traffic now comes from outside the United States;
- employees can upload videos that can damage an organization's reputation;
- these damaging videos can easily go viral;
- Domino's Pizza funded a marketing campaign that was ruined by an employee prank;
- there is nothing to stop unhappy customers posting video reviews, eg Dave Carroll's video criticizing United Airlines;
- many employers are still not taking steps to protect their online reputation on YouTube.

Twitter:

- there is legal uncertainty as to ownership of the followers that have been amassed;
- problems arise where an employee or third party is paid to tweet as part of their job role;

- employers may argue that Twitter followers are a customer database with a monetary value;
- many employers fail to exercise any control over the content of tweets;
- the threat is that an employee could tweet something libellous;
- libellous tweets made in the course of employment could lead to the employer being sued.

Recommendations:

- review any policy that bans social media use at work, as it may be counterproductive;
- organizations should create a comprehensive media policy;
- check to see that existing policies cover the following areas:
  - why a social media policy is necessary;
  - the organization's position on personal use of social media at work;
  - what staff may and may not post on social media;
  - a ban on any behaviour classed as cyberbullying;
  - what disciplinary sanctions apply to any breach of the policy;
  - who owns any LinkedIn contacts and Twitter followers made through work;
  - information on what internet or e-mail monitoring is carried out;
  - the identity and function of any social media manager appointed.

Chapter 9 looks at information security and the impact of cybercrime. It also looks at how to protect key information such as know-how, and how to comply with data protection requirements.

Information security

09

Introduction

The growth of the internet has brought many benefits to organizations, such as a global trading platform at little cost, but it also has brought downsides, the main one being cybercrime. In 2011, research by Detica entitled 'The cost of cyber crime' estimated that it cost UK businesses a total of £21 billion per year (mainly due to intellectual property theft). Also, international research carried out in 2012 by the Ponemon Institute on behalf of Hewlett-Packard (HP) found that the average time taken by companies to resolve a successful cyberattack had increased from 14 days in 2010, through 18 days in 2011, to 24 days in 2012. Its research looked at the experiences of 199 companies based across the UK, the United States, Germany, Australia and Japan. It found that the problem is not the technology but the lax behaviour displayed by staff. This chapter explore exactly how their activities can leave an employer vulnerable to an attack, for example through sharing passwords or by falling victim to social engineering (how human interaction can be exploited to trick people into breaching security rules and procedures). It also considers how information should be protected generally in terms of data protection and know-how.

Cybercrime

Dangers of 'social engineering'

In this context, social engineering is used to gain access to a computer network by tricking an employee into divulging their password. It plays on human traits in different ways, depending on the objective. In one instance, it may appeal to an employee's desire to be helpful by pretending that immediate network access is required in order to prevent a much bigger problem. In other cases, scare tactics are used in order to persuade the user to run software that infects their machine with malware and/or steals personal information. A newer trick that emerged in 2013 was the vanity scam, which targets a narrow demographic. One was a spear-phishing campaign aimed at business executives in what was known as the 'Top 100 Executives' con, in which victims received e-mails from a fake publication that claimed to be compiling a list of the most distinguished business people.

Naturally, this was designed to appeal to vanity. A link was included to a registration form on a bogus website, where visitors were asked to type in personal details such as home and mobile phone numbers, company name and job title. Once this information had been entered, cybercriminals either used it to commit identity theft or to create fake e-mails purporting to come from the executive. These e-mails contained attachments containing malware, but were opened as the employees believed them to come from a trusted source. Unfortunately, experts believe that social engineering will remain the greatest security threat. So any assessment must acknowledge that this is probably high-risk for many organizations. Whilst the solution to these and other IT-related problems are the domain of the IT department, HR has a pivotal role in making the workforce aware of what the current threats and vulnerabilities are – and how to deal with them. This should be done via induction programmes as well as ongoing training, and must be supported by robust policies. These measures can be supported by regular reminders being sent out to employees to be alert to any possible instances of cybercrime.

Passwords

One area of ongoing vulnerability for employers is the lax attitude often displayed by staff towards IT password security. This includes employees leaving their computers logged on when they take a break or when going home. It also includes those who habitually leave login and password details visible on their desk or in an unlocked drawer. Another problem is the tendency to share passwords with colleagues in case their computer needs accessing whilst they are out of the office. Although convenient, such complacency provides easy pickings for cyberattackers. You only need to consider the third parties who have legitimate access to offices (such as temporary workers, equipment repair personnel and many others), who could obtain password details and sell them on. In other cases, passwords can easily be stolen over the phone. All someone needs to do is ring up and pose as an IT network administrator requiring password information. The larger the organization, the easier this will be to pull off.

Even where there are strict rules in place for password confidentiality, problems can still arise. One is where employees create something easily remembered by using personal information to achieve this, such as the name of a pet or a birth date. Unfortunately, social-engineering techniques can unearth this information quite easily. Another is where the same password is reused several times for different types of system access – anyone using software programs to crack passwords will be well rewarded for their efforts in these instances. There is also the fact that where users have a free choice in the password used, they tend to choose ones that are shorter with minimal combinations of letters, numerals and capitalization. Even where the system has been set up to require complex passwords, staff will often use the password-remembering facility unless this option has been disabled by IT.

Any employee risk assessment incorporating IT security threats should review the entire process, from allocating passwords to new starters through to what happens when staff leave. Employees across the organization should also be surveyed to see what they do with passwords and why. Depending on the organization, anonymous surveys may be better than face-to-face interview. This is because they will obtain a more accurate picture of what really goes on, rather than interviewees giving what they think to be the desired response. Given the importance of the topic, never assume that workers will act in the way they are supposed to. Another benefit of mapping out behaviours is that it will help when it comes to re-educating employees on any new procedures that will be introduced. It should also assist in achieving a balance between protecting the employer from cyberthreats whilst not subjecting its workforce to an unnecessarily complex password regime.

In this instance, HR's role will be a more supportive one due to the technical nature of the area under review. In other words, any recommendations for the process behind tightening up password access should come from IT. However, HR should take ownership of how any revised computer-use policy is communicated to the workforce, including an explanation of the rationale behind it. Equally, HR has a key role to play during induction and in any extra training that may be rolled out. The policy should be underpinned by disciplinary sanctions for any breach and, once again, HR should be taking the lead in how managers are briefed and supported on this.

Bring your own devices (BYOD)

One area of emerging concern is the rapid rise in what is known as 'BYOD' (bring your own devices). It refers to those who bring their own equipment to work, such as smartphones and tablets, and connect them to the employer's network (this includes self-employed consultants and volunteers, not just employees). Whilst this trend reflects the increased blurring between an employee's work and home life, it does present new areas of vulnerability for organizations, the main one being data security: the second that data is transferred from an employer-owned device to one that is privately owned, it can be lost or misused. In fact, according to Dell, 50 per cent of its customers who operate BYOD have experienced security breaches. This is because they have not controlled which devices may be used.

There is also the risk that third parties unconnected to the organization, such as family members, could gain access to data. Apart from the loss of confidential information, UK employers must also be aware of how the Data Protection Act (DPA) 1998 applies to BYOD. This has now been clarified by the Information Commissioner's Office (ICO) in its 2013 publication entitled 'Bring your own device (BYOD)'. It makes it clear that the employer remains in control of all personal data that they are responsible for: this applies even though it may be stored and accessed on a device that they do not own. The reason for this is the seventh data protection principle that says 'appropriate technical and organizational measures shall be taken against unauthorized or unlawful processing of personal data and against accidental loss or destruction of, or damage to, personal data'. With this in mind, the ICO makes it clear in this publication that all the following points should be assessed:

- what type of data is held;
- where it may be stored;
- how it is transferred;
- the potential for data leakage;
- the blurring of personal and business use;
- the device's security capacities;
- what to do if the device owner leaves their employment;
- how to deal with the loss, theft, failure and support of a device.

Whilst these points are a legal requirement, they are not the only problem to overcome. The other is how an employer can gain access to a BYOD in order to carry out its role as a data controller. Unless the owner of the device gives consent first, access will not happen. After all, the individual may have legitimate concerns about the privacy of any personal material that he or she has stored on it. The best way to approach this is to use the eight points listed above as the basis for any assessment on how BYOD are actually used by staff and then to work through the following five stages:

- **Stage 1:** begin by identifying what categories of staff may be transferring information. Weak IT controls may mean that temporary workers, self-employed consultants, interns and volunteers are able to access and transfer information. Then review the type of information that can be transferred and identify who has this access.

- **Stage 2:** depending on the outcome, decide who genuinely needs to be able to transfer work data to their personal devices. It is likely that more staff have access than is desirable. If so, the IT department may need to restrict the ability to transfer data on certain pieces of equipment, eg those used by non-employees such as temporary workers and volunteers. As part of this review, consider if it would be better to extend the use of company-owned equipment instead.

- **Stage 3:** next, IT should advise on what devices can go on a 'safe list' for BYOD use. This is a crucial stage as it cannot be assumed that all those devices owned by staff are secure. For example, in 2013, the Communications–Electronic Security Group (CESG) rejected Blackberry's 10 platform and accompanying software as not being secure enough for UK Government departments (it was designed to allow users to keep work and personal accounts on their phones separate).

- **Stage 4:** work with IT to create a BYOD policy as they can advise on the technical aspects, such as Wi-Fi use, and on how to delete data on personal devices. This can be an add-on to any existing IT policy, but it must incorporate the eight bullet points listed above. Particular focus should be given to individual responsibility and data-security concerns. It should emphasize that any data obtained from the workplace remains the employer's property and must be permanently removed when the employee leaves the organization. Beef up the policy by making any infringement a disciplinary offence.

- **Stage 5:** given the implications of BYOD to employers, briefings should be carried out on the policy. This should focus on why it is necessary and the legal reasons behind its introduction. It will be necessary to include all those who are believed to have transferred data to their own devices, especially if access is to be denied in future. Don't forget to include homeworkers and others who may work remotely, such as sales staff. Play it safe and get staff to sign to confirm that they understand and will abide by the policy. If an individual misses a briefing and cannot get to another one for any reason, then their line manager should go over it with them.

Cloud computing

Whilst the cloud offers fantastic opportunities to save storage space, it presents its own set of vulnerabilities. The main one is data leakage, especially that of commercially sensitive information. Without sufficient controls in place, there is nothing to prevent data migrating to end-user's personal devices. Apart from the fact that these devices may themselves not be secure, control over what happens to this information once it is downloaded is lost. A second vulnerability was found by AIIM, the professional body for information management. In 2013, it surveyed over 500 of its members and found that one-quarter of organizations had employees who were using unofficial cloud-based file-sharing services such as Dropbox. This was for the purposes of file sharing and collaboration, often with third parties. Only 16 per cent of those surveyed had an official, cloud-hosted file-sharing system for employees to use.

Another problem involves ownership of data stored in the cloud, including files stored on non-official cloud-hosting services. The more remote from the employer's control a file is, the greater the potential will be for argument over its ownership. Despite this, any work produced by an employee in the course of employment will most likely belong to the employer, irrespective of where it is stored. Nonetheless, this is an area that any risk assessment concerned with information security should review. It should examine whether or not IT policies have been updated to incorporate legal issues surrounding the adoption of cloud computing. Also, the assessment needs to confirm that the data controller is aware that responsibility for files stored in the cloud remains with the employer (this works in the same way as it does for BYOD).

Again, the technicalities of risk mitigation will be mainly in the domain of an organization's IT department, along with the data controller. Yet, given that some of the information at risk could belong to HR, and that it is the workforce who could access and disseminate this information, it is a legitimate area of concern. Also, as with BYOD and other policies, it will be the HR function that will be instrumental in bringing the new or updated policy to the attention of staff. What recommendations are made will obviously depend on how well the use of cloud is being managed, but they could include the following:

- if the relevant IT policy does not include a section on cloud computing, include one;
- tighten up on what information is being transferred to the cloud;
- set out clearly that staff may only use approved cloud-hosting services;
- clarify ownership of any files transferred to the cloud.

Note

A document entitled '10 steps to cyber-security' (BIS *et al*, 2012) has been jointly produced by three government departments including CESG (the information security arm of GCHQ) and the Centre for the Protection of National Infrastructure (CPNI). It can be downloaded free from http://www.bis.gov.uk.

File downloads

Illegal file sharing

File downloads onto work computers and mobile devices are another potential danger for employers. However, the specific threat will depend on what type of material is downloaded and this is a trend that changes over time. Currently, one hotspot is illegal file sharing of copyrighted material, especially music downloads. One explanation for this is the faster broadband speeds that are found at work as opposed to an employee's own package. This is a potentially serious issue as the relevant authorities are more likely to pursue employers than the employee – due to the fact that they are much easier and more solvent targets. Also, for UK employers, the concept of vicarious liability applies, so it could be argued that an employee was acting 'within the course of their employment' when making illegal downloads. As this principle has been widened in recent years, it means that most illegal file downloads on work equipment and in work time will qualify.

In fact, this happened to the engineering company, Honeywell. In June 2007, the BBC reported that the British Phonographic Industry (BPI) assisted police in what was the first-ever raid of a UK-based business whose employees were involved in illegal file sharing. The raid took place in Scotland, where it was found that several thousand music files were involved. A tip-off had been received from an employee who had also helped provide vital evidence leading up to the raid. Otherwise, it would have been difficult for such wrongdoing to come to light without having access to an employer's computer network. Luckily, Honeywell did have anti-piracy policies in place, which would have helped in any defence it had to mount. Although the eventual outcome appears to be unknown, several employees were involved in police enquiries.

Although this example is an old one, it is vital that any assessment incorporating IT threats and vulnerabilities should cover this area. The main reasons are the penalties that could be levied for copyright theft. For the most serious breaches that would be heard in a Crown court, there is an unlimited fine and up to 10 years' imprisonment. For those dealt with in a magistrates' court, the maximum penalties are fines up to £5,000 and up to six months in prison. In extreme cases, it is possible for company directors and business owners to also face these penalties if they were found to have aided and abetted their staff in some way. There are other dangers too. Apart from the time-wasting and loss of productivity involved, any illegal file sharing on a large scale can slow down network speeds considerably. This will reduce productivity for all those who use computers for work, not to mention management time spent in trying to identify the cause. Finally, network security can be compromised if the files being downloaded illegally contain malware.

If any shortcomings are found, any recommendations should focus on tightening anti-piracy provisions. Doing so will help defend any claim that could find its way into a director's in-tray. This can either be through a standalone policy or via an add-on to an existing policy, such as on internet use. The policy must make it absolutely clear that downloading, copying and distributing material such as music and films is banned and explain why. As with other policies, educating staff is a priority as they must understand the possible consequences, not only for themselves but for the organization. Concentrate minds by explaining that any breach could expose both themselves and directors to the risk of both civil and criminal proceedings, and describe what the penalties are. After the briefing, get staff to sign and date to confirm that they understand and will comply with the policy on acceptable web use.

> **Key point**
>
> It is important that disciplinary procedures adequately reflect the damage that illegal file sharing can cause an employer – so make it a serious disciplinary offence.

Downloading pornography

This was one of the first problems that employers encountered once internet use became widespread. At its height, 70 per cent of internet porn traffic occurred between the hours of 9am and 5pm. Yet whilst many employers dealt with the problem by introducing policies, it may still be an issue. The problem arises when pornographic images are downloaded to work computers and disseminated via e-mail. Unfortunately for UK employers, a female employee does not have to see an image for sexual harassment to occur. This follows the Employment Appeal Tribunal decision in *Moonsar v Fiveways Express Transport Ltd* [2004] UKEAT/0476/04/TM. It was held that being present in an office where images were being downloaded and circulated was enough. This is because it can reasonably be seen as being degrading or offensive to an employee as a woman – so it follows that it is potentially less favourable treatment and a detriment, which can amount to sexual harassment. The fact that Moonsar did not complain at the time of the actual harassment was not enough to prevent her claim from succeeding.

In the UK, there is no maximum upper limit on the compensation that can be awarded, since sexual harassment comes under the umbrella of discrimination, which is covered by the Equality Act 2010. Another reason for revisiting this topic is because pornographic images, if downloaded in large enough quantities, will slow down a computer system and reduce productivity. This is what happened to the Driver & Vehicle Licensing Agency (DVLA). So many pornographic images had been e-mailed on its network that the server was affected and slowed down considerably. Following an investigation, at least

14 employees were dismissed and over 100 were disciplined. Pornographic images are also well known for carrying malware, which can quickly infect a network and therefore present a security threat.

An assessment should examine what restrictions there are to sites containing pornographic material (including child porn, which is illegal in many countries). This should be on all work devices, including mobiles. It should also look at how successful these measures have been and whether they need to be improved upon. Checks should be made to see whether or not the relevant policies are tough enough. The easiest solution is to place an outright ban on accessing such sites, just in case IT controls cannot block access to them all. Plus, any breaches should be considered a disciplinary offence. If there have been previous problems, checks should be made to ensure that all offenders have been treated equally. Failure to do this can easily lead to allegations of discrimination. If procedures need tightening, any recommendations can be along the same lines as those described earlier in this chapter.

Hate websites

Other download problems involve hate websites. These include content that may incite violence or some other form of prejudicial action against a protected individual or group. This is most likely to be via the content displayed on the site, as well as on an accompanying internet forum. However, the distinction must be made between websites that are merely offensive in nature as opposed to those that are illegal. In England and Wales, it can be a criminal offence to stir up hatred on the grounds of sexual orientation, race or religion. A website's content can also be illegal if it harasses or threatens an individual or group. According to the True Vision website on hate crime (part of the Department for Communities and Local Government: **http://www.true-vision.org.uk/**), hostility based on disability and transgenderism may also be considered a hate crime. This is likely where the website content calls for violence against these groups or glorifies it in some way. A range of online media is included such as videos, music, cartoons, text and online forums.

The employee risk assessment should approach the use of hate websites in the same way that it treats the downloading and dissemination of pornography. It should confirm that use of them has been specifically included in any IT policy. If they have, it is worth double-checking that there is a statement that makes it clear that many of these websites are illegal. In terms of recommendations, it is easier to introduce a complete ban on access to these sites. Attempting to differentiate between those that might be classed as offensive – as opposed to illegal – is unnecessarily time-consuming and confusing to employees. Also, as the example of pornography shows, a website does not have to be illegal in order to cause employers other problems, such as discrimination-based claims.

Online gambling

Internet growth has also witnessed an explosion in online gambling sites and with it a vast increase in those using them. Unfortunately, this may also have repercussions for organizations should their employees have a flutter during working hours. Although there is little research into its impact on employers, what there is suggests a serious problem. In the UK, most of this research seems to have been undertaken in 2007 as this was the year that online gambling was formally legalized. Although it was carried out seven years ago, research by Morse revealed that 30 per cent of office workers had either bet online or knew someone who had. They calculated that this would cost employers over £300 million per year in lost productivity. It was also estimated that there were already 1 million users of these websites. Given that an account can be set up in minutes, and that there are now hundreds of gambling applications that can be downloaded to phones and tablets, figures for 2014 are likely to be higher.

Although employer awareness of the dangers of online gambling should have improved in recent years, a 2006 case shows that there is no room for complacency. It involved a bookkeeper jailed for siphoning £1 million from his employer's bank accounts to fund his gambling addiction. Not only did the employer, Charminster Limited, lose this money, it also went into liquidation as a result. The fact that the guilty party received a jail sentence was probably of little comfort to the employer, or all those who lost their jobs. Yet whilst losing a business is most unusual, having even one employee with such an addiction can cost an organization dearly in terms of lost productivity. Another concern is that in the current economic climate, employees could see online gambling as a way of boosting their income to help pay the bills.

An IT manager with the energy company GDF Suez unfortunately took this several steps further, swindling his employer out of £19 million, which was not only used to fund his online gambling habit, but also used to purchase a £500,000 home. According to newspaper reports, he ordered computer equipment, which he then sold on over a three-year period. It was these proceeds that funded his gambling addiction. Even though he was arrested and granted bail on the condition that he stopped gambling and sought professional help, he continued. Allegedly he would bet as much as £300,000 on a single sporting fixture. He was jailed for seven years.

In Australia, the dangers of online gambling appear to be viewed as being an occupational health-and-safety problem. According to an article written by Jason Dowling in *The Age* newspaper on 9 November 2012, 'Push to ban online gambling at work', the Victorian Commission for Gambling and Liquor Regulation sees it as a health risk akin to smoking. As a result, workers are to be offered education and training to reduce the likelihood of developing a problem. This is definitely a softer stance to an issue that many other countries would consider to be a straightforward misconduct issue. In fact, in the first case quoted above, the employee was sentenced to five years in prison (with half to be served in the community), but was also seeking help from Gamblers Anonymous.

For these reasons, online gambling is an area that should be reviewed by any employer that does not already have adequate measures in place. Physically blocking access to these sites online is not enough as staff could also use mobile phones to place bets. Plus, there is always the chance that online gambling sites may open up that are outside any access restrictions set up by IT. Due to these shortcomings, any risk assessment should look for the existence of a policy that bans gambling during working hours. Depending on its contents, the recommendations should suggest that any form of gambling be banned during working hours and on all work equipment. This will include any laptops, tablets and mobile phones issued to an employee for work use. There should also be a link to disciplinary procedures so workers understand that they will be disciplined for breaching the policy. If an employee's productivity declined due to spending their time gambling instead of working, this would also count as misconduct (in exactly the same way that breaching an alcohol policy would).

Data protection

Although the Data Protection Act (DPA) is long established (since 1998), many UK-based organizations still breach its requirements. This can prove expensive because the ICO can levy fines of up to £500,000 for the most serious offences. Given that it posts details of employers served with monetary penalty notices on its website as well, the offence can also be damaging to an organization's reputation: the media trawl this site and the potential reputation damage can be far greater if they decide to publish the details in a national newspaper. A quick look at **http://www.ico.gov.uk/enforcement** shows that the Bank of Scotland was fined £75,000 in August 2013. Apparently, customers' account details were repeatedly faxed to the wrong recipients. This unfortunately included account details, payslips and full contact details. In July 2013, the now dissolved NHS Surrey was fined £200,000 after medical information belonging to thousands of patients was found on computer hard drives sold on an online auction site.

Until April 2010, the maximum fine for breach of the DPA was a paltry £5,000. Yet a study carried out before the maximum was increased to £500,000 revealed that many employers had not informed workers about this development. The research, initiated by Cyber-Ark Software, surveyed 500 workers in the City of London. It found that 65 per cent were unaware that they could now cost their employers up to £500,000 if their actions were found to have caused a 'deliberate or negligent' breach of personal data. It also found that 64 per cent carried customer information on mobile devices, with only 12 per cent using encryption to protect it; 38 per cent did not even have basic password protection. Given that the DPA applies to any data capable of identifying an individual 'data subject', such practices are lax in the extreme. Yet, this is also another example of where employers were (and still are) failing to keep up to date regarding emerging threats and vulnerabilities.

Any risk assessment that looks at how well its workforce is complying with the DPA should go back to the absolute basics. So, select several departments across the organization to see how well they currently comply. These should include those that handle third-party data such as customers, patients and suppliers. The first task will be to check that all the data covered by the DPA has been correctly identified. So it includes: 1) all personal data that contains enough detail to identify an individual (the 'data subject'); and 2) 'sensitive' personal data, such as medical records and trade union memberships. The second task will be to assess compliance against the eight data protection principles. As a reminder, these provide that the data must be:

1. fairly and lawfully processed;
2. processed for limited purposes;
3. 'adequate, relevant and not excessive';
4. accurate;
5. kept for no longer than is necessary;
6. processed in line with employee rights;
7. kept securely;
8. not transferred to non-EU countries without adequate protection.

Another area where some UK employers are still vulnerable is in forgetting (or being unaware) that the DPA applies during recruitment. Unsuccessful candidates can make a 'subject access request' for disclosure of copies of any notes made during the hiring process. If a request is made, copies must be made available within 40 calendar days. The fact that this type of request is being made suggests that a discrimination claim is being contemplated, such as age or disability. Unfortunately, given the increase in serial litigants (see Chapter 5), full compliance with disclosure requirements is essential. This means responding in a timely manner, with accurate information. If this is not forthcoming, the individual making the request can ask the Information Commissioner to investigate on his or her behalf.

For this reason, any risk assessment should check that those responsible for interviewing resist the temptation to make discriminatory or derogatory comments on any document connected with the recruitment process. This also includes any doodles or jottings on scrap paper. So any comments along the lines of 'looks pregnant, so a real no-no', or 'can't do the job as obviously disabled' must be avoided. The assessment also needs to look at whether or not those responsible for dealing with subject access requests know how to respond. The ICO produces numerous free publications that can help employers get back on track. In the meantime, and depending on what weaknesses are revealed in the current approach, any recommendations can focus on the real basics as follows:

- always keep securely any files containing both personal and confidential information;
- only allow authorized employees to have access to this data;
- log any personal and confidential data that is removed from the office where it is stored;

- use a logging system for this purpose;
- never give personal data to third parties without first getting permission from the data subject.

Confidential information and 'know-how'

In recent years, there has been greater awareness of the need to protect confidential business information and 'know-how' from competitors. This is due to a realization of how easy it can be to transfer copies of sensitive documents via e-mail or memory stick (portable digital device) in a few mouse clicks. The range of information that organizations need to safeguard is now extremely diverse. It includes tangible assets such as blueprints for new designs, trade secrets, instruction manuals and formulas for new products, as well as intangible assets such as work processes, and marketing and pricing strategies. As such, it represents highly sensitive information that is critical not only to future business success, but often its continuing viability. Despite this, many organizations are leaving themselves badly exposed as they fail to adequately safeguard this information.

This reveals not just a failure to safeguard against unauthorized access to data, but also how easy it is to steal it. For example, in 2013, Edward Snowden, a former National Security Agency contractor, was able to steal highly classified information using a memory stick. Although these devices were prohibited to most staff, it seems that there were insufficient controls to prevent downloading of material for those such as Snowden who did have legitimate access. So if one of the most secure spy organizations in the world was able to lose such sensitive information, it begs the question as to how easy it would be for a typical business. The answer, according to research commissioned by the technical training company QA, is worryingly simple. In 2013, QA surveyed 1,197 British workers and found that 29 per cent admitted to transferring work files to and from home; 35 per cent also used their own personal devices to access their work e-mails and documents. Whilst employers will hope that nothing untoward is happening with this information, the fact that such data transfer is possible makes an organization vulnerable. After all, what is to prevent an employee from downloading and selling customer details to a competitor?

This is what allegedly happened to Dyson, the developer of the dual-cyclone vacuum cleaner. An article in the *Telegraph*, written by Duncan Gardham on

25 November 2012, reported that one of Dyson's former employee's had been caught selling details of its know-how to a German competitor. It is alleged that this individual was paid over £11,500 over a 16-month period in return for passing on details of new technology related to high-speed brushless motors that power Dyson's vacuum cleaners and hand dryers. Such information was critical to Dyson's future product development and it is said to have invested £100 million on developing this technology. Unfortunately, the issue only came to light after this individual's dismissal for gross misconduct in June 2012. Otherwise, it may have gone unnoticed for many more months, even permanently.

In order to reduce the likelihood of this happening elsewhere, there must be collaboration between different departments and teams to ensure that there is not only a detailed computer-use policy in place, but that it is followed by anyone with computer access. Some larger organizations will have knowledge managers (or equivalent posts) as well as a sizeable IT presence, so the skills to facilitate this process already exist. It also provides a good opportunity for HR to be seen to take the initiative if threats or vulnerabilities are already suspected. It can do this by recognizing the role that each individual plays in protecting data security. This is vitally important, given the fact that many employees now use personal and work devices interchangeably (see BYOD above).

This means that the risk assessment should review what provision has been made in contracts of employment to protect this confidential information (this refers to trade secrets that are integral to business success). In particular, it needs to look at whether senior and specialist staff contracts are covered. Sometimes, people can move internally within an organization and the contractual provision can lag behind the realities of the new job. If so, it could have devastating results if a new post-holder can access confidential information for the first time, but no contractual clause has been inserted into their updated employment contract. Several contracts should be reviewed from across the organization from different departments, as applicable. Where self-employed contractors and consultants are concerned, this can be covered by reviewing contract-for-services or consultancy agreements for current or recent hires. It is important that the self-employed are covered, as they job-hop and could end up working for a competitor in the future. Where necessary, these should be updated, for example by an in-house contract specialist or retained law firm.

Chapter summary

Dangers of social engineering:

- it is seen as one of the greatest IT security threats;
- it is an easy way for cybercriminals to gain access to a computer network;
- it uses everyday social interaction to get employees to divulge computer passwords;
- a new threat is the 'vanity scam';
- employees do not realize the value of the information they have access to.

Employees lax on password protection:

- often leave computers on and logged in overnight and during breaks;
- tend to leave login and password details on their desk or in unlocked drawers;
- will share passwords with colleagues;
- create easy-to-remember passwords based on easily obtainable personal details.

Bring your own devices (BYOD):

- represents data-security threats to confidential information;
- are vulnerable to third-party access, such as by family members;
- could infringe the Data Protection Act 1998;
- an employer remains legally responsible for any of its data stored on a BYOD.

Cloud computing:

- is vulnerable to data leakage of commercially sensitive information;
- may be transferred to end user's personal devices;
- could lead to loss of employer control over what happens to confidential information;
- AIIM research found employees were using unofficial cloud-hosted file-sharing systems;
- employers are still responsible for data wherever it is stored in the cloud.

File downloads:

- can lead to illegal file sharing of copyright material on work computers; for financial reasons, copyright owners are more likely to pursue employers – the worst-case scenario for copyright theft is an unlimited fine and up to 10 years' imprisonment;
- slows down computer networks;
- downloaded material often contains malware that can introduce viruses;
- sex discrimination claims can ensue if pornography is downloaded;
- online gambling can reduce employee productivity; in the worst cases, an online gambling addiction can lead to theft from an employer.

Data protection:

- there are fines of up to £500,000 in the UK for the most serious data-protection offences;
- details of employers served with monetary penalty notices are posted on the LCO website;
- any serious breach of the DPA has potential to damage an employer's reputation.

Protecting confidential information and know-how:

- many organizations are not adequately protecting business-critical information;
- information can be easy to steal, such as via memory sticks;
- many staff send work information to home computers via e-mail;
- ease of third-party access to know-how, such as agency staff and contractors, can pose a security risk.

Recommendations:

- HR should work closely with IT on reviewing and creating robust IT policies, eg in respect to use of cloud computing;
- incorporate a section on BYOD into IT policies or introduce a standalone policy;
- review and restrict what information is transferred to cloud-hosting sites;

- require staff to only use approved cloud-hosting services;
- clarify ownership of any files transferred to the cloud;
- ban the downloading, copying and distributing of copyrighted material;
- outlaw access to pornographic and online gambling websites;
- ban access to hate websites and those that encourage harassment against specific groups;
- make any breaches a disciplinary offence;
- download the free UK Government document '10 steps to cyber security';
- HR to take a pivotal role in raising awareness via induction, training and communicating policies;
- assess basic compliance with the eight data protection principles across the organization;
- always keep securely all files containing both personal and confidential information;
- only allow authorized employees to have access to this data;
- log any personal and confidential data that is removed from the office where it is stored;
- use a logging system for this purpose;
- never give personal data to third parties without first obtaining permission from the data subject;
- implement interdepartmental collaboration to create a detailed computer-use policy;
- review employment contracts to protect confidential information and know-how.

Chapter 10 examines the HR function itself and the threats and vulnerabilities it can introduce into an organization due to a lack of business acumen. It also highlights three areas to show the negative impact that this can have.

Impact of HR function

10

Introduction

One function already mentioned is HR itself. Chapter 1 briefly outlined how employee risk management can help enhance HR's reputation, whilst Chapter 2 focused on how its status is mainly determined by the prevailing organizational culture. This chapter builds on both themes and looks at how HR can introduce its own threats and vulnerabilities into an organization. These could arise by failing to keep abreast of employment law changes, or by marginalizing itself due to poor business acumen. It then shows how this lack of commercial awareness can affect areas that HR is largely responsible for. Three key topics have been chosen. First is learning and talent development, in order to show how costly poorly targeted training can be. Second is performance management, in order to highlight the dangers of a culture of late intervention. The third is whistle-blowing, due to the reputational damage that can result from a failure of internal reporting mechanisms. Various recommendations are made that will build on how HR can enhance its value and status within the organization even further.

Role of HR

Perception of HR

Apart from the organizational culture, the key determinant of how HR is regarded depends on how it presents itself in terms of the perceived quality and relevance of its output. For example, any failure to keep up to date with employment law changes, emerging HR threats and evolving good practice will impact on employee behaviour. This perception is important as research carried out by KPMG International found that only 17 per cent of respondents maintain that HR does a good job of demonstrating its value to the business. This research, entitled 'Rethinking Human Resources in a changing world' (2012) was based on a global study of 418 executives: 32 per cent were based in Asia-Pacific, 30 per cent in Europe, 28 per cent in North America and 10 per cent in Latin America. The question asked was in what areas respondents believed HR to excel. Unfortunately, no area rated better than 39 per cent and this was for managing costs. HR's ability to manage a changing workforce, such as retiring workers, only scored 22 per cent. Given that 58 per cent of the respondents stated that their role was primarily HR, these figures seem lower than expected.

These findings are supported by research undertaken in 2013 by the management consultancy Orion Partners. They polled 67 senior HR professionals in UK organizations with a combined total of 1.1 million employees and found that:

- 70 per cent say that HR decision making is not supported by 'robust management information';
- 54 per cent stated that there are no mechanisms for evaluating HR's effectiveness;
- 37 per cent believe that the purposes and values of their department are poorly defined;
- 30 per cent think that new HR initiatives are not communicated in a way that describes their relevance to business objectives;
- 26 per cent of HR directors describe their own function as ineffective.

If these findings are not only representative of UK HR practitioners, but also of those globally, they give cause for concern. In particular, the high proportion of those admitting that their decision making is not based on hard facts explains why HR is often seen as 'woolly' rather than business-savvy. Given that its people strategy should be closely aligned to wider business strategy, this is not possible if decisions are made on assumptions and 'gut feelings'. Neither of these will cut any ice with the C-suite or equivalent decision makers, many of whom will come from fact-based disciplines, such as finance or law. In fact, this point returns to the research mentioned in Chapter 2 on how many top HR jobs are being filled by those outside HR. Part of the problem is that those entering HR do so as it has always been seen as a home for a 'people person', rather than attracting those with analytical skills who are confident around data. This means that some potential employee threats may be overlooked as a result.

One recommendation is to look at recruiting an individual with good IT and analytical skills into the HR team. This could be someone already working in an organization's IT department who is seconded to HR. Alternatively, it could be a newly created post with someone taken on specifically to bridge this skills gap. Apart from assisting with the employee risk management process, he or she can also analyse data for the HR department generally. The costs of their appointment could be justified through the potential cost savings to be made as a result of the work that they will carry out. This still applies even if an organization does not have the means to be able to interrogate 'big data' sets. What this individual can do instead is create an inventory of what data already exists via departmental surveys. They can then identify what information could be useful to HR and analyse it, not only in terms of cost savings, but in other areas too, such as a review of the return on investment in recruiting. This could compare the costs of recruitment campaigns across different mediums with the number of suitable candidates yielded. Apart from cost savings, this analysis also allows for the identification of talent shortages in order to aid with succession planning.

A related problem is the image that still persists of many HR departments as having a negative 'can't do' attitude. It can also sometimes be seen as a function that justifies its existence through the creation of bureaucratic procedures that bear little relation to business needs. One explanation for this is the high number of HR practitioners that lack business qualifications and/or much experience in other functions. Many organizations tried to resolve this by reinventing their HR adviser roles as business partners. This met with mixed success, partly for the reasons already mentioned, but also because HR lacked the skills to define its contribution to business strategy and its own 'value proposition' to its organization. In turn, this impacts on how HR is viewed. For example, is it seen as an integral, value-adding part of the business or merely a support function, separate from the real decision making? If the latter, there is a chance that no matter how well-drafted its policies are, they will often be ignored or only followed when it suits local management.

Legal compliance

How HR interprets ever-changing employment law legislation and updates managers on compliance issues is important. So, the risk assessment should look at how legislative changes are interpreted and disseminated, as well as good practice and case law updates. Do not limit the risk assessment to high-profile employment law changes – include any updates that are less topical but still capable of causing problems. Start with a point at which there was awareness within HR that new developments were coming and then track progress from that point forward. This process could usefully include a review of the following:

- What employment law qualifications, if any, are held by those responsible for disseminating legal changes. Also check what employment or related law courses are attended by HR staff and when. In other words, is their knowledge current?

- The information sources used by HR, such as subscription-based products, newsletters from law firms and any updates from an in-house legal team. Based on previous experience, do these information sources meet the organization's needs?

- How the details of employment law changes or key tribunal rulings and their implications for the organization were interpreted by HR. Also, what thinking goes into how this often dull information is presented to staff in an engaging way?

- The methods used to circulate these updates. These may include established media such as newsletters and memos, or newer methods such as via podcast on an organization's intranet.

- Was this information tailored to the needs of different recipients? A one-size-fits-all approach is not going to work as a department head, for example, will need different information to a team leader.

- Whether there are any monitoring mechanisms in place capable of assessing how effective the process was in terms of getting the message across to staff.

Whilst the recommendations will depend on the specific findings from the employee risk assessment, they are likely to focus on improving the knowledge of employment law of those with responsibility for updating others in the organization. This may involve building more regular employment law course attendance into annual appraisals. Luckily, there are plenty of law firms that tailor these types of courses specifically to the needs of HR practitioners and will carry out in-house training. Another recommendation may be to review the existing employment law sources that are currently used and whether they continue to meet the organization's needs. If the assessment feedback is that the information on employment law updates needs improving, HR could seek advice from any internal communications or PR function on how to best present the information.

Self-regulation

Issues of self-regulation are closely connected to legal compliance. Amongst the criticisms levelled at HR is the lack of formal regulation. This means that if there are concerns internally as to how well HR keeps itself abreast of employment law changes and evolving ideas of good practice, there is no independent body to go to. So it is not surprising that the above research found that so many senior HR practitioners have no framework in place to evaluate HR's effectiveness. Whilst an employee risk management approach will not be a solution to every problem, it can be useful as a self-audit tool. If done well, it should help alleviate any concerns that may exist, especially if the findings are made available across the organization. It will also help where an image-conscious HR team is aware that the lack of regulation could be damaging to its reputation internally. This is even more important where employment tribunal claims have been lost and the employer's reputation and brand has suffered as a consequence. If this applies, part of the risk management exercise must involve project team members from outside HR, as it will otherwise lack credibility.

To successfully self-regulate means HR being proactive and not just relying on a tick-box exercise as a job well done. Again, this is where the monitoring and review mechanisms of this approach can help, in that it forces hard questions to be asked on matters such as the operational effectiveness and relevance of procedures produced by HR staff. With cost and time pressures that are so typical of today's working environment, this can easily be neglected. One activity that will need reviewing is how information learned from training courses is cascaded within the HR team itself. It cannot be assumed that those attending courses, for example on employment law, will automatically take the initiative in disseminating the content to his or her colleagues. Neither is it a given that it will be done in an effective way. As with other HR-focused questions, any review of HR should be carried out by a non-HR member of the project team.

Demonstrating business acumen

HR is often criticized for its lack of business awareness and understanding of how the wider organization works. As mentioned in Chapter 1, HR can use corporate governance requirements as a way of justifying greater business involvement. Whilst the precise regime will vary depending on the country of operation, the principles will centre on risk management. Even though the main drivers will be financial compliance, there is still a 'hook' for HR to latch on to: this is the negative impact that the workforce can potentially have on the bottom line. Taking the example of a disengaged workforce, HR can use data to apply costs to sickness absence, management time spent dealing with grievances and possibly underperformance (depending on how measurable this is in practice). Unhappy staff are more likely to be actively looking for new employment opportunities. If so, this is likely to mean time spent surfing online job boards during work hours. Regular research is carried out into the time that employees spend online surfing at work, so approximate hourly rates can be set against these.

Combine this with the reputation damage that resentful employees can cause employers via social media – and you have a deadly mix. Together, these problems will be costly, both in terms of money and management time spent dealing with them. It means that valuable people and financial resources are being diverted from adding value to the organization, be it a charity or a multinational company. Depending on the costs involved, these issues are of legitimate concern to shareholders. The same principle applies to other stakeholders, such as the tax payer if the employer is public sector. Also, since 2008, many employers have had to consider their 'risk profile'. This is an outline of the threats and vulnerabilities that they face and the degree of risk attached. It became necessary as the global economic downturn revealed various operational weaknesses and there was a greater awareness of risk. This new awareness is a trend that will likely continue, given the ongoing economic uncertainty. As part of this process, employers will also need to start identifying where they are storing up problems for themselves in the future.

HR can show its business credentials by becoming part of this process and taking the lead in flagging up issues within its own sphere of influence. For example, there could be latent threats such as underlying staff stress and presenteeism problems due to a toxic management culture. Equally, there could be emerging threats of a new kind, such as an ageing or increasingly unhealthy workforce. Turning a blind eye to this will not make these problems go away. Instead, it will most likely lead to increased costs and labour shortages in the not too distant future. This will become evident when there is sufficient employee confidence that the labour market is showing sustained signs of improvement. In fact, according to the CIPD/Halogen *Employee Outlook for October 2013*, gradual signs of job market recovery are already in evidence and nearly one-quarter of UK employees are actively seeking new job opportunities.

Involvement in new areas

Apart from taking ownership of the concept of employee risk management, HR can also use it to enhance its standing in certain strategic areas. This would be done via the promotion of specific recommendations made in the risk assessment. For example, if high staff turnover included a disproportionate number of new employees leaving within six months, HR could take the initiative and promote employer brand management as an activity that it should be leading. This refers to how an organization markets its offering to both existing and future employees. It is still an emerging discipline, so has considerable potential for HR practitioners going forward (see Chapter 5), as it focuses on how organizational values, people strategy and HR policies connect to the corporate brand. The logic behind this is that an organization's brand success relies on the actions of its workforce – and HR is ideally placed to obtain employee buy-in. Given that the process involves defining and promoting the employer brand on a day-to-day basis (eg through employee involvement initiatives), the HR function is well placed to take strategic ownership of it.

Another area that HR could exploit is to create a role for itself in embedding corporate social responsibility (CSR) throughout the organization. Obviously, the push for this will depend on the nature of the findings from the employee risk assessment. However, given the impact of organizational culture on risk taking, it should not be difficult to work into the recommendations (see Chapter 2). Apart from the topicality of this subject after the recent banking crisis, the importance of HR's contribution to the corporate responsibility agenda was the subject of CIPD research. Its publication *The Role of HR in Corporate Responsibility* (2013) found that focus in this area was gradually increasing for 22 per cent of those surveyed. Arguably, this is a low figure and suggests that HR is justified in putting the topic on the agenda at senior level.

This is particularly the case given the 'reality gap' between where HR would like to be in terms of leading the corporate responsibility agenda and where it actually is. Only 56 per cent of the 523 general managers surveyed consider the HR contribution in this area as vital, whereas 81 per cent of the 353 HR managers surveyed believe it to be so. Part of this 25 per cent discrepancy could be explained by a lack of awareness of HR's suitability in this area by general managers. But it could also be explained by their perception that HR is not really a business function. If so, the risk assessment's recommendations must sell the fact of how well-placed HR is to take the lead in this area: for example, by pointing to HR's ownership of the induction process, its strategic role in learning and development and its role in driving organizational change programmes.

Part of the corporate responsibility agenda includes how ethical an organization is, or is seen to be, in terms of the goods or services it produces. Many organizations face challenges over their working practices, how they are funded or what they produce. For example, the retail industry has faced allegations over appalling working conditions and pay in India; pharmaceutical and cosmetic companies over animal testing; McDonald's over promoting obesity and dead-end jobs; and the tobacco industry is criticized on health grounds. Whilst the main problem is front-line staff having to field difficult questions from the public, any employee could be on the receiving end. This could also be from family and friends. If employees are not given the tools to be able to deal with sustained criticism, they can become disengaged and demotivated. If so, and no management intervention is forthcoming, it could lead to declining productivity and a higher staff turnover rate.

It is this that offers HR an ideal opportunity to become part of the solution. For example, an organization's PR team may send out brief updates on how a particular problem or scandal is being dealt with. But this is unlikely to be more than sound bites. If so, it will not be enough to help employees counter the flak that has or will come their way. Also, unprepared staff could, through no fault of their own, cause further reputation damage to their employer, for example by not knowing enough to be able to give a strong response to those who challenge them, or by giving the wrong information. Instead, what HR could do is liaise with the PR team. Its purpose would be to ensure that staff, especially those who are customer-facing, are given sufficient information and training to communicate on the organization's behalf – in order to be able to state the correct position taken up by the organization, or to describe what is being done to rectify a situation. Having staff act as ambassadors in this way should also be a cheap means of boosting employee engagement.

Learning and talent development

Introduction

For many organizations, the humble training function has changed rapidly in recent years. It evolved to become learning and development, but has more recently reinvented itself to become learning and talent development (LTD). The CIPD (2013) describes this as being 'an organizational strategy that articulates the workforce capabilities, skills or competencies required to ensure a sustainable, successful organization and that sets out the means of developing these capabilities to underpin organizational effectiveness'. A good part of this evolution is due to HR's desire to be seen as having become more business focused in how it aligns its LTD initiatives to business strategy.

Correctly identifying the business need

Whilst sounding like a positive development in theory, there are still weaknesses that can be inbuilt into any LTD strategy. These will be administered by those with responsibility for commissioning training solutions in this area. Unfortunately, they can have serious implications for the organization, which is why the topic is being covered here. The main problem is failing to properly define the underlying business need from the outset. According to KnowledgePool, the managed services learning provider, this may be a more common occurrence than expected. In its business white paper 'How to reduce training wastage' (2011), it found that '25 per cent of all training fails to yield significant performance improvement'. This was based on over 10,000 responses to their learning outcomes evaluation surveys, which were issued three months after the completion of training. Yet, what is more interesting is the belief that this figure of 25 per cent is actually an underestimate.

The author of the white paper, Kevin Lovell, KnowledgePool's Learning Strategy Director, says the feedback revealed that the real figure is actually much higher. Comments from learning and development professionals put the figure of training failing to have the desired effect at 50 per cent or possibly 60 per cent. However, this was anecdotal so could not be evidenced in any way. Yet no matter what the true figure is, it shows that a lot of organizations are financing training programmes that fail to deliver the planned benefits. If an external course provider has been used, the wasted costs could be considerable, not to mention the loss of productivity involved in planning and attending the courses. Where such courses are rolled out across an organization over a period of months, and involve middle to senior management, these costs could easily run into six figures. The other problem is that the workforce, based on previous experience, could come to view such courses as a waste of time.

For these reasons, a review of the LTD process could usefully form part of a wider employee risk management assessment. Also, with tight budgets, it would also help show HR as keen to play its part in improving value for money. However, in order to utilize this opportunity, there must be honesty in unearthing any hidden agenda at the commissioning stage. A second KnowledgePool white paper entitled 'From conspiracy of convenience to virtuous circle' (2011), called this a 'training conspiracy'. The idea behind this is that all the training stakeholders have vested interests in approaching commissioning in a certain way. It starts with a manager who sees training as a safe solution to a problem. For example, instead of having to confront employee performance issues, the manager knows he or she will not be criticized for asking for a training solution. It is an easy answer and it makes the manager look good for trying to resolve matters.

The second stakeholder is the department responsible for providing LTD solutions. They want to provide a good service to their internal customers and quickly. But doing this means agreeing to a request without discussing whether or not training is the right solution. In their eyes, challenging the manager could result in them going to a third-party provider who will happily give them what they want. Therefore, the vested interest continues and the belief that training is a good thing becomes reinforced. Those providing the actual training represent the third stakeholder. For internal training delivery teams, the more training they provide, the busier they are and the more secure their jobs become. Equally, if the training is outsourced to a third-party provider, keeping their client happy will keep them in work and earning money. So once again, there is a vested interest in maintaining the status quo and not asking if training is appropriate.

Any employee risk assessment of training will need to identify if this practice goes on. One way of finding out is to interview employees who have been on courses in the last two years in order to obtain their feedback. Another way (depending on the numbers involved) is to send out a brief survey for employees to complete. The questions should identify the course they were sent on, the reason for it and whether or not the employee has transferred what they have learned to their work. Any employees who have left employment in this period should also be included in the figures. If there is evidence of a training conspiracy, it means that training is being used as a costly solution to the wrong problem. It also means that the underlying issues remain unresolved. The assessors will need to interview managers who have commissioned training as well as those responsible internally for providing it. This is in order to identify their motives for opting for an LTD solution.

The risk assessment will need to reveal the managers' decision-making process, so should ask what thought was given to other possible solutions, such as on-the-job coaching. Depending on the findings, any recommendations for change will revolve around altering the mindset of those involved in commissioning LTD. This could be done by holding workshops on performance management in order to reinforce the need to be proactive. It can also increase managers' awareness of the options available to them for doing this. This recommendation also has the added benefit that it can be sold on the basis that there will be cost savings from reducing the amount of wrongly targeted training given to staff. A rough cost estimate can be made by taking the feedback from any staff surveys carried out. For example, if 40 per cent of staff say that they have not used what they learned, then their time spent on the course can be set against their gross hourly rate. Then the costs of training can be factored in. Any money saved can then be directed at better LTD initiatives.

Training and learning needs analysis

In many cases, a training-based initiative will prove to be an appropriate response to learning needs. However, the next challenge is to ensure that it will meet the needs identified. If not, it could result in a considerable waste of both time and money. The organization could also suffer as its workforce has not received the right learning and development for it to remain competitive. This is where a training and learning needs analysis (TLNA) comes in. Proactive in nature, it looks at the current skills and behaviours that employees possess and how best to develop them to: 1) meet the organization's strategic objectives; and 2) to support an employee's career progression. It can also look at department or team needs as well as at specific occupational groups. So it is both versatile and flexible.

However, even if those responsible for learning and development use a TLNA or similar, there is still room for mistakes. Therefore, the assessment should look at how those who have input into a TLNA go about it. For example, incorrectly identified needs could result in the development of an excellent course, but it will still be time and money wasted if it does not meet actual requirements. So the assessors should look at what methods are currently used to identify training needs within their organization. Ideally, it will be a mixture of some or all of the following:

- outcome of employee annual or biannual appraisals;
- feedback from TLNA questionnaires issued across the organization;
- face-to-face interviews with managers, supervisors and staff;
- observing employees at work in order to look for training gaps, eg customer service staff;
- focus groups set up to discuss how well training needs are identified and met.

The question also needs to be asked as to how well any identified LTD needs are prioritized, to ensure that resources only go where they are most needed, rather than focusing on the easiest 'solution'. The risk assessment also needs to examine whether or not its format is suitable for its intended audience. Apart from educational level, suitability needs to consider English language proficiency, especially amongst organizations that rely heavily on immigrant staff for low-skilled positions. For example, in some cases such as safety training, pictorial-based learning and development will be more effective than a lengthy presentation accompanied by hand-outs. Another question for those responsible for LTD commissioning is how well it fits the preferred learning methods of those attending. Everyone has their own preferences, and if the training mode is the opposite to this, the required learning experience will not take place: one good example of a mismatch is where a formal training format is used for those who are not at all academic.

The assessment also needs to look at how the LTD given is translated into a business benefit. This is the entire point of the training, but is where so many initiatives fall short. Unless those attending actually apply what they have learned into their job role, it is money and time wasted. The KnowledgePool research found four reasons why learning is not converted in post-training performance:

- lack of support from the line manager after the learning intervention;
- receiving unsuitable training, ie, pitched at the wrong level;
- sending an employee on a course they will not use, just to 'keep them happy';
- poor timing in that the training was given too early or too late for the employee's needs, or changing work circumstances that prevented them from applying their learning.

As part of the risk assessment, these four points could be turned into questions to be asked of both managers and those attending courses. Equally, if a survey is going to be used, they can be added on to it. Depending on the culture of the organization, it may increase the survey response rate if those returning them are allowed to remain anonymous (although this would only work if the questions were generic and did not refer to specific courses). In terms of recommendations, it is also likely that those in HR with responsibility for LTD will need to refocus the process of commissioning training interventions. Once again, the solution will largely come down to changing the behaviour of line managers: this is because the above four bullet points come back to them in some way. For example, instead of sending an unhappy employee on a training course to 'keep them happy', their manager should be looking at resolving the source of the discontent, such as giving the employee new duties.

Managing poor performance

The framework for managing poor performance within an organization is usually created by HR and is a good example of an activity that greatly influences business performance. Yet, it is an area that can be poorly managed. Part of this is down to a lack of sufficient emphasis by HR for early line manager intervention in resolving performance problems. However, it can also be explained by the reluctance of many line managers to proactively performance-manage their staff. Unfortunately, failure to do so can lead to several problems. The main ones are as follows:

- A decline in individual or team performance becomes the new 'normal': the longer it goes unchallenged, the harder it will be to turn around.
- After a sufficient time lapse, any performance management intervention by the line manager is likely to be met with a grievance, as the employee will feel picked on.

- Resentment from colleagues who believe that they are carrying someone who is not pulling their weight. If not dealt with, this can damage team cohesion and productivity levels.
- Time spent by others on rectifying mistakes made by the individual or team. This takes them away from their role and is likely to reduce their output.
- If the employee or team have customer-facing roles, there could be a loss of satisfaction, or in the worst cases, a loss of customers.
- The result could be damage to the organization's reputation, for instance if a disgruntled customer vents their anger on social media (see Chapter 8).

In order to be effective, performance management interventions must be triggered as soon as it becomes obvious that the problem is not a temporary blip. The warning signs to look out for are evidence of: 1) making basic mistakes several times in a row; 2) poor timekeeping; 3) regular bouts of a loss of concentration; 4) failing to meet targets; 5) missing deadlines; and 6) customer complaints. There will usually be one of three possible explanations for declining performance. The first is capability, where the employee cannot do the job. This may be due to being given new duties that he or she is unable to fulfil due to lack of training or experience. Similarly, the problem could follow a recent promotion that the employee was not qualified for. A second explanation is conduct, where the employee chooses not to do their job to the standard required. This can also arise through disengagement from both the job and/or the employer. If so, it requires a different approach. The third explanation is where personal reasons are a factor, such as a bereavement or money worries.

Unless the problem is serious enough to warrant capability proceedings (formal measures to help an employee improve their performance) any intervention should be informal. For UK employers, this is the approach recommended by Acas. It works on the principle that the sooner a manager has a quiet word, the easier and faster it will be to resolve a problem. If the risk assessment covers this area, a sample of managers should be asked for their views on performance management. They should also be asked if they intervene early when problems appear and, if so, what form their intervention takes. Where they show resistance to tackling performance problems, the reasons for this must be explored and not glossed over. It might be that they feel awkward in raising the fact that there is a problem, especially if they have a good relationship with the employee concerned. Alternatively, they may have previously experienced a lack of support from their own managers and/or HR in providing help to employees in the past, such as extra training.

A second problem is that once formal intervention is unavoidable, the process gets dragged out. If so, this can also prove damaging for an organization as it gives the wrong message to staff. It is also inefficient from a business perspective. So one area that a risk assessment can usefully examine is what time frames HR have set for sustained performance improvements to occur by. A period of between four to eight weeks after capability proceedings have started should be sufficient in most cases. Such a time frame balances the employer's need to resolve the problem against giving the employee a reasonable chance to improve. If the period provided for is much longer than this and the capability procedure has contractual status, then amending it will be more complex. For example, it will require consultation, be it with employees or trade unions (if they are formally recognized by the employer). In all cases, the reasons for shortening the period of improvement should be explained, such as improving business efficiency in what may still be challenging operating conditions.

In some cases, this four- to eight-week time frame may not be suitable. Thus the risk assessment should consider if HR has built sufficient flexibility into the process. For example, the longer the employee has been employed, the more reasonable it will be to extend the period of improvement. The same applies if their work is normally of a good standard. Equally, shorter periods may be acceptable if the role is customer-facing, or if it is industry practice. In all cases, it is important that the end of the improvement period is marked with a formal review. This should be supported by a letter that acknowledges progress, but clearly states that the employee must not allow their performance to deteriorate again. Any assessment into this area should examine whether:

- the aims of the process are made clear to the employee;
- the employee is made aware at the outset that if dealing with the problem informally fails to achieve the necessary improvement, capability proceedings will be the next step;
- goals/targets for improvement have been created using SMART or similar objectives (see Chapter 3);

- interim reviews take place at different stages of the performance process and how effective they are at keeping the underperforming employee on track;
- feedback is obtained from relevant third parties, such as those providing mentoring;
- the employee is given a chance to provide feedback on the process throughout;
- line managers adhere strictly to the agreed time frame – the danger of being too willing to extend it is that it undermines the whole process.

Where the answer to any of these bullet points is in the negative, they should be added to the section on recommendations. If necessary, another is to review the relevant budget so that any suggested initiatives to support an employee can actually happen. Without this, any attempt to penalize an individual via capability proceedings could be met with a grievance. This would be for failure to offer promised support. Depending on the findings, one last recommendation could be that HR reviews how performance management is carried out across the organization in order to ensure consistency of approach and fairness.

Whistle-blowing

Whistle-blowing arises when a worker reports suspected wrongdoing in the workplace. Although a fairly universal concept, the way it is approached varies from country to country. For example, in the United States and Canada different laws will apply depending on the subject and the state or province where the whistle-blower works. In Great Britain, it is the opposite, as whistle-blowing activities are covered by a piece of legislation: the Public Interest Disclosure Act 1998 (PIDA), which covers: 1) criminal offences; 2) failure to comply with a legal obligation; 3) miscarriages of justice; 4) environmental damage; and 5) health and safety concerns (Northern Ireland is producing its own legislation). With a few exceptions, such as the military and the self-employed, PIDA covers a wide range of workers who are 'making a disclosure in the public interest'. Where such a disclosure is made, it does not have to be 'in good faith'. However, the individual is protected both from dismissal and from being subject to any other detriment.

Any employee risk assessment should look carefully at whistle-blowing: the threat to employers comes from the fact that a worker is not required to raise concerns internally first. Yet the outcome can prove highly damaging for an organization's reputation and bottom line, as penalties can run into millions. Two examples reported from the United States in 2013 include a US $39.3 million judgement against Tuomey Healthcare System, relating to the paying of illegal referral fees to doctors. In this case, the whistle-blower was also a physician. However, this was eclipsed by an even bigger fine of US $3 billion levied by the US courts against GlaxoSmithKline, the UK's biggest drug manufacturer. Four former employees blew the whistle on the mismarketing of medicines in the United States. So, the starting point for any risk assessment is to look at whether or not there is an internal whistle-blowing framework in place and how effective it actually is.

In November 2013 the UK charity Public Concern at Work (**http://www.pcaw.org.uk**) published the outcome of research of over 164 senior staff in 30 different industry sectors. It found that in the UK, one in three respondents believed that their arrangements for whistle-blowers are ineffective. This is despite the fact that 93 per cent of those surveyed have formal measures in place. The research also found that: 1) 54 per cent said that they do not train those employees responsible for dealing with concerns; 2) 44 per cent confuse protected disclosures with grievances; 3) only 30 per cent tell staff how to go about approaching a regulator; and 4) 10 per cent admitted that their arrangements are not clearly endorsed by senior management. These findings are likely to be similar to those found in many countries, so a risk assessment should concentrate on the following areas:

- **Credibility:** in many cases, a whistle-blowing policy will be drafted by HR, possibly with input from other departments. If so, the first question to ask is if it has the genuine support of senior management, or if it really exists only as a tick-box exercise.
- **Organizational culture:** a candid view needs to be taken of the existing organizational culture and how supportive it really is to those who raise concerns. For example, have genuine attempts been made to get workers to come forward, or is this discouraged, such as in the NHS?
- **Framework:** any policy must be clear on how concerns are raised and to whom. It should state that bullying or harassing whistle-blowers, or subjecting them to a detriment, will not be tolerated (as a result of legal changes in 2013, in England, Scotland and Wales employers must take steps to prevent this).

- **Training:** the assessment must also look at what training any designated contacts are given, not just on how whistle-blowing legislation (such as the PIDA) operates, but on how to carry out investigations when concerns are raised. Also, some sectors, such as banking and health and social care, are more likely to experience certain types of whistle-blowing, so a look at what sector-specific training is provided is recommended.
- **Confidentiality:** checks should be made on how an employee's wish to preserve confidentiality is handled. This should look at the circumstances where this both can and cannot be done, eg such as where their evidence may be needed in court.

Depending on the findings from the risk assessment, any recommendations can be built around the above points. For example, where necessary, any whistle-blowing policy must be revised by HR so that it clearly sets out the process for raising concerns. Second, any training needs identified by the assessment should be followed up. One aspect of the training may involve clarifying the difference between whistle-blowing and raising a grievance. The distinction is that whistle-blowing affects others and the whistle-blower is a witness to alleged wrongdoing. In contrast, a grievance is personal to the individual raising it, as it relates to their own employment situation. Another recommendation is that a named director should sponsor the whistle-blowing policy in order to give it credibility.

> **Note**
>
> In November 2013, the Whistleblowing Commission produced a report with 25 recommendations. The main one is for a Code of Practice to be developed by the UK Government that could be taken into account in any whistle-blowing cases heard in court. More information can be found at http://www.pcaw.org.uk/whistleblowing-commission-public-consultation.

Another option to consider is using a third party to manage an anonymous whistle-blowing service. This works by an organization signing up and designating a senior manager to be responsible for answering messages. Once employees have been informed about the service and need to use it, they can register via their work e-mail address. This is only to enable recognition and matching to the right employer by the third-party provider's software. If an employee has a concern they can then send a message to this designated senior manager that is routed through the third-party's software. A two-way anonymous dialogue takes place until both parties decide that the issue has been resolved. At that point, the employee reporting the concern can decide if they want the conversation to be available to others. One of the few examples of this type of service is SpeakInConfidence (**http://www.speakinconfidence.com**).

Chapter summary

How HR is perceived as a function:

- is influenced by how relevant its output is deemed to be;
- KPMG research found that only 17 per cent think that HR does a good job of showing its value;
- depends on how it relates its initiatives to business objectives;
- is 'woolly' as its decision making is often not supported by hard facts – as a result HR personnel are often overlooked by the C-suite for the top 'people' jobs;
- HR can be perceived negatively due to the lack of a regulating body for HR professionals;
- HR has a tendency to still lack business acumen.

How employee risk management can enhance HR's reputation:

- as a self-audit tool on compliance and good practice, as HR has no regulatory body;
- it helps demonstrate business acumen;
- it contributes to the creation of an enterprise risk profile;
- by involvement in new areas, eg employer branding and corporate responsibility.

Learning and talent development (LTD) pitfalls:

- failing to define the business need for specific training from the outset;
- research found that 25 per cent of LTD fails to yield significant performance improvement – feedback on this research revealed the figure to be as high as 50–60 per cent in reality;

- the wasted costs involved in poorly targeted training could be considerable;
- stakeholders arguably have a vested interest in approaching LTD in a certain way – if so, these vested interests may mean that LTD is a costly 'solution' to the wrong problem;
- high risk that the workforce have not received the right input to remain competitive;
- wrong methods can be used to identify LTD needs;
- poor prioritizing of LTD needs leads to the budget not being used to its best effect;
- training may be given in the wrong format for its intended audience;
- where the LTD fails to be translated into a business benefit.

Poor performance problems can result when:

- HR fails to emphasize the importance of early line manager intervention;
- a lack of proactive performance management leads to:
  - a sustained decline in performance, which becomes the new 'normal';
  - the employee raising a grievance as matters have been allowed to drift;
  - resentment from colleagues, which can damage team relationships;
  - time spent by others correcting mistakes;
  - loss of customer satisfaction;
  - in the worst-case scenario, damage to an organization's reputation.
- an overgenerous time frame is given to staff for them to improve their performance;
- insufficient support is given to managers who try to performance manage;
- managers procrastinate over performance-managing staff.

Whistle-blowing dangers:

- in the UK, a whistle-blowing disclosure no longer has to be in 'good faith';
- the individual making the disclosure is protected from suffering a detriment;

- no legal requirement is in place for the employee to raise concerns internally first;
- lack of an effective internal whistle-blowing framework;
- failure to train employees who are responsible for dealing with concerns raised;
- creating a policy that is not genuinely supported by senior management;
- having a culture that discourages employees from coming forward;
- poor standard of investigation carried out once whistle-blowing has occurred;
- failure to protect employee confidentiality.

Recommendations:

- HR departments to second or recruit an individual with good IT and analytical skills – costs of the appointment can be offset against savings made from data analysis;
- where necessary, HR staff to attend more employment law updates;
- review the employment law resources used to see if they still meet organizational needs;
- talk to internal communications/PR on how to improve readability of legal updates;
- employee risk management is offered as a means of auditing HR;
- depending on the assessment findings, HR to push for involvement in:
  - employer brand management as an activity that it is well placed to lead;
  - embedding corporate social responsibility initiatives;
  - promoting the workforce as brand ambassadors.
- Where training solutions are overused by managers:
  - look at changing their mindset to find more appropriate solutions;
  - a workshop may be necessary to make them aware of better options;
  - sell it on the cost savings that will arise from reducing unnecessary training;
  - refocus these cost savings on more appropriate initiatives.

- to carry out a training needs analysis;
- to ensure that the LTD given is translated into a business benefit;
- to create a culture of early but informal intervention with poor performance;
- with formal intervention, four to eight weeks should usually be enough time to improve;
- make employees aware of how the performance management process will work;
- undertake interim progress reviews throughout;
- to ensure that any support promised to an underperforming employee is forthcoming;
- the employee is told that failure to improve will result in action being taken;
- a whistle-blowing policy must state how concerns must be raised and to whom;
- provide training to those responsible for handling whistle-blowing concerns;
- a named director should sponsor the whistle-blowing policy;
- use a third-party provider to manage an anonymous whistle-blowing service;
- this review of HR functions should be carried out by someone outside HR.

Chapter 11 looks at the end of employment and the broad principles that employers in any legal jurisdiction should follow when dismissing staff. It also covers other areas, such as providing references.

End of employment

11

Introduction

As with recruitment, an employee's departure from an organization is far from risk free. The main problem arises when they have been dismissed. This occurs: 1) where a contract of employment is terminated with or without notice; 2) the employee terminates their contract of employment due to the employer's unreasonable conduct (known as constructive dismissal in the UK, Canada and New Zealand, and constructive discharge in the United States); and 3) a fixed-term contract expires but is not renewed. But rather than focus on dismissal generally, this chapter targets the areas that employers still get wrong. So, its focus is more on the principles that employers should be following. It then moves on to the elements of a sound disciplinary investigation, as many organizations still make mistakes. Even where the employee chooses to resign, there is still a potential minefield to navigate. This chapter includes the main considerations, which include giving references, retrieving company property and being able to enforce post-employment restrictions. Whilst some of the points included here are more UK-focused, many of the principles behind them can also be applied to other jurisdictions.

Unfair dismissal

The concept of unfair (or unjust) dismissal is understood in several countries, including the UK, Canada, Australia, Germany and New Zealand (known as wrongful dismissal in the United States). It is a statutory creation built on the concept of fairness. However, the protection given to employees varies from country to country. Therefore, the focus of this chapter is on following good principles based on the life cycle of a potential dismissal situation. Some examples may be more UK-centric (England, Wales, Scotland and Northern Ireland), or relevant to Great Britain (GB) (England, Wales and Scotland). Yet they will also provide good practice points for other jurisdictions, especially those in the Commonwealth. In terms of overall approach, the employee risk assessment should look at how any previous employment tribunal claims were dealt with as well as how managers currently tackle the disciplinary and dismissal process. It is important that the assessors reassure interviewees that the exercise is not designed to penalize them for not following procedures in the past. With regard to method, it may be helpful to break down the assessment process into distinct stages, as set out below.

Preliminary assessment

When a potential disciplinary situation arises, begin by designating it as either misconduct or capability: the two problems have different origins and should be treated differently. Misconduct is where an employee 'won't do', whereas capability issues arise where the employee 'can't do'. This could be due to: 1) ill-health problems; 2) inability to carry out certain tasks; 3) inexperience; or 4) lack of training. In these circumstances, it is unfair to penalize an employee, which is what adopting the disciplinary route would do. So the assessment should start by asking managers if they know the difference between the two. In some cases, employee wrongdoing will involve both misconduct and capability, so the assessors should check that the manager has separated them out for different treatment. In larger organizations it is good practice, in order to ensure fairness, for different managers to investigate the two areas separately. Generally, the problem should fit into one or other category.

Investigation

Investigations still catch out many employers, which can lead to protracted disputes and employment tribunal claims. The weak links are the managers tasked with carrying out the investigations, as it is their evidence that will form the basis of the disciplinary hearing. What should happen is that the investigation is proportionate to the seriousness of the allegations and the implications for the employee. So with allegations of gross misconduct, a more detailed investigation is required as the outcome could be dismissal. Equally, a briefer investigation is justified for a first-time 'offence' over timekeeping, which is likely to result in a warning. The assessment should also examine: 1) if any witness-evidence favourable to the employee is routinely considered; and 2) where the evidence conflicts, or reveals no case to answer, that proceedings will be dropped.

Employers also come unstuck with a lack of transparency and keeping the employee updated over new developments to the investigation. For example, any delays to its progression should always be relayed to the employee with an explanation of the reasons behind them. The employee will need to have an interview, so the risk assessment should check that they are given enough notice of any meeting as well as its purpose. Also, where there is no legal right to have a companion present at an investigation meeting, such as in England and Wales, this should be explained to the employee. At this point, it would be useful to review paperwork from previous investigations in order to assess its quality and how objective and fair-minded the investigator was. When interviewing the employee, remember that it is an investigatory meeting, it is not a disciplinary hearing. Unfortunately, some managers get carried away and forget this.

Fair procedure

Once the investigation is complete, it will be known whether or not there is a case against the employee. If not, then proceedings should be halted, but if there is, the organization's disciplinary procedure must be followed. For employers in GB, this should be based on the Acas Code of Practice (2011). Whilst there is no legal requirement to follow this code, employment tribunals will take it into account when assessing individual cases. Other jurisdictions will likely follow a broadly similar process. So any assessment should continue to focus on what those responsible for the disciplinary and dismissal process do in practice. This means reviewing the process leading up to any dismissals that have previously taken place, especially those that end up in the tribunal system. In particular, the assessment should look for evidence of the following:

- **Disciplinary procedures:** the organization's disciplinary and dismissal procedure should be checked to ensure that it is both readable and clear for managers and staff to follow. It should also be regularly reviewed to ensure that it complies with the relevant standards or codes of practice; relevant case law findings should also be incorporated.
- **Training:** all those involved in carrying out investigations and/or disciplinary hearings should have received training on how to carry

them out in a manner that minimizes the threat of a subsequent claim. Depending on the findings from this part of the risk assessment, it may be necessary for one recommendation to be for some in-house training, preferably from a law firm with a good team specifically focusing on employment law.

- **Timely:** as well as carrying out a prompt investigation, no undue delay should arise in holding meetings, reaching decisions or notifying the employee of the outcome. Records from a sample of previous hearings should be checked to see that this is the case. Where there have been delays, the reason should be noted.

- **Suspension:** any period of suspension should be paid as it is not meant to be a punishment in itself. There should also be evidence that alternatives to suspension were considered, such as a temporary transfer to another nearby site. Where the decision to suspend was made, there should be reasons given in the documentation as to why. Suspension should last no longer than is absolutely necessary.

- **Companion:** where there is a statutory right to be accompanied to a disciplinary hearing, the employee should be informed of this in writing. Also, since the Employment Appeal Tribunal ruling in *Toal and another v GB Oils Ltd* [2013] EAT/0569/13, employers in England and Wales must recognize that an employee's choice of companion no longer has to be reasonable. This is providing that their choice fits in with one of the accepted categories of companion – such as a trade union representative certified for the purpose – and there is no conflict of interest in their choice.

- **Employee no-show:** the risk assessment should check that where an employee does not turn up to a disciplinary hearing: 1) enquiries are made as to why; 2) a second hearing is scheduled; and 3) the employee is given at least three days' notice (more if the reason for non-attendance is for a medical problem). As employees do abuse the system by not turning up, the risk assessment should check to see how many times a hearing will be rescheduled before it goes ahead in the employee's absence. Look at proceeding on the third occasion where there is no good reason for the no-show, but write to the employee advising them of this.

- **Hearing format:** the hearing should follow a logical format that is explained to the employee and their companion (if one is chosen) at the start. The manager conducting it should set out the nature of the complaint and review the evidence. Afterwards, it is the employee's turn to present their case and respond to the allegations. They should also be given a reasonable opportunity to ask questions and call their own witnesses.

- **Witnesses:** anonymous witness evidence should only be allowed in exceptional circumstances. This is where there are reasonable grounds to fear retribution from the employee facing dismissal, such as violence. In such cases, this evidence should be subject to extra scrutiny and be verified by a third party wherever possible. Doing otherwise leaves the employer vulnerable to challenge, especially if the decision to dismiss was largely based on anonymous evidence. The assessment should check policy content on dealing with anonymous witnesses and clarify when they are allowed.

- **Consistency:** when deciding on a course of action, the employer should look at how similar cases have been dealt with previously. Many employees often succeed in an unfair dismissal claim because they can show that they have been dealt with unduly harshly. So it would be useful for the risk assessment to review any previous dismissals in order to check for consistency with similar cases.

- **Decision to dismiss:** this should only be made by a manager with the express authority to dismiss. Whilst appropriate for gross misconduct offences, such as theft and violence, consideration should also be given to other options such as demotion. The letter to the employee should set out the reasons for dismissal and remind them of their right to appeal.

- **Appeal:** employees must be given the right to appeal a decision, which should be duly considered. Employees should state the grounds of their appeal in writing. Ideally, the appeal should be heard by a manager who has had no prior involvement in the case. Again, the risk assessment should check this point.

- **Audit trail:** weaknesses are often introduced into the disciplinary and dismissal process due to poor record keeping and the lack of a good audit trail of paperwork. If this is found to be a problem, consider purchasing computer software specifically designed for case management purposes. Its costs could be outweighed by the savings in management time alone. One that is highly configurable depending on the type of organization and its needs is by Workforce Metrics (**http://www.workforcemetrics.co.uk**). In the United States, a similar product has been created by Column Resources (**http://columncasehr.com**).

On July 29, 2013, a new charging system was introduced for employment tribunals and the Employment Appeal Tribunal in England, Wales and Scotland, resulting in claimants having to pay to bring claims. For example, at the time of writing, it will cost £250 to lodge a claim for dismissal and another £950 if it is accepted for a full hearing. Unsurprisingly, the quarterly tribunal statistics produced for October to December 2013 (published March 2014) show that 79 per cent fewer claims were brought in this period when compared to the same quarter in 2012. In addition, a new early conciliation service is being launched by Acas on April 6, 2014. This requires claimants to contact Acas before they can bring an employment tribunal claim against an employer, the idea being that Acas intervention will help resolve the dispute and avoid the claim going to tribunal. Should the process fail or one of the parties refuses to cooperate, the claim can still proceed, but only after Acas provides a certificate to the claimant. Taking these two developments together, many commentators expect this decline in the number of tribunal claims to be maintained.

From an employer's perspective, this looks to be good news. However, there is a danger of becoming too complacent. Problems could arise if the employer takes the view that it does not have to take early conciliation seriously, for example because the employee will be unable to afford to take them to a tribunal if it fails. Another danger lies in the potential damage to employee engagement that could result. For example, any employer that is dismissive of employee grievances and complaints could find that staff may retaliate in other ways against them. This could take the form of loss of productivity, industrial espionage or other activities calculated to damage the employer in some way. Also, trade unions will often pay tribunal charges for cases they take on behalf of their members, so this could result in a growth in union membership. Equally, employers should not overlook the existence of the Fee Waiver Scheme which allows claimants who cannot afford tribunal fees to apply for an exemption. Finally, there is also the possibility that the fee charging regime could change or be scrapped entirely, especially if there is a change of government in the UK in 2015.

Key point

Any attempts at corner-cutting and unfair treatment in disciplinary cases may have a negative impact on employee engagement if it became widely known amongst the workforce.

Is the reason fair?

If the decision is taken to dismiss and that decision is upheld following any appeal by the employee, it follows that it must be for a fair reason and reasonable in all the circumstances. What counts as fair will vary from country to country, but in the UK it must fall into one of the following categories:

- **Capability:** continued inability to carry out the requirements of the post, despite attempts at performance management. Dismissal can arise where there is no other suitable job for the employee to do. The assessment will need to ensure that any employee put through capability proceedings is given any support promised and is given a fair chance to improve.
- **Conduct:** dismissal most likely arises with gross misconduct offences, such as violence at work or theft. It may also occur when an employee has breached the terms of a final written warning. However, the workforce must know what behaviour counts as gross misconduct – and its penalties. So the assessors must check that this is actually the case. If not, a list of examples should be given along with a statement that they are not exhaustive. That way, if there is something not on the list but deemed equally serious, dismissal is still possible.
- **Statutory restriction:** this is less common but usually occurs when continuing to employ someone will break the law. One example is someone employed to drive, such as a delivery driver, but who has lost their licence and there is no other suitable work available for them.
- **Some other substantial reason:** this is a catch-all category, but is most often used when the working relationship has irretrievably broken down. However, for an employer to succeed in this, the relationship must be genuinely beyond repair.
- **Redundancy:** (see separate section below).

Where employers often get caught out is with automatically unfair dismissal. This arises when employees do not need the usual qualifying period of service before they can claim for unfair dismissal. For UK employers, this is either one year's continuous service, or two years where employment started on or after 6 April 2012. In the UK, most employees are protected from their first day of employment. Any attempt to persuade an employee to waive their right to this statutory protection will be void and struck out by a tribunal.

So, it is important that the risk assessment can confirm that managers are conversant with the areas covered by automatically unfair dismissal and are updated on any changes.

> **Key point**
>
> For UK employers, a free, succinct and regularly updated summary on unfair dismissal can be found at: http://www.xperthr.co.uk/quick-reference/automatically-unfair-reasons-for-dismissal/104812/.

Constructive dismissal

Constructive dismissal arises when an employee resigns following an alleged breach of their employment contract by their employer. It may involve one single breach of a serious nature, or a sequence of less serious events leading to one that was 'the final straw'. Unfortunately, many employers still overlook the fact that the final straw can be quite minor. What matters is whether or not the employer's actions amounted to a fundamental breach of the employment contract. Where this happens, the following four events must occur: 1) the employer breaches the employee's employment contract; 2) the employee resigns by considering themselves constructively dismissed as a result; 3) the resignation is in response to the breach; and 4) is timely in that the employee resigns within a reasonable time frame from the last event. In the UK, constructive dismissal usually arises in the following circumstances when the employer:

- unreasonably increases an employee's workload;
- changes the location of their workplace at short notice;
- breaches the implied duty of trust and confidence, eg by allowing an employee to be bullied, harassed or discriminated against;
- reduces their wages/salary without agreement;
- makes them work in dangerous conditions;
- demotes them unlawfully.

The key point is that constructive dismissal is a situation that the employer will usually have prior warning of. Managers turning a blind eye will not be a defence. Therefore, any risk assessment should review any previous constructive dismissal cases that have been brought against the organization in recent years. Apart from the outcome, the assessment should review the reasons behind any claims, which managers were involved and how the situation was dealt with. The purpose of this exercise is to identify trends. One trend could be that line managers are the weak link due to a lack of training in the type of behaviour and actions that can lead to constructive dismissal. Another is that the culture in a given department or site may be one of bullying, with staff leaving as a result. Depending on the findings, recommendations could be as follows:

- Ensure that all managers know what constructive dismissal is, along with the dangers of ignoring employee complaints or formal grievances.
- From a tactical standpoint, ensure that managers understand the value in responding to grievances quickly. If they do so, and the employee rejects any reasonable attempt to resolve the issue, the organization can use that refusal to its advantage. This would work by arguing that it would have tried to rectify the alleged breach of contract, but this opportunity was denied them. Therefore, there is no reasonable basis upon which the employee could resign.
- Build a culture where employees are encouraged to raise matters informally and managers understand the need to act promptly.
- Train line managers in conflict management. This should do much to reduce the likelihood of a constructive dismissal situation taking place.
- Always check the terms of employment contracts before altering them. Anything other than a trivial change can only be made with employee consent. For example, a cosmetic change to a bonus scheme such as a name change is trivial. However, an attempt to unilaterally alter the terms of a contractual bonus scheme is an entirely different matter.
- Ask any in-house employment law specialist (or external firm) to review employment contracts. The purpose is to see whether additional flexibility can be built in, at least for new hires (existing employees will need to be consulted prior to any changes being made to their contract). For example, to look at adding a new clause that retains the right to transfer an employee between different sites, provided that they are within a specified distance of each other.

Forced retirement

Since the default retirement age was abolished in the UK, it is hard for employers to successfully justify having a fixed retirement age. Those that try are likely to be sued due to misunderstandings over how the limited exceptions work in practice. For example, attempting to justify set retirement ages purely on the basis of an organization's own situation will not succeed in direct discrimination cases. This applies even if they are based on solid business grounds. Instead, justification must be argued on one or both of the accepted social policy objectives set out by the European Court of Justice (ECJ). The first is the aim of intergenerational fairness, which concerns the need to provide recruitment and promotion opportunities for younger workers. The second is to preserve personal 'dignity' by avoiding the embarrassment of having to performance-manage older workers. Unfortunately, employers can face difficulties with both aims if they cannot show that they have experienced problems: forcibly retiring someone on the basis of what *could* happen is insufficient.

These points were considered by the Supreme Court in *Seldon (Appellant) v Clarkson Wright and Jakes (A Partnership) (Respondent)* [2012] UKSC 16 on appeal from: [2010] EWCA Civ 899. This long-running case involved the partner of a law firm who was forced to retire at the age of 65. Whilst admitting to direct age discrimination, Seldon's employer had three reasons for insisting on this fixed age, arguing that all three were a proportionate means of achieving various legitimate aims: 1) abiding by the principle of intergenerational fairness – in this case by ensuring that younger solicitors were given partnership opportunities after a reasonable period; 2) maintaining the dignity of older workers by reducing the likelihood of having to performance-manage them if they could no longer do their job properly; and 3) allowing for future workforce planning. The employment tribunal had accepted all three were valid and rejected Seldon's claim. He appealed and his case proceeded through the legal system until it reached the Supreme Court.

The Supreme Court agreed with the lower courts that the employer had identified legitimate aims that were capable of justifying compulsory retirement for partners. It then clarified the current legal position, which has changed since this case first entered the tribunal system, and sent the case back to the original employment tribunal. The question for it to consider (based on the points outlined by the Supreme Court) is whether or not a fixed age of 65 was a proportionate means of achieving the law firm's stated aims. The employment tribunal ruled that in these circumstances, a mandatory retirement age of 65 was proportionate. However, its decision was based on the legal position in 2007, which was prior to the abolition of the default retirement age. A case brought now could easily have a different outcome. For this reason, UK employers must think carefully before implementing a fixed retirement age. It should also be noted that in the intervening years, the employer's third argument of allowing for workforce planning was disallowed. This was because it did not fall within a social-policy ground laid down by the ECJ.

> **Note**
>
> Whilst relating to the UK, the principles outlined in this ruling could easily apply to any other legal jurisdiction that decides to dispense with fixed retirement ages.

Wrongful dismissal

In the UK and countries such as Canada, wrongful dismissal arises where the employer breaches one or more contractual terms. The most common mistake employers make lies in not giving the correct notice when dismissing an employee. Often, the motivation for this is financial, for example timing a dismissal to prevent an employee from gaining entitlement to a contractual bonus payment, or from accruing another year's service towards an enhanced company redundancy scheme. Another pitfall is thinking that money can be saved by not providing the correct pay in lieu of notice (PILON). Under these circumstances, the employee will likely claim for the outstanding amount plus any other contractual benefits owing, such as accrued holiday pay. Also, there are costs to include such as management time in defending a claim. There is usually no minimum period of employment required before an employee can bring a claim. However, in the UK, the right to a minimum notice period is not triggered until the employee has completed one month's continuous employment.

One area that the risk assessment could usefully review is employee notice periods. Whilst longer periods, such as three months or more, may be necessary for senior or specialist staff, they are unlikely to be for many others. Equally, the organization may be operating on notice periods of six months, when three would do. If so, one recommendation can be to reduce the period of contractual notice that needs to be given. In turn, this would reduce any PILON that would need to be made. From the employee's perspective, shorter notice periods are likely to be more attractive as it enables them to move on to a new job quicker. Although more of a problem for smaller organizations, it is worth checking that those with the authority to dismiss staff are aware of the importance of complying with notice periods and other contractual obligations. If not, any knowledge gaps can be plugged by management briefing on this topic.

End of fixed-term contract

A fixed-term contract (FTC) either: 1) runs for a defined period of time, such as one year; 2) lasts for the duration of a specific project; or 3) specifies a precise end date at the outset. Recruiting staff on this basis offers employers the advantage of buying in extra expertise without having to add to headcount permanently. However, it is not unusual to find that those in charge of hiring and managing the contract are still introducing unnecessarily high risks into the organization due to some basic misunderstandings about how FTCs operate. These almost always relate to how the end of a FTC should be treated. The first point to note is that for UK employers, the Fixed Term Employees (Prevention of Less Favourable Treatment) Regulations 2002 provides that if an individual's total period of employment with one employer exceeds four years, the FTC will automatically become a permanent contract. Whilst the employer can try to objectively justify why it should remain on a fixed-term basis, this argument will rarely succeed.

However, a bigger problem is the misconception still held by some employers that an employee engaged on a FTC does not accrue unfair dismissal rights. This is incorrect, as those who work on one or more contracts continuously can gain the necessary continuity of service to qualify. For those engaged on or after 6 April 2012, two years' continuous service will be required instead of one year. Also, the end of a FTC is a dismissal for legal purposes, even one specified to end on a specific date. This means that where the employee has gained the relevant one or two years' qualifying service, an employer must be able to show that: 1) a fair dismissal procedure has been followed; 2) dismissal was reasonable in all the circumstances; and 3) consideration has been given as to whether or not the employee can be redeployed in the same or a different department.

If an organization wishes to avoid an employee accruing unfair dismissal rights, the conventional advice has been to limit the FTC to six months, which should then be followed by a break of two weeks between each contract. The idea behind this has been to break the continuity. However, this is not a risk-free strategy as these gaps may not be enough to break it if they are for a short duration in comparison to the overall length of employment. For example, five or six contracts lasting six months with a fortnight's break each time may look like an obvious means of avoiding a fixed-term employee from gaining protection against unfair dismissal.

Nonetheless, this is the only way that continuity can be avoided. Another issue is the need to protect the organization by including an early termination clause. This enables the contract to be brought to an end sooner than originally intended, but in a way that avoids a breach of contract claim. If this type of clause is not included, it is likely that the employee would claim for damages. These would equate to what they would have received under the full contract. Apart from pay, this would also include benefits.

Redundancy

Introduction

Redundancy arises when an employee's dismissal is wholly or mainly due to: 1) the organization closing down; 2) the site where they work is closing; or 3) there is a reduced need for a particular type of work to be carried out. Whilst fewer redundancies are now being made globally than in 2008–09, the threat still remains. For example, according to research by consultancy Aon Hewitt, one-third of UK employers either made or considered making redundancies as recently as 2013. Whilst devastating for those losing their jobs, redundancies are a potential legal minefield for employers. Plus there is the impact of social media to factor in as well. HMV found this out to its cost when its handling of redundancies at its head office in 2013 was broadcast live by staff via the company's Twitter feed. It went viral very quickly. For these reasons, employers in any legal jurisdiction must exercise care in how the process is carried out. However, particular care must be taken with the following areas.

Making excessive redundancies

Redundancies are still a possibility for some organizations, but get the process wrong and an employer will not only find itself in an employment tribunal, but it can do lasting damage to its business reputation. This is not just in the eyes of those being made redundant, but also for those employees who remain and may become less engaged and motivated as a result. A major problem is when senior management panic and adopt a 'slash and burn' strategy. Such a tactic may achieve the main objective of cost savings, but it is often only a short-term benefit. This is what KPMG found when it embarked on a large-scale redundancy programme in 2002–03. According to its UK head of people, it constrained growth when the economic upturn arrived, as the business lacked the highly specialist people to fulfil the increased demand for its services. KPMG's experience was also that it had inadvertently created an 'inward looking focus' at its leadership level. In other words, cutting headcount was at the expense of looking outwards to the marketplace and supporting its clients.

If a redundancy programme has already been undertaken within the last few years, the employee risk management review should include an honest assessment of how well it worked. Equally, if redundancies are envisaged in future, there are weaknesses that can be built into the process (see below). So, it is advisable to be aware of them now rather than be taken to a tribunal later. Another problem with making excessive redundancies is that the HR function is put under greater pressure to manage them. As a result, corners are likely to be cut, especially with regards to staff consultation and in devising legally compliant selection criteria. In turn, this could lead to an increase in employment tribunal claims. This is what happened in the UK in 2009–10 when unfair dismissal claims relating to an unfair redundancy process increased by several thousand.

So the starting point for any employee risk management assessment should be to examine the rationale behind any decision to make redundancies. This would require input from members of the board into what approach would be taken. Where redundancies have previously been made, it would review the approach taken in order to evaluate its effectiveness. These questions will need to cover the following areas:

- **Financial models:** what exercise in financial modelling has or would take place in order to assess the impact that any redundancies would have on the bottom line? This should look at what impact making different types of staff redundant would have on the organization. For example, cutting front-line employees will reduce sales turnover, whereas reducing headcount in the warehouse is likely to increase delivery times to customers.

- **Opportunity cost:** this is connected to the above point and refers to the cost of not being able to do something because another course of action has been pursued instead. As a result, the possible benefits of that first activity have been lost. So questions need to be asked in relation to what analysis would be undertaken into this: for example, the loss of front-line sales staff reducing a company's ability to service a specific market.

- **Impact on support functions:** the desire to cut budgets for health and safety, marketing and training. What impact assessment would be carried out? For example, into the greater risk of safety infringements, or loss of sales due to poorly trained staff.

- **Costs of redundancy:** have the full costs of a redundancy exercise been factored in? In the rush to realize short-term savings, senior management may overlook the true costs involved. Apart from calculating what a statutory or a contractual redundancy package would amount to, this should include other elements such as PILON, National Insurance contributions and accrued holiday entitlement. However, it also needs to include other costs that may be overlooked, such as outplacement services and the money involved in retraining employees who can be redeployed elsewhere.

- **Alternative options:** what alternatives to redundancy were considered and why were they rejected? This could include restructuring and retraining staff to service emerging markets. It could also include offering sabbaticals and the option for staff to go part-time, at least on a temporary basis.

Weak selection criteria

Another area of vulnerability for employers is creating redundancy selection criteria that are not sufficiently objective or non-discriminatory. This can result in tribunal claims for unfair dismissal as well as those based on discrimination law. These threats tend to arise through indirect discrimination, such as using sickness absence as a criterion. For example, if it includes absences that are pregnancy-related or disability-related, a claim under the Equality Act 2010 for sex-based or disability-based discrimination will likely arise for UK employers. Also, selection criteria must be objective, so any assessment must confirm that a range of criteria (or selection matrix) is used. Acceptable criteria include timekeeping, attendance and disciplinary records, performance reviews, ability to take on extra duties, as well as possessing relevant skills and knowledge. The more comprehensive and varied the criteria used, the fairer any system will be.

Following the Court of Appeal ruling in *Rolls-Royce plc v Unite* [2009], 'LIFO' (last in, first out) can still be used by UK employers, providing it is one of several criteria. Using it on its own or giving it a disproportionate weighting is potentially age discriminatory. So, those carrying out the risk assessment should delve into how 'LIFO', would be used if redundancies ever become necessary. They should also see how it is described in any HR policy. A good description is one making it clear that its use has a legitimate aim, which is to reward loyalty and long service whilst reinforcing the appeal of a stable workforce. The assessors should also consider if the redundancy criteria is used to its best advantage, ie if the scoring matrix is optimized to use poor performance as a means of getting rid of certain employees. If not, they can recommend that a weighting factor is added that will highlight poor performance. In practice, this means that if a system is used where those with the highest overall score will be made redundant, a disproportionately high weighting to poor performance should be given.

Providing that the process is conducted fairly, it is reasonable to focus on poor or barely acceptable performers, assuming that steps have been taken to rectify the situation. If they have not, the employee is likely to claim for unfair dismissal. This is another reason why effective performance management at an early stage is so important (see Chapter 10). Also, where formal capability proceedings have proved necessary, a good audit trail must be kept. This information can then be used to support any redundancy decision taken that involves an emphasis on poor performance. However, a good mix of employees must be included in the redundancy pool. If this is not done and only 'undesirables' are targeted, there could be legal challenges, as those affected may work out what is happening, such as where pregnant women or those on maternity leave are disproportionately affected (see below).

> **Key point**
>
> Where possible, avoid giving redundancy criteria contractual status; this way it can be amended as necessary.

Pregnancy/maternity discrimination

Another weak point concerns pregnancy/maternity discrimination. Some employers still see redundancy as an easy way of managing this group of employees out of the organization. They then come unstuck because they do not realize how transparent their real motives are. The legal position in many jurisdictions is straightforward in that any redundancy that arises because an employee is either pregnant or on maternity leave, will count as an automatically unfair dismissal. There will also be the risk of a sex discrimination claim. Whilst redundancy is possible in this type of situation, great care must be taken in how it is managed. So any risk assessment should focus on how pregnant employees and those on maternity leave have been treated in the past and how they would be dealt with in future. Those carrying out the assessment should be looking for a process that incorporates the following stages:

- **Stage 1 – creating redundancy criteria:** the first task is to create redundancy criteria that can stand up to scrutiny as being both objective and non-discriminatory. As mentioned above, the fairest method is to use a matrix based on several different factors.

- **Stage 2 – exclude pregnancy-related factors:** the redundancy criteria must not penalize a woman for reasons connected with either pregnancy or maternity leave. So time off for antenatal appointments or pregnancy-related sickness absence must be excluded from any figures used. If not, the redundancy criteria will fall at the first hurdle.

- **Stage 3 – selecting the 'pool':** choose which employees will form the 'pool'. Again, some employers encounter problems as they define the pool too narrowly. Apart from including those working in the area where redundancies are anticipated, include similar job groupings from any other sites in close proximity, as well as any shift workers. Do not target women simply because they are pregnant or are young enough to start a family.

- **Stage 4 – suitable alternative roles:** as with any employee at risk, an employer must consider if there is a suitable alternative role. However, for UK employers, it is the law that where a suitable vacancy exists, an employee on maternity leave must be given first refusal. This applies even where there are better candidates for the role. If this does not happen, any dismissal through redundancy will be automatically unfair.

What counts as a 'suitable alternative role' depends on several factors. Apart from similar pay and working hours, the proposed position should be of a similar status to the current role. Whether or not it is suitable also depends on its location. If the working location is different, any additional travelling time and cost will influence its viability as a 'suitable alternative role', as will the employee's own particular circumstances. Should the employee reject the offer and bring an unfair dismissal claim, the test of suitability will be for a tribunal to decide. However, it is the employer's responsibility to show that an offer of alternative work has been made. This must be done before the existing employment contract ends and should be documented in writing.

If an employee who is pregnant or on maternity leave is made redundant, employers must show that there is no suitable alternative role for her. Generally, the larger the organization, the harder this will be, due to the greater number of options available. As a result, any risk assessment should look at the process that has or would be undertaken in order to reach this conclusion. This will require the assessor looking for evidence that a review has been carried out into the employee's skills, experience and relevant qualifications. Against this, any decision to support redundancy should be documented, eg based on poor appraisals or a record of being unsuccessful in applying for promotions/lateral moves. Where the job role needs to change due to restructuring, this should also be recorded. So in order to complete this part of the exercise, assessors need to look for an audit trail.

Consultation

Consultation is another area where employers can come unstuck. The first problem concerns compliance with statutory time periods. In the UK, the position is that where 20 or more employees face redundancy, collective consultation must take place. This must be with either recognized trade unions or elected employee representatives. Since 6 April 2013, the minimum period for collective redundancy consultation – ie where an employer proposes to make 100 or more employees redundant – was reduced from 90 days to 45 days. The minimum period of 30 days currently remains unchanged where it is proposed to make 20–99 redundancies. But what some employers fail to realize is that collective consultation is a two-way process. So it should be a genuine opportunity for elected representatives to put their ideas across on how to prevent or reduce the number of proposed redundancies. Employers must also consult with individual employees and give reasonable warning that redundancies are on the agenda.

Redundancy consultation should take place in good time and before the need to make redundancies is a certainty (which is the point of consultation). UK employers must not overlook the fact that the maximum compensation for failing to properly collectively consult is up to 90 days' gross pay per employee. This refers to actual pay, so it can add up for organizations looking to make large numbers of staff redundant. There is also the damage to the employer's reputation to factor in as well. Another problem for employers lies in ignoring consultation rules altogether and dismissing staff via text message. The claims firm, Accident Group, did this in 2003 when it sacked over 2,000 staff. If the company had not collapsed and gone into administration, its exposure to compensation claims would have been huge.

UK employers must be aware that collective consultation requirements are now triggered if they propose to make 20 or more employees redundant across the entire organization within a period of 90 days or less. It is no longer 20 employees per site. Another problem for employers in both the UK and the European Union has been in pinpointing exactly when collective consultation should start. The Court of Appeal attempted to finally resolve this question by referring a case to the ECJ (*United States of America v Nolan* [2012] IRLR 1020 ECJ). However, the ECJ refused to hear the case as it concerned the United States, which is not covered by the relevant Directive (this case concerned a US military base in the UK). Until this is clarified, the safest option is to begin consultation as soon as it is believed that redundancies are likely. Where collective consultation is necessary, it must be completed before notice of dismissal is served on any employee. If there are no recognized trade unions or employee representatives, it is the employer's responsibility to organize the election of representatives by employees for the purpose of consultation.

> **Key point**
>
> With fixed-term contracts, the obligation for UK employers to consult collectively will arise if the contracts are to be terminated early due to redundancy.

Once any required representatives have been elected, the employer is required to provide them with the following information:

- the reason why redundancies are necessary;
- the number of the proposed redundancies;
- the job types involved;
- the total number of employees affected;
- the selection methods;

- what procedures will be followed;
- how redundancy payments will be calculated.

> **Key point**
>
> Individual employer consultation is required where less than 20 redundancies are likely.

Other concerns

References

Giving references can present problems for many employers. The main one is where the subject of the reference objects to what has been written about them and sues the employer. For example, bringing a civil court claim for damages where a job offer has been withdrawn as a result of negative comments made in a reference. As a result, the standard advice has always been to be true, accurate and fair. So if a prospective employer asks whether or not any disciplinary proceedings have been brought against the employee within the last two years, it is safe to confirm that they have, providing this is actually so. What would be unfair is to state that no proceedings had been brought within that time frame, but that they had 10 years ago. In such circumstances, unhappy employees have still litigated against employers but have used allegations of discriminatory treatment. However, in the UK, whether or not an employee can bring a claim for such post-employment victimization has yet to be clarified. This is due to what appears to be a drafting problem under the Equality Act 2010 with the result that there have been contradictory Employment Appeal Tribunal findings on this point.

Due to these dangers, any risk assessment should review the organization's policy on providing references in order to seek out potential weak points. In particular, it should look at:

- the type of information that is provided in response to reference requests;
- whether or not only designated staff are allowed to provide references;

- if staff have been briefed on the type of information that can be given;
- whether or not a policy exists on the giving of telephone references;
- where more detailed references are provided, that they are given consistently and not unreasonably withheld.

One possible recommendation is that only standard or basic references are provided. This is where information is pared down to the minimum to confirm: 1) employment dates; 2) salary; and 3) the position(s) that have been held. In other words, the reference avoids subjective topics such as performance and relationships with colleagues. The reason is that these topics can lead to employment tribunal claims. If this recommendation is made, it should be accompanied by a second one to the effect that a written statement should be included with the reference. This should state that providing a standard reference is now company policy and that no negative inference should be drawn from the fact. Do not rely on using disclaimers as a 'get-out' clause against providing inaccurate references. They will not protect against negligent misstatements.

Restrictive covenants

A restrictive covenant refers to a specific type of clause found in employment-related contracts. Its purpose is to prohibit a contracting party, such as an employee or director, from engaging in: 1) similar employment; 2) for a specified period of time; and 3) within a defined geographical area. They are included in this book due to the problems that so often arise in their drafting. The problem (certainly in the UK) is that if they are drafted too widely, a court will strike them out in their entirety, not just the wording that it dislikes. This is in an attempt to balance the employer's right to protect their business with the right of the employee to be able to earn a living. However, in doing so, this can deprive the employer of sufficient legal protection if senior employees set up in direct competition following their departure from the organization.

On this, the case of *Romero Insurance Brokers Ltd v Templeton & Anor* [2013] EWHC 1198 (QB) has provided some much-needed guidance to employers. Whilst it is a UK case, its principles can also offer guidance to organizations in other jurisdictions experiencing similar problems. In this case, Templeton (T) was employed as an insurance broker. After his departure from the business to a new employer, he tried to contact his old clients. Unsurprisingly, his former employer sought an interim injunction against him in order to enforce a restrictive covenant. This covenant imposed a 12-month restriction on T in terms of entering into business with any of its clients that had been a client in the last six months and with whom T had dealt with. The only question for the high court was whether or not the 12-month period was more than was reasonably necessary to protect Romero's relationship with its clients. In deciding this, the onus is on the employer to prove that it was reasonable.

In this case it was, but only due to how the insurance industry works. Most insurance contracts are subject to annual renewal and the renewal date is the most likely time that customers will switch providers. Therefore, a 12-month restriction on the contracts of insurance-broking employees is a common practice. As a consequence, Romero was entitled to damages for T's breaches of the restrictive covenant from his date of departure to the date of the high court ruling. The court used this opportunity to helpfully distil some key issues for employers to be mindful of when creating restrictive covenants:

- Whether or not a term in the covenant is too restrictive depends on the individual facts and the context of the claim.
- Employers must be able to identify exactly what interests need protecting and why. These interests must then be clearly defined.
- Timescales must be no longer than necessary. The longer the restriction, the better the explanation must be to justify it and the harder this will be.
- One determinant of this is to look at what is the accepted industry practice.
- One-size-fits-all clauses must be avoided. They may be convenient in the short term, but they will not fit the individual circumstances and are likely to be struck out if challenged.

Key point

Tactically, it is better to be cautious and draft a restrictive covenant for a shorter period of time. This way, it has a better chance of surviving a legal challenge.

Another point still overlooked by some employers is that it is possible that there are circumstances surrounding a dismissal that could render any restrictive covenants void. This arises where the employer dismisses the employee unfairly or wrongly without notice and without any PILON that they are entitled to. If so, the employer will be deemed to have repudiated the contract. As a result, the employee will be freed from any obligation to honour their contractual obligations, which will include any restrictive covenants. So yet again, this reinforces the importance of ensuring that any dismissal is carried out legally. After all, the loss of key clients could prove far more costly to an organization than the time and expense involved in following a fair dismissal procedure and PILON. Any risk assessment covering this area needs to review any existing restrictive covenants that are used and check their provisions against the above bullet points.

Vengeful former staff

Given the increase in redundancies and a greater unwillingness in the last few years to 'carry' poor performers, there is an increased likelihood that organizations will encounter a former employee with a serious grudge. This is what happened to a UK financial services firm in late 2011 when an ex-employee managed to get past security and access his old offices. He then set off fire extinguishers, activated sprinklers and threw various items through a tenth-floor window, including computers, a fire extinguisher, chairs and a desk. Considerable damage was said to have been caused, as well as unwanted publicity for the organization concerned. However, it does raise the question of whether employers are leaving themselves vulnerable to vengeful former employees and, if so, how? As such, this is a legitimate area for a risk assessment to review. In particular, the following should be checked:

- Are departing employees and those on temporary passes (such as self-employed contractors) required to hand back any security passes and keys that may be in their possession?
- Do the same rules apply for the return of equipment owned by the employer, such as laptop computers and smartphones?
- Is computer-network access suspended as soon as someone leaves? This is in order to prevent a former employee being able to access confidential information or damage their former employer's reputation via unauthorized use of their old work e-mail account.

Depending on the findings from the assessment, one recommendation could be the introduction of an inventory. This will help track what has been issued to a worker during their employment.

Chapter summary

Following a fair dismissal process:

- decide whether the issue is conduct-based or capability;
- if capability, identify the source of the problem, eg ill health or inexperience;
- where both conduct and capability are involved, separate them out for different treatment;
- always be transparent and keep the employee informed over new developments;
- if there is a case to answer, follow a fair procedure – this should be based on any Code of Practice or other relevant jurisdictional requirement;
- the process should be timely from the investigation through to notification of outcome;
- any suspension should be paid, as it is not punishment in itself;
- suspension should be for as brief a period as possible;
- consider other alternatives to suspension, eg a temporary transfer to another site;
- advise the employee in writing of any right to be accompanied to a disciplinary hearing;
- in England and Wales the choice of accepted companion no longer has to be reasonable;
- if the employee is a no-show at the hearing, reschedule it at least once;
- give at least three days' notice before the rescheduled hearing;
- at the hearing, give the employee reasonable opportunity to present their case;
- anonymous witness evidence should only be allowed exceptionally;
- subject any anonymous witness evidence to extra scrutiny;
- be consistent with any disciplinary sanctions levied;

- decisions to dismiss should only be made by a manager with the express authority;
- other options such as demotion should also be considered;
- the employee must be informed in writing about the reasons for dismissal and right of appeal.

For UK employers, a fair dismissal must be for one of the following reasons:

- conduct;
- capability;
- statutory restriction;
- some other substantial reason;
- redundancy.

Constructive dismissal pitfalls:

- a claim can result from a minor incident that is the 'last straw' for the employee;
- employers forget that it can arise from a breach of the implied duty of trust and confidence;
- managers overlooking the warning signs that there is a problem;
- managers are often a weak link due to a lack of awareness of the legal position.

Forced retirement in the UK:

- it is extremely difficult for employers to justify a fixed retirement age;
- arguing the case on business grounds will be unsuccessful;
- instead, the case must be argued on one or both social policy grounds;
- if these arguments are to be used, problems must already have arisen.

Wrongful dismissal:

- arises where the employer breaches one or more contractual terms;
- the most common mistake is not giving the employee the correct period of notice – the motive for this is often to prevent employees gaining the right to a payout, eg bonus;
- the employee is entitled to receive contractual benefits during his or her notice period.

Redundancy dangers:

- making excessive redundancies constrains growth when the economy improves;
- 'slash and burn' strategies encourage an inward focus rather than outwards;
- excessive redundancies may lead to corners being cut, eg over employee consultation;
- underestimating the full costs of making redundancies;
- failing to adequately consider other options;
- weak selection criteria that is not objective or non-discriminatory;
- weak selection criteria can result in tribunal claims for unfair dismissal and discrimination;
- giving extra weighting to poor performance without having first tried to rectify the problem;
- failing to include a good mix of employees in the redundancy pool;
- using redundancy to dismiss pregnant employees or those on maternity leave – leaving the organization vulnerable to an automatically unfair dismissal as a result;
- failing to offer a woman on maternity leave a 'suitable alternative role'.

Consultation traps for employers:

- failing to comply with the statutory time periods;
- not carrying out collective consultation where 20 or more face redundancy (UK employers);
- not appreciating that consultation is a two-way process;
- failing to consult individually with employees;
- UK employers are liable to financial penalties for failing to properly collectively consult;
- these penalties are up to 90 days' gross pay per employee;
- serving dismissal notices before collective consultation is completed;
- failing to appoint employee representatives if there are no recognized trade unions;
- failing to provide unions/employee representatives with the necessary information.

Other concerns:

- any references given must be true, accurate and fair;
- employees have sued where poor references have led to job offers being withdrawn;
- restrictive covenants must not be drafted too widely as it will invalidate them;
- unfairly dismiss an employee and they will cease to be bound by any restrictive covenants;
- wrongly dismissing an employee will also free them from any restrictive covenants;
- harm can be caused to an unprotected organization by vengeful former staff, eg property damage.

Recommendations:

- ensure that managers know the difference between conduct and capability;
- in larger organizations it is good practice for different managers to investigate the two areas;
- an investigation should always be proportionate to the allegations facing the employee;
- witness-evidence favourable to the employee's case should always be considered;
- where evidence conflicts or reveals there is no case to answer, that proceedings are dropped;
- give the employee enough notice of any investigative meeting and its purpose;
- never allow an investigative meeting to become a disciplinary hearing;
- ensure disciplinary and dismissal procedure is readable and clear to follow;
- review disciplinary and dismissal procedure regularly and update with new case law;
- those involved in investigations and disciplinary hearings should be trained first;

- always advise the employee of any delays and the reason for them;
- if suspension is deemed necessary, record why this is;
- for no-shows at disciplinary hearings for no good reason, proceed as intended with dismissal on the third occasion;
- clarify the limited circumstances where anonymous witness evidence is permissible;
- appeals should ideally be heard by a different manager to the one directly involved in the dismissal;
- maintain a good audit trail of paperwork documenting reasons behind any decisions;
- consider purchasing a dedicated case management system;
- ensure that a record of automatically unfair reasons to dismiss is regularly updated;
- introduce management briefings on constructive dismissal to include:
  - the need to respond to grievances promptly;
  - always check the terms of contracts before trying to alter them;
  - train managers in conflict management;
  - review contracts to see what extra flexibility can be built into them.
- UK employers should take extreme care before implementing fixed retirement ages;
- review notice periods to see if their length can be justified, if not reduce them;
- where necessary, introduce manager briefings on wrongful dismissal pitfalls;
- include early termination clauses with fixed-term contracts (FTCs);
- use a range of different redundancy criteria that is objective and non-discriminatory;
- add a weighting factor to the redundancy scoring matrix that highlights poor performance;
- avoid giving redundancy criteria contractual status – so that it can be amended easily;
- exclude pregnancy-related factors from any redundancy-scoring criteria;

- to elect employee representatives in good time so that consultation can be carried out;
- limit the writing of references to designated staff;
- consider providing basic references with limited but non-contentious information;
- do not rely on disclaimers as a 'get-out' clause against providing inaccurate references;
- with restrictive covenants:
  - identify exactly what interests need protecting and why;
  - ensure timescales are no longer than absolutely necessary;
  - consider industry practice when drafting them;
  - avoid one-size-fits-all clauses.
- on an employee's last day at work:
  - require them to hand back security passes and keys before they leave;
  - the same applies to handing back laptops and smartphones;
  - suspend computer network and e-mail access as soon as they leave.
- introduce an inventory to track what has been issued to a worker during employment.

Chapter 12 looks at the main problems that could arise when carrying out an employee risk assessment, when they are likely to arise and how they should be dealt with.

Avoiding common problems

12

Introduction

As with any project, things can go wrong and often do so because problems that should have been anticipated have not been. This final chapter looks at what these problems are and when they are most likely to arise. It starts by covering common project management pitfalls and then moves on to the need for effective change management. Without this, any attempt at embedding proactive employee risk management across the organization will fail. It requires culture change at all levels and managing this transition will not occur without leadership from the top. An organization must also know what a good risk culture looks like and how it can be achieved. Without this, the necessary transition cannot occur, as no one will know how to get there. Another mistake is to assume that change will happen simply because senior management wants it to. This chapter troubleshoots these problems by looking at what can be done to prevent or otherwise manage them. In doing this, it also covers the importance of maintaining good communication throughout.

Project management pitfalls

Whilst project management has already been covered (see Chapter 3), there are various pitfalls that even experienced project teams can fall into. If these are not anticipated and avoided, they can have a negative impact on the entire exercise. The main pitfalls are:

- **Insufficient stakeholder support:** it is vital that the project has board-level buy-in from the outset. Without this, it would be difficult (if not impossible) to secure the cooperation of site managers and heads of department for their staff to be involved. Also, it is important that the project manager is savvy enough to actively involve senior management in determining project scope and direction. If this is lacking, it is likely that senior management will only pay lip service to it, due to their own lack of buy-in.

- **Lack of authority:** those forming the project team will need sufficient authority and credibility in order to successfully carry out all aspects of the project. Simply relying on a project manager to have good influencing skills is not enough on its own. In some cases, such as those where the assessment will examine organizational culture and ethics, there is value in having more remote input. Ideally, this will be from an individual at senior level, such as a non-executive director or trustee who can join the team for this part of the project.

- **No accountability:** if there is a lack of individual accountability it can introduce a blame culture into the project. This will be characterized by an unwillingness to admit to mistakes, attempts to cover them up, or to shift the blame on to a colleague. This kind of behaviour can prove toxic to any project as it erodes trust and cooperation. Avoid this by defining individual and team responsibilities from the outset and reinforce these throughout the project.

- **Project team conflict:** conflict within the team can easily occur if the wrong people are involved. The obvious personality types to avoid are those who are poor communicators, as well as non-team players. Others can also disrupt it, such as the individual who sees the exercise as an opportunity to settle old scores. However, some mild disagreement amongst the team can be beneficial. Avoiding a groupthink mentality usually results in the use of lateral thinking and more innovation in how the project is handled.

- **Ignoring project risk:** even though this project concerns the management of employee risk, the fact that risk must also be factored into the project itself must not be overlooked. In other words, risk management principles should be embedded into it from the beginning. If this is done well, the wasting of time on fire-fighting foreseeable problems will be avoided. So brainstorm where the pitfalls are likely to be, such as uncooperative interviewees and insufficient planning, and identify ways of overcoming them.

- **Excessive project scope:** although employee risk management covers a vast area, do avoid the temptation to try to do everything at once. If team members are trying to deal with too many different areas simultaneously, the quality of their work will decline. Instead, break down the project into manageable steps. Whilst there will be an overlap with other areas, creating some boundaries will also allow for a better allocation of resources.

- **Time-wasting meetings:** many projects contain meeting overload. For instance, a two-hour meeting involving four people but convened for no real purpose will effectively waste eight hours. That equates to one working day. So for each meeting planned, ask the following questions: is the meeting being scheduled to make decisions or to plan and discuss progress? If not, what are its objectives? Unless there is an objective that is central to the project, do not hold the meeting.

- **Poor communication:** poor team communication can also cause problems, such as failing to give updates on any problems that arise. Apart from making team members feel isolated, it could reduce work quality. Another problem is poor communication between the project manager and the stakeholders. If good dialogue is not maintained throughout the project's life cycle, there is a risk that support and perception of its relevance could wane.

- **Lack of contingency planning:** even the best-prepared projects can go wrong if unforeseeable events or challenges arise. For this reason, contingencies should be built into the project. The main one to factor in will be in allowing extra time to complete it. Another will be to appoint a reserve for the project team, just in case of illness.

- **Ignoring the opportunities:** understandably, it is easy for attention to be focused on trying to eliminate or reduce any threats and vulnerabilities found. What is less common is to use this process to look for opportunities. For example, there may be new ways to enable a process under review to be carried out more efficiently.

Failing to manage change

After the employee risk assessment is complete, recommendations will be made and a number of these should be approved. Yet successful implementation will require more than procedural modifications. Instead, a widespread change in attitudes and behaviours across all levels of the organization will be necessary. This is because all will revolve around the need to change the organization's risk culture in some way. Here, the danger lies in assuming that the desired changes will happen simply because the board says so. Under these circumstances, change may happen, but it will be disengagement, due to the fact that employees have not been given the opportunity of buying into a new risk culture, nor had the need for it explained to them. Instead, staff will: 1) require training on why such a move has been deemed necessary; 2) need to understand what it involves and what will be expected of them in terms of participation; and 3) need to be equipped with the tools to make this cultural shift.

Mapping out the transition to the desired future state

Unfortunately, carrying out a change management programme can be difficult and can fail if the right questions are not asked at the outset. So, the first step is to understand the current culture and its approach to risk management. Honesty is best, so if the truthful answer is 'we don't bother until something goes wrong', say so. Equally, if the culture is risk averse to the extent that raising concerns is frowned upon, this must be recognized. If not, making the necessary cultural shift to an environment where staff feel that they can come forward with concerns will not be possible. Without this, any change management initiative will be starting from the wrong place and will likely fail. The next question is: what does our target culture look like? Answering this will require input from the board and key stakeholders. Only when these questions have been answered can a strategy be created for making the transition from the present to the desired future state.

Ideally, a move to integrate employee risk management into an organization's culture will be part of a move to embed risk management generally: this exercise provides a fantastic opportunity to facilitate wider change. But even if this is not the case, it will still require commitment from the board, in respect to both time and resources. The process will also require regular reviews in order to track progress. Also, those responsible for seeing this process through should not underestimate the fact that it is a change management project in its own right. Yet, in order to make this transition, several questions need answering first. Some will be more contentious than others. They are as follows:

- Is there clarity over exactly what changes need to be made?
- Is the board aware of its role in leading the changes?

- Is the desired outcome known?
- Are the changes urgent or is there a more relaxed timescale?
- Is there consensus over how the changes will be introduced?
- How well does the workforce tend to deal with change?
- Who are the key stakeholders driving this initiative?
- Is there sufficient trust in the senior team?
- Who will be the sponsor of this project?
- How will staff be informed (eg via team briefings)?
- How will staff be involved in the process?
- Will the informal organizational networks (see Chapter 2) help or hinder the process?

Dealing with resistance to change

Being realistic, it is likely that some employees will resist change. The best way to deal with this is to appreciate the reasons behind it. Only then, can it be countered. The main reasons are: 1) a fear of the unknown; 2) concerns that employees will suffer in some way; 3) previous experience of poorly handled change; 4) a perception of change for the sake of it; or 5) employees feel that they lack the skills to cope with what is coming. It is also important that the proposed changes are introduced in a way that fits with the existing culture. For example, those used to working in a strict 'command and control' environment will struggle to deal with focus groups suddenly wanting their input and opinions. So it is important to state why changes are being introduced and to show how employees will benefit. This is most important where engagement is poor. Also outline the proposed changes and the format they will take, and tailor this to the needs of different audiences.

This is not a one-off exercise, especially where the intention is a widespread cultural shift to a more proactive and risk-aware culture. Instead, continual reinforcement of the changes and the reasons behind them will be necessary. Unlike organizational restructuring, this is far more of a gradual change that can be actioned in the following ways:

- having a named director as sponsor;
- building employee risk into existing operational meetings;
- adding employee risk management to job descriptions, even if just to report concerns;

- extending the use of staff suggestion schemes to include ideas on how to manage risk;
- including articles about employee risk in staff newsletters, explaining how problems have been overcome.

Creating a risk-aware culture

In order for an employee risk management approach to be successful, it must be embedded into an organization's culture. It will not work if it is perceived as an add-on. This is why it is a task that must initially be driven from the top and cascaded downwards to all levels of the workforce. Its purpose is to emphasize that risk management is part of every individual's job role on a daily basis. The board (or equivalent) must be highly visible here, not just at the outset but throughout the roll-out and beyond. In order to maintain a high profile, someone at director level (ideally) will sponsor this process and be seen to lead it as a figurehead. Success will only be achieved where: 1) management and staff proactively look for existing and emerging threats and vulnerabilities; and 2) managers habitually assess the potential risk impact that their decisions could lead to.

In order to be successful, training at all levels will be necessary, but it is especially relevant for management. Many managers have little appreciation of the benefits that a wider risk management approach can offer them at both the strategic and operational levels. One option is for members of the project team to train up others so that they can cascade the training throughout the organization. If so, workshops will need to be tailored to their audience, which will mean progressively less theory on risk management the further down the organizational hierarchy that the training goes. But what is important for all levels is to include exercises based on day-to-day activities in the organization. Ideally, where one or more risk managers are employed by the organization, they could also provide some input. Their value would be optimized by giving practical examples of what can happen when things can go wrong and when they go right (do try to include positives wherever possible). However it works, this segment should include the following points:

- why a formalized process of employee risk management is important to an organization;
- examples of what can go wrong when it is not managed effectively;

- what it can cost an employer – the bringing down of Barings Bank is one example;
- what it can offer managers and staff, eg a time-saving device, as having to deal with issues reactively is more time-consuming;
- the importance of integrating it into any decision-making process in the same way that budgeting and scheduling would be;
- the role each individual plays in being proactive in reporting any concerns;
- what is expected of managers in terms of dealing with concerns reported to them;
- how any threats and vulnerabilities that have been identified will be recorded and what the process is for reviewing and managing them.

> **Key point**
>
> Build risk management into job descriptions throughout the organization for both managers and staff. Where appropriate, add it to forward objectives and discuss at appraisals.

Poor communication

A common theme in avoiding problems lies in having good communication channels in place across the organization. This is essential at the best of times and its importance in managing risk is no exception. After all, identifying potential threats and vulnerabilities is only part of the process. What they are and the strategies for reducing or managing them must also be communicated to the workforce. However, this is not enough on its own. To be effective, communication needs to be two-way rather than being restricted to a one-way stream of information from the decision makers at the top. Managing risks on a day-to-day basis involves the entire workforce. Therefore, it is important that a culture is embedded into an organization whereby risk management is seen as the responsibility of all staff (albeit to different degrees). After all, in many cases, the first people to be aware of a problem are those at the 'coalface'. Yet in some organizations these people have no formal voice.

By introducing a formal communication structure, employers will benefit from leveraging the knowledge and expertise of those who may be able to suggest solutions to problems. This information can then be shared across the organization and reworked where necessary, depending on local site conditions and needs. Establishing good communication channels does not need to be complicated. However, it does need some planning. For a risk management programme, the best way forward is to look at how it can be embedded into an existing communications structure wherever possible. In many cases, this will be better than creating an extra layer of meetings. Apart from the extra bureaucracy involved, the problem is that to many staff, risk may be seen as an add-on rather than something that is fully integrated into the business (this can still be seen with some safety committees). Examples of how this integration can be done include the following:

- **Board meetings:** these will already discuss various threats and vulnerabilities facing the organization, eg as part of existing corporate governance requirements. If necessary, its remit can be extended to include the topic matter covered in this book.
- **Risk management meetings:** if organizations are large enough to justify their own dedicated risk team and/or internal audit function, look at how the findings from other meetings in the organization can feed into these.
- **Team meetings:** in order to gain buy-in across the organization, use team meetings as an opportunity for two-way dialogue. Managers can explain what is being done to manage known or perceived threats, and employees can use these meetings as a forum to offer their ideas and potential solutions. Providing opportunities for staff involvement in this way should have the added benefit of helping to improve employee engagement generally.
- **Training:** where appropriate, risk management can be formally built into in-house training sessions. The time to start this is during induction training for new starters.
- **Staff newsletters/intranet:** reinforce the message by including updates on risk management initiatives. One option is to focus on a specific issue and offer prizes or some other form of recognition to an employee that comes up with a solution to a particular problem.

Once a formal communication structure has been put in place for risk management, its details need to be added to any policy in place on how risk is managed. Similar to a health and safety policy, this will also describe those individuals responsible for risk management and their remit. It will also explain: 1) the organization's overall approach to threats and vulnerabilities; 2) the process for identifying and managing them; and 3) the process for review. This policy should then be brought to the attention of all staff and third parties, as appropriate. As with any other policy, it should also be subject to regular review and updated as necessary.

Final thoughts

Depending on the employer, the key to maximizing the value of an employee risk management approach is to embed it firmly within the organization, rather than treating it as a one-off exercise. That way it can be integrated seamlessly with other risk management initiatives and related processes. However, for this to work, there must a culture shift that is actively managed from the top down. It will also require a change in attitude and behaviours throughout the workforce, not only towards employee risk, but towards how risk is perceived generally. In other words, the tone in the middle and at the bottom also needs managing. This is important as there is a danger that too much emphasis can be placed on the mechanics of the process at the expense of the behavioural changes needed to make it work. Sitting back and hoping for the best is not enough. Get this right and the result will be a flexible process that can evolve and adapt along with organizational needs, both now and into the future.

Chapter summary

Project management pitfalls:

- lack of stakeholder support for the project;
- those forming the project team lack the authority and credibility;
- no individual accountability of group members;
- conflict amongst the project team due to personality type;
- ignoring project risk;
- drafting the project scope too widely;
- time-wasting and unnecessary meetings;
- poor communication within the team;

- poor contingency planning;
- ignoring the opportunities that may present themselves.

Failing to manage change:

- do not assume change will happen automatically;
- employees become disengaged if they are denied the opportunity to 'buy-in';
- can result in:
  - failing to grasp the current culture and its approach to employee risk management;
  - a good chance that any change management initiative starts in the wrong place;
  - not mapping out the transition to the desired future state;
  - not recognizing that this is a change management initiative in its own right;
  - lacking sufficient support from the board;
  - making no effort to deal with employee resistance to change.

Poor communication:

- there can be poor communication channels in general in an organization;
- results in not relaying information to staff on how threats and vulnerabilities will be managed;
- where communication does exist, it sometimes only flows one way from the decision makers;
- in some organizations employees have no formal voice.

Recommendations:

- obtain board-level buy-in from the outset;
- secure the cooperation of heads of department/site managers to the project;
- actively involve senior management in determining project scope;
- appoint a project team with enough authority;
- set out individual and team responsibilities from the outset;
- factor project risk into the project to avoid having to fire-fight foreseeable problems;

- brainstorm where the likely project pitfalls will be;
- break down the project into manageable steps;
- question the point of holding meetings in order to avoid time-wasting;
- have good communication between project team members and with stakeholders;
- always contingency plan, especially building in extra time for project completion;
- whilst contingency planning, always look for opportunities;
- be brutally honest about the current culture's shortcomings;
- when planning a culture change, break down the transition into several stages;
- equip staff with the tools to make this cultural shift happen;
- reinforce the new risk culture by:
  - having a named director as sponsor;
  - building employee risk into existing operational meetings;
  - adding employee risk management to job descriptions;
  - extending the use of staff suggestions schemes to include ideas on managing risk;
  - including articles on employee risk in staff newsletters.
- the board must be highly visible in driving through a new risk-based culture;
- train managers on the benefits of employee risk management and what is expected of them;
- use the project team to train others in order to cascade training throughout the organization;
- tailor workshops to the needs of the audience, ie less theory for junior/manual staff;
- workshops should include:
  - why an employee risk assessment approach has become necessary;
  - practical examples of what can happen when things go wrong (and right);
  - what doing nothing can cost an employer, eg Barings Bank;
  - what it can offer managers and staff;
  - the importance of integrating it into the decision-making process;

- the role each individual plays in being proactive in reporting any concerns;
- what is expected of managers in terms of dealing with concerns reported to them;
- the process for dealing with any threats/vulnerabilities that have been identified.

- introduce a formal risk communications structure or extend an existing one;
- embed employee risk management into an existing communications structure by:
  - adding it to board meetings by including it as part of corporate governance;
  - feeding concerns into meetings held by the risk team and/or internal audit function;
  - encouraging discussions on the subject at team meetings;
  - build risk management into in-house training sessions, including induction;
  - reinforce the message by including updates in staff newsletters/intranet;
  - add details of this new/revised communication structure to any risk policy in place.

The appendices include two checklists on project management and on compiling a business case, as well as two sample risk assessments.

APPENDIX 1
Project management checklist

1. Project planning		
Have the following questions been answered:	✓	✗
• What are we trying to achieve?		
• What are the intended project outcomes?		
• What key issue(s) will the project address?		
• What resources do we need as a minimum?		
• What level of resourcing would be desirable?		
• What are the main threats that could affect this project?		
• Have we chosen a potential project sponsor amongst senior management?		
• How long is the project likely to last for?		
• When will it start?		
• Who must be informed about it?		
• Who needs to give final approval?		
• How will project changes be managed?		
• Who needs to approve them?		

1. Project planning		
Have the following questions been answered:	✓	✗
• How will the project be broken down into distinct stages?		
• Where is the project plan?		
• Who is responsible for updating and maintaining it?		
• Who can offer extra support, eg internal audit or IT?		
• What skills do we need in the project team?		
2. Project scope		
Has the draft project scope been broken down by:		
• Category of 'employee', eg director, employee or contractor?		
• Different types of working practice, eg remote working?		
• 'Employee' characteristics, eg age or disability?		
• Organizational factors, eg culture?		
• Employment law issues, eg discrimination law?		
• HR-related policies and procedures?		
• Core business issues, eg performance management and reward?		
• Health issues, eg sickness absence and well-being?		
Where areas have been excluded, are there good reasons for doing so?		

3. Project objectives		
Are the objectives:	✓	✗
• Aligned with organizational objectives?		
• Designed to yield the optimum return on investment (ROI)?		
• Specific?		
• Measurable?		
• Achievable?		
• Relevant?		
• Time bound?		
• Evaluated and reviewed?		

4. Project links		
Where appropriate, can the project link to:		
• Work of interest to other departments, eg IT or health and safety?		
• ISO 31000: 2009?		
• Total quality management (TQM)?		
• Six Sigma?		
• Lean thinking?		

APPENDIX 2
Business case checklist

1. Creating a business case		
Have the following stages been completed:	✓	✗
• Defining the proposed project's scope?		
• Identifying its boundaries?		
• Setting distinct objectives?		
• Linking each objective to business drivers/organizational objectives?		
• An assessment of project risks, such as:		
– Time overrun?		
– Cost overrun?		
– Project team illness/resignations?		
– Lack of cooperation from interviewees?		
• The following costs estimates as a:		
– Best-case scenario?		
– Expected-case scenario?		
– Worst-case scenario?		
• A review of data sources to justify the project such as:		
– Number of applications for each vacancy?		
– Overall recruitment costs?		

1. Creating a business case		
Have the following stages been completed:	✓	✗
• A review of data sources to justify the project such as:		
– Demographic data, eg on workforce age?		
– Diversity breakdown?		
– Training costs?		
– Training course feedback?		
– Scoring/outcomes from appraisals?		
– Productivity data?		
– Profitability data?		
– Customer satisfaction surveys?		
– Employee surveys?		
– Wage bill?		
– Distribution of performance pay-related awards?		
– Sickness absence figures?		
– Grievances (subject matter and outcome)?		
– Disciplinary hearings (subject matter and outcome)?		
– Breakdown of employment tribunal claims?		
– Length of service?		
– Resignations?		
– Dismissals?		

APPENDIX 3
Employee engagement risk assessment

Issue	Threat/problem	Risk L/M/H	Proposed control measures	Done by whom	Deadline	Done Y/N
Disengaged workforce	An emotional detachment from work and colleagues that has led to declining productivity.	High	• Survey staff to find out reasons for disengagement (do anonymously to encourage a response). • Review working hours and the level of support provided to staff.			
	Higher staff turnover expected as employees gain more confidence in the labour market. If so, costs will increase due to having to recruit new staff. There is also the loss of employee know-how.	High	• Revisit existing staff communications to see whether or not it is genuinely two-way. If not, look at building in formal feedback via team meetings and encouraging dialogue via the staff intranet. • Introduce focus staff groups to get feedback on how new engagement initiative(s) are working. • Initiative to have a director-level sponsor. • Senior management to become more visible throughout the organization.			
	Company reputation has suffered recently with unprepared staff having to field difficult questions from the public, family and friends. This can lead to disengagement and declining productivity.	Medium	• Liaise with PR team to ensure that employees are given sufficient information and training to communicate effectively on the organization's behalf. • Prioritize customer-facing staff for these briefings.			

APPENDIX 4
Reputation risk assessment

Issue	Threat/problem	Risk L/M/H	Proposed control measures	Done by whom	Deadline	Done Y/N
A potentially 'toxic' organizational culture	A robust management culture that can be perceived as bullying. Staff could use social media to publicly criticize the company.	High	• Review and strengthen the Dignity at Work Policy. Brief managers and staff on its importance and the sanctions for breaching it. • Bring it to the attention of third parties, such as contractors.			
	Long working hours now being seen as the norm. This can lead to sickness absence and/or presenteeism. Again staff can criticize via social media.	Medium	• Monitoring of employee working hours and checking on whether opt-out has been signed by individuals (where applicable). • Review of staffing levels across the business.			
	Increasing numbers of grievances being raised. If not managed properly these could result in tribunal claims and adverse publicity, eg from local media sources.	Medium	• Train managers on the need to resolve issues informally, how to do it and when to intervene. This should be backed up by revised procedures that managers are fully briefed on. • Look at whether there are problems with individual managers.			
	Poor communication with staff is leading to disengagement. This could harm our reputation with customers through poor service.	Medium	• Review internal communications strategy in conjunction with marketing team. Look at creating staff newsletters and improving feedback mechanism for team briefings.			

Issue	Threat/problem	Risk L/M/H	Proposed control measures	Done by whom	Deadline	Done Y/N
Weak and badly applied HR policies can lead to reputation damage due to:	Failure to manage employee use of social media, such as personal blogs and Twitter.	High	• Review our social media policy to see what controls we exercise over what employees can post about us. • Train staff on new policy requirements and retain right to levy disciplinary sanctions over any breaches.			
	Not managing the content uploaded to business social media channels.	High	• Whilst avoiding micro-management, ensure those responsible for uploading content adhere to guidelines on what message we want to get across.			
Non-compliance with employment law requirements:	Use of unpaid internships could tarnish our image due to bad press and accusations of slave labour, eg Tesco experience.	Medium	• Ensure that any internship offered is genuine and not 'work' in disguise. • Update our policy to reflect the latest employment tribunal position and brief supervisors/managers on the changes.			
	Insufficient understanding of employment law requirements, which can lead to tribunal claims reported in the media.	Medium	• Review current level of training of those responsible for updating and disseminating employment law updates and HR policies. • Look at internal/external employment law courses and updates.			
	Inappropriate employee monitoring can lead to complaints to the Information Commissioner and/or the charity – Liberty.	Low	• Look at data protection policy and provide extra management training if necessary on the Information Commissioner's Employment Practices Code.			

GLOSSARY

Acas Advisory, Conciliation and Arbitration Service (**www.acas.org.uk**).

Big data This refers to a collection of data sets that are so extensive and complex that processing them on traditional data-processing applications is difficult, if not impossible.

Capability An employee's ability or qualification to do their job.
CIPD Chartered Institute of Personnel and Development. This is the UK's main professional body for HR and people development (**www.cipd.co.uk**).
CLERP 9 Australian legislation entitled Corporate Law Economic Reform Program (Audit Reform & Corporate Disclosure) Act 2004.
Conduct An employee's behaviour in the workplace.
CSR Corporate social responsibility.
C-suite Senior executives who all have 'chief' in their job title, such as chief executive officer or chief information officer.

EAT Employment Appeal Tribunal. Its main role is to hear appeals from decisions made by employment tribunals.
ECJ European Court of Justice. The Court of Justice interprets EU law to make sure it is applied in the same way in all EU countries. It also settles legal disputes between EU governments and EU institutions.
EU European Union. Now comprised of 28 countries.
EURIBOR The average inter-bank interest rate at which a large number of banks on the London money market are prepared to lend one another unsecured funds in European euros.

Gap analysis A technique used to determine what steps an organization must take in order to move from its current situation to a preferred future state.

HMRC Her Majesty's Revenue & Customs.
HR Human Resources.

IRM Institute of Risk Management.

Know-how Informal practical knowledge, experience and ability.

LIBOR   London inter-bank offered rate. This is a global benchmark interest rate that is used to set a range of financial deals. It is also a measure of trust in the financial system and the faith that banks have in each other's financial health.

Malware   Short for malicious software and is a catch-all term for viruses, spyware and worms. It is usually installed without the user's knowledge.

NMW   National minimum wage.

PIDA   Public Interest Disclosure Act 1998.
PILON   Pay in lieu of notice.
Presenteeism   Refers to attending work whilst ill, but being less productive or engaged as a result.

Risk   The likelihood of an organization being harmed by a threat or a loss of some kind and how serious the harm could be.
Risk register   Acts as a central source for all risks that have been identified by an organization. Often includes information such as risk rating, impact, control measures and risk owner.

Sarbanes–Oxley   US federal law that sets standards for all US public company boards, management and public accounting firms. It is named after its two sponsors, US Senator Paul Sarbanes and US Representative Michael G Oxley.

Wilful blindness   A legal principle stating that knowledge will be inferred if someone deliberately blinded themselves to the existence of a fact that they should have been aware of.

Zero-hours contracts   A type of on-call arrangement where an employee only gets paid for the hours worked.

REFERENCES

Acas (2011) *Code of Practice 1 – Disciplinary and Grievance Procedures* [online] http://www.acas.org.uk/index.aspx?articleid=2174

Acas (2011) *Discipline and Grievances at Work: The Acas Guide* [online] http://www.acas.org.uk/index.aspx?articleid=2179

Acas (2011) *Working Without the Default Retirement Age* [online] http://www.acas.org.uk/media/pdf/d/4/Working_wtihout_the_DRA_Employer_guidance_-_MARCH_2011.pdf

Aon Consulting (2010) News release: one billion man hours lost to sickies across Europe each year [online] http://aon.mediaroom.com/index.php?s=25776&item=63933 (accessed 2 December 2013)

Aon Consulting (2010) The European sick leave index: fresh insights into sick leave absence [online] http://img.en25.com/Web/AON/Aon-ESLI-Report.pdf (accessed 2 December 2013)

BIS (2006) Union membership rights of members and non-members [online] http://www.bis.gov.uk/assets/biscore/employment-matters/docs/06-558-union-rights-members (accessed 10 September 2013)

BIS, CPNI, The Cabinet Office *et al* (2012) Executive companion: 10 steps to cyber security [online] http://www.bis.gov.uk/assets/BISCore/business-sectors/docs/0-9/12-1120-10-steps-to-cyber-security-executive.pdf (accessed 16 September 2013)

Bupa (2009) Healthy work: challenges and opportunities to 2030 [online] http://www.bupa.com/media/58510/health-at-work-report.pdf (accessed 30 November 2013)

Bupa (2010) Health work: evidence into action [online] http://www.bupa.com/media/35337/healthy-work-evidence-into-action-report.pdf (accessed 27 November 2013)

Canada Life (2013) Untitled research into presenteeism [online] http://www.canadalife.co.uk/group/intouch-whats-new/documents/G2881ASTradereleasepresenteeismfinal.pdf (accessed 8 December 2013)

Centre for Mental Health (2011) Managing presenteeism: a discussion paper [online] http://www.centreformentalhealth.org.uk/employment/presenteeism.aspx (accessed 7 December 2013)

CIIA (2013) *Effective Internal Audit in the Financial Services Sector: Recommendations from the Committee on Internal Audit Guidance for Financial Services*

References

CIPD (2012) *Work Audit 2012 – Counting the Cost of the Jobs Recession* [online] http://www.cipd.co.uk/binaries/5795workauditWEB.pdf

CIPD (2013) *Employee Outlook: Focus on Rebuilding Trust in the City* [online] http://www.cipd.co.uk/hr-resources/survey-reports/employee-outlook-focus-rebuilding-trust-city.aspx

CIPD (2013) *Employers are from Mars, Young People are from Venus* [online] http://www.cipd.co.uk/pm/peoplemanagement/b/weblog/archive/2013/04/25/employers-are-from-mars-young-people-are-from-venus.aspx

CIPD (2013) *The Role of HR in Corporate Responsibility* [online] http://www.cipd.co.uk/hr-resources/research/role-hr-corporate-responsibility.aspx

CIPD/Halogen (2013) *Employee Outlook for October 2013* [online] http://www.cipd.co.uk/hr-resources/survey-reports/employee-outlook-autumn-2013.aspx

Court Approved Consent Decree for Abercrombie & Fitch case (2005) [online] http://www.afjustice.com/pdf/20050422_consent_decree.pdf (accessed 10 July 2013)

CRF/People in Business (2013) Employer Brand Research Results – Infographic [online] http://www.top-employers.com/en/news-and-insights/Blog/2013/07/employer-brand-research-results-infographic/ (accessed 15 August 2013)

Deal, T and Kennedy, A (2000) *Corporate Cultures: The rites and rituals of corporate life*, Basic Books, Cambridge MA, 2000 Edition

Detica and Cabinet Office (2011) The cost of cyber crime: a Detica report in partnership with the Office of Cyber Security and Information Assurance in the Cabinet Office [online] https://www.gov.uk/government/uploads/system/uploads/attachment_data/file/60943/the-cost-of-cyber-crime-full-report.pdf (accessed 28 May 2013)

Ellipse and Professor Cary Cooper, CBE (2012) Sick notes: how changes in the workplace and technology demand a rethink of absence management [online] http://www.ellipse.co.uk/images/pdf/SickNotesReport.pdf (accessed 9 December 2013)

Equality Act 2010 [online] http://www.legislation.gov.uk/ukpga/2010/15/contents (accessed 15 October 2013)

Groysberg, B, Kelly, LK and MacDonald, B (March 2011) 'The New Path to the C-suite', *Harvard Business Review*, pp 3–10

High Pay Centre (2013) Banks will not rebuild public trust until they tackle bonuses [online] http://highpaycentre.org/bigpay/banks-will-not-rebuild-public-trust-until-they-tackle-bonuses (accessed 2 September 2013)

Home Office/UKBA (2012) Summary guide for employers on preventing illegal working in the UK [online] http://www.ukba.homeoffice.gov.uk/sitecontent/documents/employersandsponsors/preventingillegalworking/currentguidanceandcodes/summary-guidance.pdf?view=Binary (accessed 17 July 2013)

ICO (2013) Bring your own device (BYOD) [online] http://www.ico.org.uk/for_organisations/data_protection/topic_guides/online/byod (accessed 28 May 2013)

IRM (2011) *Risk Appetite & Tolerance* [online] http://www.theirm.org/knowledge-and-resources/thought-leadership/risk-appetite-and-tolerance/
IRM (2012) *Risk Culture: Resources for Practitioners* [online] http://www.theirm.org/knowledge-and-resources/thought-leadership/risk-culture/
IRS Employment Review, Issue 924 *KPMG Avoids Redundancies Through Flexible Working*
KnowledgePool (2011) Business white paper: 'From conspiracy of convenience to virtuous circle'
KnowledgePool (2011) Business white paper: 'How to reduce training wastage'
KPMG (2012) Rethinking Human Resources in a changing world [online] http://www.kpmg.com/Global/en/IssuesAndInsights/ArticlesPublications/hr-transformations-survey/Documents/hr-transformations-survey-full-report.pdf (accessed 15 July 2013)
Krivkovich, A and Levy, C (May 2013) Managing the people side of risk, McKinsey Insights [online] http://www.mckinsey.com/insights/risk_management/managing_the_people_side_of_risk (accessed 5 June 2013)
Medibank (2011) Sick at work: the cost of presenteeism to your business and the economy [online] http://www.medibank.com.au/Client/Documents/Pdfs/sick_at_work.pdf (accessed 2 January 2014)
Melbourne Newsroom (2009) Freedom to surf: workers more productive if allowed to use the internet for leisure [online] http://newsroom.melbourne.edu/news/n-19 (accessed 21 August 2013)
Minchington, B (2010) Communicate your EVP to attract and retain talent [online] http://www.brettminchington.com/files/communicate_your_EVP_to_attract_and_retain_talent.pdf (accessed 15 July 2013)
OECD (2012) Obesity update 2012 [online] http://www.oecd.org/health/health-systems/49716427.pdf (accessed 9 December 2013)
Orion Partners (2013) Over a quarter of senior HR professionals think their HR function is ineffective [online] http://www.orion-partners.com/a-quarter-of-hr-directors-say-their-own-hr-function-is-ineffective/ (accessed 3 December 2013)
Ponemon Institute (2012) Cost of cyber crime study: United States [online] http://www.ponemon.org/local/upload/file/2012_US_Cost_of_Cyber_Crime_Study_FINAL6%20.pdf (accessed 3 June 2013)
Ponemon Institute (2013) Cost of data breach study: global analysis [online] http://www.ponemon.org/local/upload/file/2013%20Report%20GLOBAL%20CODB%20FINAL%205-2.pdf (accessed 3 June 2013)
PwC (2013) 16th Annual Global CEO Survey: dealing with disruption adapting to survive and thrive [online] http://www.pwc.com/gx/en/ceo-survey/2013/assets/pwc-16th-global-ceo-survey_jan-2013.pdf (accessed 24 May 2013)
PwC (2013) The rising cost of sickness absence [online] http://pwc.blogs.com/press_room/2013/07/rising-sick-bill-is-costing-uk-business-29bn-a-year-pwc-research.html (accessed 16 November 2013)

QA (2013) New QA research reveals major cyber security flaws in working practices [online] http://www.qa.com/about-qa/news/2013/new-qa-research-reveals-major-cyber-security-flaws-in-working-practices/ (accessed 4 June 2013)

Talent, Q (2013) The vicious circle of volume recruitment [online] https://www.talentqgroup.com/media/89692/volume-survey-report-the-vicious-circle-of-volume-recruitment.pdf (accessed 11 September 2013)

Womack, J and Jones, D (2003) *Lean Thinking: Banish Waste and Create Wealth in Your Corporation*, Free Press, New York

Work Foundation (2013) Beyond the business case: the employer's role in tackling youth unemployment [online] http://www.theworkfoundation.com/DownloadPublication/Report/336_Employer's%20Role%20FINAL%202%20July%202013.pdf (accessed 15 November 2013)

World Health Organization (2013) Comprehensive mental health action plan 2013–2020 [online] http://apps.who.int/iris/bitstream/10665/89966/1/9789241506021_eng.pdf (accessed 3 December 2013)

XpertHR (2010) Return-to-work interviews survey 2010: line managers' effectiveness [online] http://www.xperthr.co.uk/survey-analysis/return-to-work-interviews-survey-2010-line-managers-effectiveness/105161/ (accessed 4 December 2013)

FURTHER READING

AIRMIC, ALARM & IRM (2010) *A Structured Approach to Enterprise Risk Management (ERM) and the Requirements of ISO 31000*

CIPD (2013) *Megatrends: The trends shaping work and working lives*

Financial Reporting Council (2012) The UK Corporate Governance Code [online] http://www.frc.org.uk/Our-Work/Publications/Corporate-Governance/UK-Corporate-Governance-Code-September-2012.aspx (accessed 20 November 2013)

Heffernan, M (2011) *Wilful Blindness: Why we ignore the obvious at our peril*, Simon & Schuster, London

ICO (2011) The Employment Practices Data Protection Code [online] http://www.ico.org.uk/for_organisations/data_protection/topic_guides/~/media/documents/library/Data_Protection/Detailed_specialist_guides/the_employment_practices_code.pdf (accessed 28 May 2013)

Infosecurity Magazine (2012) The 2012 cost of cyber crime report says successful attacks doubled [online] http://www.infosecurity-magazine.com/view/28664/the-2012-cost-of-cyber-crime-report-says-successful-attacks-doubled-/ (accessed 3 June 2013)

Smith, G (2012) *Why I Left Goldman Sachs: A Wall Street Story*, Grand Central Publishing, New York

Steare, R (2013) *Ethicability: How to decide what's right and find the courage to do it*, Roger Steare Consulting Limited

INDEX

NB: page numbers in *italic* indicate figures or tables

'10 steps to cyber-security' (2012)   157

Abercrombie & Fitch   70–71
   and class action *Gonzalez v Abercrombie & Fitch*   70–71
Accident Group claims firm   211
accountability, lack of   224
Advisory, Conciliation and Arbitration Service (Acas)   184
   Code of Practice (2011)   195
   early conciliation service (2014)   198
ageing population, realities of   93–94
   census figures, US (2010)   94
   figures from Australian Bureau of Statistics (for 2012)   94
   figures from Office for National Statistics (2013)   93
ageing workforce (and)   29, 93–98
   age-related insured benefits   97–98
      see also employment tribunals
   declining performance: risk assessments   94–96
      appraisal history   95
      recommendations   95–96
      sickness absence records   94–95
      training   95
   succession planning   96
anti-piracy   158–59
Apple   12, 66
articles/papers (by/on)
   'From conspiracy of convenience to virtuous circle' (KnowledgePool, 2011)   180
   'How to reduce training wastage' (KnowledgePool, 2011)   179
   'Managing the people side of risk' (McKinsey Insights, 2013)   19
      see also Krivkovich, A *and* Levy, C
   'The New Path to the C-suite' (*Harvard Business Review*, 2011)   16
      see also Groysberg, B; Kelly, L K and MacDonald, B
   'Push to ban online gambling at work' (Jason Dowling in *The Age*, 2012)   162
   selling of 'know-how' by Dyson ex-employee (*The Telegraph*, 2012)   165
   'Vast Mexico Bribery Case Hushed Up by Wal-Mart After Top-Level Struggle' (*New York Times*, 2012)   20
      see also Barstow, D
   'Why I am leaving Goldman Sachs' (Greg Smith, *New York Times*, 2012)   15
audit trail organizations
   in UK: Column Resources (http://columncasehr.com)   197
   in US: Workforce Metrics (http://www.workforcemetrics.co.uk)   197
Australia   17, 108
   anti-discrimination laws in   71
   Victorian Commission for Gambling and Liquor Regulation   162
Austria 108
avoiding common problems   *see* common problems

banks/banking   14–17, 106–07
   Bank of Scotland   163
   Barings Bank   1, 77, 229, 233
   Co-op   77
   crises   13–15, 177
   Deutsche Bank   16
Barstow, D   20
Belgium   123
below the line activities   67
Bercow, S   135
blogs/blogging   50, 56, 133, 136, 138–39, 144
Border Agency (UKBA)   81, 82, 83, 91
   quarterly naming and shaming reports   81
   Summary Guide for Employers on Preventing Illegal Working in the UK   91
Branson, R   12
BRIC (Brazil, Russia, India, China) countries   68
bring your own devices (BYOD)   154–57, 166 *see also* information security
Business, Innovation and Skills, Department of (BIS)   76 *see also* reports
   and policy of naming and shaming   105
business case checklist   238–39

Index

business case format   37–39
  costs   39
  data sources   38
  methods   38
  project risks   39
  purpose   38
business networking   133
business reputation, safeguarding   7–8
  and threat trigger points   8

Canada   17, 108, 120, 135, 193
  social media in   137
  whistle-blowing laws in   186
  wrongful dismissals in   203
Canada Life   126
case study: drafting business case – using data to develop compelling business case   39–40
Centre for the Protection of National Infrastructure (CPNI)   157
change   225–28
  dealing with resistance to   227–28
  and transition to desired future state   226–27
chapter summaries (for)
  avoiding common problems   231–34
  employee health and well-being   128–31
  end of employment   216–21
  impact of HR function   189–92
  information security   167–69
  introduction   8–9
  organizational context   24–26
  pre-assessment groundwork   44–46
  recruitment   88–91
  social media   147–49
  types of employee and third parties   110–13
Chartered Institute of Personnel and Development (CIPD)   16, 30, 64, 83, 85, 108, 177 *see also* reports; research *and* surveys
checklists for
  business case   238–39
  project management   235–37
China   17, 68, 120
CIPD   *see* Personnel and Development, Chartered Institute of (CIPD)
Coker, B   138
collectivism/individualism–collectivism   17
common problems   223–34
  creating a risk-aware culture   228–29
  failing to manage change   225–28
    see also change
  final thoughts on   231

  poor communication   229–31
  project management pitfalls   *see subject entry*
communication, poor   225, 229–31
Communications–Electronic Security Group (CESG)   155
contingency planning, lack of   225
control measures and precautions   51
  remove threat   51
  risk acceptance   51
  risk reduction   51
  risk transfer   51
  root cause analysis   52–55 *see also* root cause analysis (RCA), stages of
Costco   141
countercultures   29, 44
court cases   *see also* Abercrombie & Fitch *and* European Court of Justice
  Hays Specialist Recruitment (Holdings) Ltd & Another v Ions v Ions & Another [2008] EWHC 745   141
  involving social media   140–45
  Majrowski v Guy's and St Thomas' NHS Trust [2006], UKHL 34   135
  Rolls-Royce plc v Unite [2009]   207
  Romero Insurance Brokers Ltd v Templeton & Amor [2013] EWHC 1198 (QB)   213–14
  Seldon (Appellant) v Clarkson Wright and Jakes (A Partnership) (Respondent) [2012] UKSC 16 on appeal from [2010] EWCA Civ 899   202
  Teggart v TeleTech UK Limited NIIT 00704/11   140
  Whitmar Publications Limited v Gamage and Others [2013] EWHC 1881 (Ch)   142
Crossrail project   75
CV-checking agency (NARIC, UK)   81
cybercrime (and)   151–53
  dangers of 'social engineering'   151–52
  passwords   152–53

Deal, T   11, 24
definitions of
  employee engagement (CIPD)   30
  employees   8
  employer value proposition (EVP)   66
Denmark   122
discrimination (and)   28, 51, 70–76 *see also* legislation (UK)
  disabilities   71, 73–74
  'fattism'   71
  hiring policies   70–72
  indirect sex   71

Index

interview questions 74
job adverts 68–70
'lookism' 71
pregnancy/maternity 208–10 *see also* redundancy/ies
race 69
against trade unionists 74–76
dismissal 93 *see also* unfair dismissal
Dowling, J 162
Dropbox 156
Dyson 165–66

employee engagement 30 *see also* definitions of
risk assessment 240
employee health and well-being 115–31
health issues 115–21
presenteeism 126–28
sickness absence 121–25
Employee Outlook: Focus on Rebuilding Trust in the City (CIPD, 2013) 16
Employee Outlook for October 2013 (CIPD/Halogen) 177
employee risk assessment (and) 47–61, 180–81
carrying out (by) 47–52, 54–56, 57–58, 48, 53, 57
choosing areas to be reviewed 49
deciding who/what may be harmed and how 50
evaluating risks and deciding on control measures 50–55 *see also* control measures and precautions
identifying threats and vulnerabilities 49–50
recording findings and implement control measures 55–56
scheduling periodic reviews; updating where necessary 56
SWOT analysis 56, 57, 59 *see also* key points
horizon scanning 58–60
incorporating IT security threats 153
sources of intelligence 59–60
employees *see* definitions of; foreign nationals *and* recruitment
employer(s)
brand 67
dignity at work policy 140
value proposition (EVP) 66–67
Employers are from Mars, Young People are from Venus (CIPD, 2013) 108–09
Employment Appeal Tribunal 198, 212
employment legislation 3, 4, 34, 59 *see also* end of employment *and* legislation (UK)

Employment Practices Data Protection Code (UK) 79–80
recommendations of 79–81
employment tribunal(s)
claims 4
Moonsar v Fiveways Express Transport Ltd [2004] 159
new (2013) charging system for 198
Toal and another v G B Oils Ltd [2013] EAT/0569/13 196
Witham v Capita Insurance Services Ltd 97
end of employment 193–221
other concerns 212–16
redundancy 205–12 *see also* redundancy/ies
unfair dismissal 193–205 *see also* subject entry
Erhardt, M (intern: Bank of America Merrill Lynch) 106
ethics 14–16
European Convention on Human Rights (ECHR) (Article 8) 140–41
European Court of Justice (ECJ) 211
and *United States of America v Nolan* [2012] IRLR 1020 ECJ 211
European Economic Area (EEA) 81
European Union (EU) 68
figures of unemployed young people in 108
external branding 67, 90

Facebook 7, 56, 68, 133, 134
employee misuse of 140–41
employer misuse of 140
on sharing passwords 79
Statements of Rights and Responsibilities: Registration and Accounts Security 78–79
figures
areas of coverage 5
carrying out an employee risk assessment 48
potential overlap with other disciplines 35
root cause analysis 53
foreign nationals 81–83 *see also* recruitment
and dismissal of non-EEA nationals 82–83
giving notice to 83
France 75, 122, 123
Société Générale 16

gap analysis 4, 57, 85
Gardham, D 165–66

Index

Germany 18, 108, 120, 122, 123, 151, 193
Glassdoor 67
   and http://www.glassdoor.com 67, 90
Goldman Sachs 15
Google 66
Greece 108, 116
greed, culture of 15–16
Groysberg, B 16

hazards, identifying 47
health (and)
   chronic diseases 29
   ill health as growing issue 29
health and safety 28, 36, 38, 47, 55, 107, 162, 186, 207, 230
High Pay Centre 16
Hindson, A 20 *see also* Institute of Risk Management (IRM)
hiring policies and 'refer a friend' schemes 72
HM Revenue & Customs (HMRC) 102, 106
Hofstede, G 17–18
   and individualism–collectivism 17
   website 18
Honeywell and illegal file sharing 158
human resources (HR) (and) 171–79
   see also legislation
   corporate social responsibility 177
   demonstrating business acumen 176–77
   enhancing profile of 6–7
   involvement in new areas 177–79
   legal compliance 174–75
   perception of 16–17, 171–73
   self-regulation of 175
Hungary 108

IBM and risk assessment for social media 7
impact of HR function (and) 171–92
   learning and talent development (LTD) 179–83 *see also subject entry*
   managing poor performance 183–86
   role of HR 171–79 *see also* human resources (HR)
   whistle-blowing 186–89 *see also subject entry*
industrial tribunal (Northern Ireland) 140
information security (and) 151–69
   bring your own devices (BYOD) 154–56 *see also* legislation (UK)
   and data protection stages 154–56
   cloud computing 156–57
   and '10 steps to cyber-security' (BIS *et al*, 2012) 157
   confidential information and 'know-how' 165–66

cybercrime 151–53 *see also subject entry*
data protection 162–65
   fines for breaches of 163–64
   recommendations for 164–65
file downloads 157–61
   hate websites 160–61
   illegal file sharing 157–59
   of pornography 159–60 *see also* legislation (UK) *and subject entry*
online gambling 161–62 *see also subject entry*
Institute of Risk Management (IRM) 20 *see also* model(s)
   and risk appetite 42
   'Risk Culture: Resources for Practitioners' (2012) 22
Internal Auditors (UK), Chartered Institute of guidance update (2013) 16
interns 105–07
   health problems for 106
   and Intern Aware (UK) 105
   NMW requirements for 105
   questions and recommendations for 106
Ireland 75 *see also* Northern Ireland
ISO 31000:2009 36
IT 36
Italy 108, 116

Japan 18, 116, 151
Jobs, S 12
Jones, D 37

Kelly, L K 16
Kennedy, A 11, 24
key points (for)
   age-related benefits 98
   corresponding with shortlisted candidates 81
   court cases and ownership of Twitter followers 145
   employing foreign nationals 82, 83
   Hofstede's website/scores on his 'dimensions' 18
   illegal file sharing and disciplinary procedures 159
   links to other disciplines and processes 37
   project planning 34
   redundancy 208, 211, 212
   and restrictive covenants 214
   risk appetite and risk tolerance 42
   risk assessment 58
   and remote workers 100
   risk-aware culture 229
   root cause analysis (RCA) 55

SWOT analysis   57–58
unfair dismissal cases   198, 200
use of data   41
KnowledgePool   179–80, 182
KPMG/ KPMG International   172, 205–06
Krivkovich, A   19

Lagarde, C (head of IMF)   13
Latvia   108
Leahy, Sir T   108
lean thinking   37
learning and development initiatives   37
learning and talent development (LTD)   179–83, 189
  identifying business need for   179–81
  and training and learning needs analysis   181–83
Leeson, N   1, 77
legal compliance, improving   4, 6, 5
Legatum Prosperity Index (2013)   108
legislation (Australia)
  CLERP 9   6
legislation (EU)
  and potential for legislation on blacklisting (2011)   75
legislation (UK) *see also* court cases
  Corporate Governance Code   6
  Data Protection Act (1998)   75, 154, 162, 167
  Employment Relations Act 1999 (Blacklists) Regulations (2010)   75
  Equality Act (2010)   28, 72, 73, 98, 159, 207, 212
  Fixed Term Employees (Prevention of Less Favourable Treatment) Regulations (2002)   204
  Malicious Communications Act (1988)   134
  Protection for Harassment Act (1997)   135
  Public Interest Disclosure Act (PIDA, 1998)   186
legislation (US): Sarbanes–Oxley Act (2002)   6
Levy, C   19
Lewis, P N   14
  and risk and ethics culture assessment   22–24
libel   *see* social media
LIBOR and EURIBOR scandal   16
LIFO (last in, first out)   207–08
LinkedIn (and)   64, 80, 133, 146
  Ions, M   141–42
  ownership of contacts   141–42
Lithuania   108
Lovell, K   179

McAlpine, Lord   135–36
MacDonald, B   16
Michalak, E   1
Minchington, B   66–67
models
  'Risk Culture Aspects Model' (IRM)   20
MySpace   79

Netherlands   75, 123
New Zealand   108, 193
Northern Ireland   140–41, 194
  industrial tribunal in   140
  legislation on whistle-blowing in   186
Norway   18, 81

obesity and discrimination   71
O'Leary, M (Ryanair CEO)   14
online gambling   161–62
  dangers of   161–62
  as occupational health-and-safety problem (Australia)   162
organizational context (and)   11–26
  how culture influences risk taking   13–18 *see also* risk taking
  improving organizational culture   20, 22–24, 21
  overview of   11–13
  significance of link between culture and risk taking   18–20 *see also* risk-taking
outsourcing   2, 3, 4, 28, 58, 64, 93, 103–04, 108, 180

performance management   29, 94, 171, 181, 199, 208
  and managing poor performance   183–86
PILON (pay in lieu of notice)   203, 215
pornography (and)
  malware   160
  sexual harassment/discrimination   159
  tough policies against downloading   160
pre-assessment groundwork   27–46
  drafting the business case (and)   37–43
    see also subject entry and case studies
    format for   37–39 *see also* business case format
    identifying risk appetite and risk tolerance   42–43
    other data sources   40–41
    terminology   41–42
    key points   34, 37, 41, 42 *see also subject entry*
    link to other disciplines and processes   34, 36–37, 35

project planning 27–34 *see also subject entry*
  trade union involvement 43–44
privacy, individual's right to privacy 140 *see also* court cases
project management checklist 235–37
project management pitfalls 223–25
  excessive project scope 225
  ignoring opportunities 225
  ignoring project risks 224
  insufficient stakeholder support 223–24
  lack of accountability 224
  lack of authority 224
  lack of contingency planning 225
  poor communication 225
  project team conflict 224
  time-wasting meetings 225
project planning (and) 27–34
  coverage 27–31
  project objectives 32–34 *see also* SMART/SMARTer objectives
  project team skills 31–32
  selection of project leader 31

race discrimination 69
recruitment (and) 63–91
  agencies 64
  candidate screening (and) 76–83
    CV/application checks 76–81
    Disclosure and Barring Service (DBS) checks 81
    employing foreign nationals 81–83
    problems and recommendations 80–81
  discrimination 70–76
    disability 73–74
    and interview questions 72
    practices 70–72
    against trade unionists 74–76
  high-volume 85–87
  hiring policies 70–76
  promoting internal candidates 87–88
  pre-recruitment (and) 63–70
    discriminatory job adverts 68–70
    employment mismatch 63–68
  skilled/senior roles 83–85
redundancy/ies (and) 205–12
  consultation 210–11
    collective requirements for 211 *see also* European Court of Justice
    ignoring 211
  LIFO 207–08
  making excessive 205–07

pregnancy/maternity discrimination 208–10
rationale behind/questions on decisions on 206–07
references 212–13
restrictive covenants 213–15 *see also* court cases: Romero
vengeful former staff 215–16
weak selection criteria for 207– *see also* court cases *and* legislation (UK)
remote workers (and) 98–100
  data security 98–100
  homeworking 99–100
  productivity concerns 100
reports (on)
  'Beyond the business case: the employer's role in tackling youth unemployment' (Work Foundation, 2013) 109
  costs of filling vacancies in UK (Annual Survey Report, CIPD, 2013) 64
  court case: Australian construction company/Electrical Trades Union (Working Life, 2013) 75
  hiring of unsuitable candidates (Talent Q, 2013) 85–86
  'Union membership rights of members and non-members' (BIS, UK 2006) 76
reputation 7–8
  damage 81, 143, 176
  risk assessment 241–42
  and threat trigger points 8, 9
research (by/on)
  'The cost of cyber crime' (Detica, 2011) 151
  educational standards (OECD) 108
  employees' knowledge of costs for breaching Data Protection Act (Cyber-Ark Software) 163
  employer brand (People in Business and CRF Institute, 2013) 68
  HR's contribution to the corporate responsibility agenda (CIPD, 2013) 177–78
  human resources (HR) (Orion Partners, 2013) 172
  redundancy and UK employers (Aon Hewitt) 205
  remote workers and data security (3M, 2010) 99
  'Rethinking Human Resources in a changing world' (KPMG International, 2012) 7, 172

time taken to resolve cyberattacks (Ponemon Institute/Hewlett-Packard, 2012)   151
   use of social media at work (University of Melbourne, Australia, 2009)   138
   whistle-blowing (Public Concern at Work, UK, 2013)   187
RIGHT: R-ules, I-ntegrity, G-ood, H-arm, T-ruth and T-ransparency   23–24
risk appetite   42–43
risk assessment (for/on)   80
   interns   105–07
   older workers   94
   online gambling in working hours   161, 162
   protection of confidential information   166
   questions   84–85
   remote and home workers   99–100
   and social media   145–47
   third parties   101–04 *see also subject entry*
   volunteers   107–08
   young people   108–09
risk and ethics culture assessment for   22–24 *see also* Lewis, P N
   employee engagement   240
   reputation   241–42
'Risk Culture: Resources for Practitioners' (IBM 2012)   22 *see also* Lewis, P N
risk mitigation   157
risk taking (and)   13–20
   culture   18–20
   dangers of 'groupthink'   13
   impact of international culture   17–18 *see also* Hofstede, G
   relationship to how HR is perceived   16–17
   role of ethics   14–16
risk tolerance   42–43
risk-aware culture   228–29
risks, project   224
The Role of HR in Corporate Responsibility (CIPD, 2013)   177
root cause analysis, stages of   52, 54–55, 53
   analyse information   54
   key point for   55
   major factors   52
   possible causes   54
   recommendations/implementation   54
   symptoms   52

Saudi Arabia   17
scams 151–52
   'Top 100 Executives'   152
   vanity   152

Scotland, Bank of   143
Scotland   158, 187, 194, 198
Securities and Futures Authority   77
serial litigants   69–70
   and reducing likelihood of claims   69–70
   website: http://www.serial-litigants.com/whatwedo.html   70
Six Sigma   36
SMART/SMARTER objectives   32–34, 185
   achievable   33
   evaluated and reviewed   33–34
   measurable   33
   relevant   33
   specific   32–33
   timebound   33
Smith, G   15   *see also* Goldman Sachs
Snowden, E   165
social media (and)   7, 113–49
   blocking access to   138
   ownership of user-generated content   136–37
   policy (on)   145–47
      content ownership   146
      cyberbullying   146
      disciplinary sanctions   146
      monitoring   147
      personal use   146
      purpose of   146
      social media management   147
   potential for libel   135–36
   reduced productivity   137–38
   reputation damage   133–34
   trolling/harassment   134–35
   user-generated content (UGC)   133–34
social networking   133
Société Générale (France)   16
Spain   14, 108, 122, 123
SpeakInConfidence (http://www.speakinconfidence.com)   189
stress   29
study: global study of 418 executives re HR   172 *see also* research
surveys (on)
   '16th Annual Global CEO Survey' (PwC, 2013)   84
   employees using unofficial cloud-based file-sharing services (AIIM, 2013)   156
   'Resourcing and Talent Planning Survey, 2013) (CIPD/Hays)   83–84
   transfer of work files to and from home (QA, 2013)   165
   workers using social media sites in US and Canada (Intelligent Office, 2012)   137

Sweden   18, 75
Switzerland   81
SWOT (strengths, weaknesses, opportunities, threats) analysis   47, 56, 57, 59

tables
  example of a SWOT analysis   57
  risk culture aspects model   21
third parties (and)   101–04
  agency staff   101–02
  self-employed contractors/consultants   102–03
  non-disclosure agreements (NDAs)   103
  outsourcing and data leakage   103–04
The Times   143
total quality management (TQM)   36, 38
trade unionists
  blacklisting of/discrimination against   74–76
training and learning needs analysis (TLNA)   181–83
Twitter   7, 133, 134, 135, 146
  and Kravitz, N/PhoneDog   144–45
types of 'employee' and third parties   93–113
  ageing workforce   93–98 *see also* subject entry
  interns   105–07 *see also* subject entry
  outsourcing   103–04
  remote workers   98–100 *see also* subject entry
  and third-party threats   101–04 *see also* third parties
  volunteers   107–08
  young people   108–09 *see also* subject entry

uncertainty avoidance (UAI)   18
unfair dismissal, fair procedure for   195–98
  appeal   197
  audit trail   197
  companion   196 *see also* employment tribunals
  consistency   197
  decision to dismiss   197
  disciplinary procedures   195
  employee no-show   196
  Fee Waiver Scheme   198
  hearing format   196–97
  suspension   196
  timely   196
  training   195–96
  witnesses   197

unfair dismissal, fair reason for   199–200
  automatic   199–200
  capability   199
  conduct   199
  other substantial reason   199
  redundancy   199
  statutory restriction   199
unfair dismissal (and)   193–205
  constructive dismissal   200–201
  end of fixed-term contract (FTC)   204–05 *see also* legislation (UK)
  fair procedure   *see* unfair dismissal, fair procedure for
  fair reason   *see* unfair dismissal, fair reason for
  forced retirement   201–03 *see also* court cases
  investigation   194–95
  pay in lieu of notice (PILON)   203
  preliminary assessment for   194
  wrongful dismissal   203
United Kingdom (UK)   17, 18, 108 *see also* legislation (UK)
  Border Agency (UKBA)   81, 82, 83, 91 *see also* subject entry
  quarterly naming and shaming reports   81
  Summary Guide for Employers on Preventing Illegal Working in the UK   91
  Department for Communities and Local Government: True Vision website   160
  Information Commissioner's Office   79
  and wrongful dismissals   203
United States (US) (and)   17, 68, 108 *see also* legislation (US)
  free speech   141
  GlaxoSmithKline   187
  judgement against Tuomey Healthcare system   187
  National Labor Relations Board   141
  social media   137
  whistle-blowing laws   186

Virgin   66
  Virgin Atlantic: employee misuse of Facebook   140
volunteer workers   107–08

Wales   70, 134, 160, 187, 194, 195, 196, 198
Wal-Mart   19–20
  and the *New York Times*   19–20
Waterstones: lack of policy on blogs   139

websites (on)
    hate crime (True Vision)   160
    Hofstede: http://geert-hofstede.com/
        countries.html   18
    litigation: http://www.serial-litigants.com
        70, 91
    what employers are like to work for
        68
whistleblowing   186–89 *see also* Canada;
        legislation (UK); research *and*
        United States (US)
    anonymous third-party service for
        188–89
    risk assessment areas   187–88
        confidentiality   188
        credibility   187
        framework   187
        organizational culture   187
        training   188
Whistleblowing Commission: report
        recommending Code of Practice   188
Womack, J   37
Wordpress   133
Working Without the Default Retirement Age
        (Acas guide, 2011)   96

young people   108–09
    Eurostat (2013) unemployment figures for
        108
    and youth unemployment   108–09
YouTube (and)   68, 133
    Domino's Pizza video   143
    United Airlines/Dave Carroll: 'United
        Breaks Guitars' video   143–44